T0149477

THE NUN *and* THE BUM

a journey, a communion, a birth

BOOK OF FICTION INSPIRED BY TRUE STORY

ADELE AZAR-RUCQUOI

BALBOA.
PRESS
A DIVISION OF HAY HOUSE

Balboa Press books may be ordered through booksellers or by contacting:

Balboa Press
A Division of Hay House
1663 Liberty Drive
Bloomington, IN 47403
www.balboapress.com
1 (877) 407-4847

Print information available on the last page.

ISBN: 978-1-5043-8894-8 (sc)
ISBN: 978-1-5043-8896-2 (hc)
ISBN: 978-1-5043-8895-5 (e)

Library of Congress Control Number: 2017914731

Balboa Press rev. date: 11/13/2017

in the face of despair, contemplate all things as they present themselves from the standpoint of redemption

~ Theodore Oderno

DEDICATION

To beloved sons, Marc and David Rucquoi

Reverend Stephan Bauman, Associate Pastor,
Annunciation church, Longwood, Florida

The Sisters of St. Joseph of St. Augustine

PREFACE

They were all writers. They all kept journals, or at least notes scribbled on loose pieces of paper. In a series of strange events, a stack of worn scribbled hardback journals was placed in my hands. Somehow, a wife, a woman writer herself, researched and found those who had known Andrew LeBoeuf, and who had played a vital role in just the right precise seconds of his life. They offered her all their kept scribbled notes, journals, and verbal memories, all describing a zero event or events in the life of this one evolved man. Some journals were fat, some in dialogue, others simply a description of someone who had lost his way, a boy who married young, too quickly entered the privilege of fatherhood.

After years of denying his enchantment, his world falls apart. He falls completely with it.

According to his wife, through divine promptings he chose to follow, he found even more meaning to life than he'd ever known. His wife, a former nun, insisted their story was begging to be told.

As an author, I am fascinated by her vast collection and see it as a rediscovery of my own need to write again. Under her direction, or without it, I settled in to write this emotional narrative. I read and reread their journals and recorded parts that lent truth to the story. It felt like a call to service. A spiritual contact. I allowed my own soul to take charge. I had no idea where it would lead, but hoped that you'd join me in discovering how and why and with whom a man had finally created a life that mattered.

the magic of love is that it finds you, no matter where you are
it'll wrap itself around you, like the light on a distant star
and it'll keep on a-glowin
making one out of every two hearts that cling to each other
that's all it asks of you
that's all it asks of you

~ Charles Mullian
Mount Dora Florida Writers Guild

CONTENTS

PROLOGUE

~Aneesa~

I run down the novitiates' wooden boardwalk stretching over Florida's shimmering St. Lucie River, feeling every one of my twenty-one years, newly clothed in sacred black, far from family, friends, everything familiar. New life awaits me, every heartbeat now in God's embrace.

At dock's end, I settle on sun-drenched wooden planks, my shiny black granny shoes dangle over schools of dancing fish, my white veil blows under the bluest of skies. Giant royal palms pirouette in unison behind me.

I'm so happy to leave the world, to be God's girl forever.

~Andrew~

Doors swung open under relentless razor-wire spun high on prison walls.

Skyline of oaks spread their welcome against the widest of bright skies, mountains of white cottony puffs sailing by. Absurdity behind, streaming sun gels smooth on my face. Blackbird warbles my high-wire song.

Life is re-gifted, new mission awaits.

CHAPTER ONE

End of Sentence

-Andrew-

Fresh Start's small bedroom is a slice of pure blue heaven. The clean white curtain blows freely over a wide window—the room's walls are powder blue, its forgiven solitude, its white painted door that won't slam shut. Can I handle this blessed silence, lost friend of so long ago? The crucifix above my bed stares down on me. It's time to abandon all old bitterness.

I shower and dress in clean second-hand Salvation Army clothes that fellow inmate Ennis had tossed my way. "You'll need better duds if you go looking for work." He laughed. That sure was Ennis, a laugh that never exactly rang true. This inmate knew the miles of walking that lay ahead. "Andy, these leather boots are your size." I'll be sure to keep them going in his name.

Downstairs, a pot of coffee simmers on the front burner. My hand shakes as I pour a fresh cup, everything coming at lightning speed. Look at this kitchen, these appliances, this tiled floor! I butter the burnt toast, spill the soft yellow gel on the floor. *What am I feeding on? Can this be freedom I'm eating?*

I take a seat near a window. One starved cat runs across the lawn from an incessantly barking dog. *You're here, Andrew, for a maximum of ninety days while you look for employment. If that doesn't*

1

work, you're on your own. The manager's meaning suggests I'll be pounding Orlando's streets in true Bumstead. Well, okay, but first I'm gonna treat myself to my dream ever since lockup. I'm heading out—there's an ocean waiting!

I hitch a ride. A baldheaded black man sits behind the wheel. He needs a listener. I put up with the droning, capable after all I took away from those blabbing inmates, just another weird encounter. *Okay*, but now I can begin to handle the unexpected. Finally, his mouth shuts as he lets me off. I put my feet to work the rest of the way.

Florida's ocean waves me a true homecoming. Blue horizon stretches above roaring surf. I can hardly breathe—winds, waves, seagulls—capture me totally. *I'm home!* One bird flies right over my head. I raise my hand to salute. "Hello, flying cousin." Everything I'd ever believed in resides right here, owned by no one. Nature has been waiting for me. I drop to my knees. The ocean's pounding rhythms escort me back to story time with my two kids at the beach. "Daddy! Daddy, read this one!" And so, I read their favorite, *Winnie-the-Pooh.*

> *Christopher Robin came down from the forest to the bridge, feeling all sunny and careless, and just as if twice nineteen* didn't *matter a bit, as it* didn't *on such a happy afternoon, and he thought that if he stood on the bottom rail of the bridge, and leant over, and watched the river slipping slowly away beneath him, then he would suddenly know everything that there was to be known.*

I remain all day, walking the shoreline, picking up shells, dusting them off, throwing them back, wishing my hands held a camera for this perfect sunset. One fisherman on the surf's edge snaps his reel, a familiar Florida sight. Thoughts of that island deliver creepy sadness to my memory. I grab a pebble, rub it, forget what needs to be forgotten, drop it in my pocket.

I curl up behind a grassy dune for the night, with mere geography of blinking stars and the fullest orange moon, glowing dusk. I'm pulled into their light, torching my faith, reminded of an old Jesuit teaching at Georgetown, St. Julian of Norwich: *All is well and all will be well.*

In the morning, waves send salty smells that awaken me. Dancing sea grasses dazzle my entire spirit under rising sunbeams. The beach is empty. No fisherman, not even early risers, nobody. Nobody except swirling sea gulls, hopping sandpipers, and vast swells watering my parched spirit. They send me back to three words I jotted the night before my release, three words to keep pondering until I got them down tight: *Slowly…Steadfastly…Patiently.* Chosen words from every pointed angle of clean crisp breathing. At last. This is what freedom tastes like.

On the highway, I hitch a ride back to Fresh Start, the place where men leaving prison are given a home for at least the time it takes to free themselves for independent living, meaning until they get money dropping into their pockets, find their own shelter, and eke out their own living style.

This time I sit in up front, a two-seater beside a silent old Hispanic, his beard sweeping the steering wheel. He owns a Pinocchio nose, eyes that play sly detective. He doesn't trust me. Of course! I'm only learning to trust myself. I'm not sure of anything, of talking, of asking questions. I'm like foreigner not knowing what to say to strangers I don't yet understand. The open window delivers salty air.

He drops me by a phone booth near a laundromat. The scent of clean clothes perfumes the air. I suck it in, take deep breaths, jangle the few coins in my hand, capture my courage, thumb and finger slide that quarter given me by guard Moses into the phone slot.

"Hello."

"Honey, it's me."

"Daddy! Daddy! Is it really you?"

And there it is—my little girl's squeal.

"Oh, Kelly, I'm out!"

She squeals again and just the sound of her voice floods the memories: my ten-year-old howling after tripping on a backyard wire, how I lifted her close, shushed her sobs, traced my finger down the perfect curve of her bruised cheek: "Daddy's here, honey. Daddy will always be here."

Kelly, my little Jiminy Cricket is a woman now, a strong fighter who from birth battled her shorter leg, her obvious limp, a foot that could not be medically repaired. She battled depression, battled the boys who desired her loveliness, battled her mother.

But never, never did she fight with me. We were buddies from the start. Poetry pals. Even after they escorted me behind bars, my years in the joint produced Kelly's recipes for healing: weekly letters, packages of poetry books, and loaves of my favorite home baked banana bread. Best of all, her words, hard as they were to hear after what I'd done. "Dad...someday, you'll find yourself again, the self that fathered me with so much loving care." More than once, Kelly had insisted that finally a right partner would come along, "a woman you deserve, not like the others, a mature woman who will love you for just who you are."

CHAPTER TWO

To Florida

-Aneesa-

If a chicken dinner landed on our table, it was Mama's singular plan for our dinner. Only twenty-seven years old, she had managed to put up the chicken coop, would daily feed the chickens but this time, she unlatched the backyard coop door behind our tiny grocery on Florida's Highway 17-92. How she did it, I'll never know but she ran after the squawking bird running for its life, grabbed it and held it by its neck, and in a circle above her head twisted and twisted again until its feathered body dropped and lay completely still, eyes closed, breathing no more.

I watched the death of that animal. I was about seven years old and puzzled. I saw how this sweet unassuming young mama who had never raised a chicken or any animal in her life could so easily kill a living thing. I didn't like what I saw but something in me knew she was doing this cruelty to that chicken not only for herself but for us, her family. and so I never cried out.

Our grocery store had just opened its doors to the neighborhood. Daddy's financial adventure now entered Orlando's business community. In that tiny grocery, Mama and Daddy stood on their feet day and night to bring in what profits a young Orlando neighborhood had to offer. That bird Mama had snapped into death

5

was created for our next meal even though the poor chicken had no choice in the matter. Maybe it was because we were hungry for that longed-for taste after eating sparsely, vegetables for lunches and dinners. According to Mama, that meal from a backyard chicken proved the tastiest nourishment we'd enjoyed in a long time. When our hunger had been satisfied that day, I observed how his remaining parts lay quietly on Mama's special wedding platter, having left the life he once knew back within the grocery store's tiny wired fence. Somehow, staring at its lonely remains, I wanted to cry, just like Mama had often done when she thought no one was looking after she left her Paterson home. She missed her home and her Mama in old Paterson, New Jersey.

The year was 1936, and my parents were struggling to build a life in the then-sleepy town of Orlando, Florida. We were a family of five: Mama, Daddy, me, and my baby brother and sister. Daddy had built our tiny home in the back of the store, and only a breezy curtain separated our business store from our home's dwelling.

I can never forget how in those early days before the roof of the two-bedroom home was finished, down it came, a strong thunderous rain literally falling on our sleeping bodies, causing Mama and Daddy first to wonder the cause of the noise but then sleepily jump up, grab us kids, and scoot into the store to hide under the store's defending roof which had been finished weeks before. I have never forgotten that night of the awakening, when my parents had braved sleeping under an open roof and our earth gave us an unforgotten story.

As for the store's beginning financial life, everything in that early investment time was apportioned around a new start. Coffee without cream or sugar, leftovers for dinner, and day old or even more old bread…which is why that chicken had been such a gift to our family's palate. My father never even ordered a newspaper.

Unlike the neighbors who lived on the street behind the store, this kind customer noticed that there was no morning newspaper lying on our store's front step. So he knew how Daddy thickly eyed his morning news when he came in for bread and milk. He kindly passed it pronto onto the store's counter after paying for his groceries. My father smiled his way, happy to have that Orlando *Sentinel* because he always checked the classified ads for real estate opportunities, hoping that a potential piece property might be available for him, that constant brain's dream of owning pieces of Orlando's developing real estate.

Yet, I remember that our Florida's geography at the start of 1936 hadn't been Orlando. Before this newly acquired hometown grocery, our first stop after Paterson New Jersey had been in the then-frontier and wildly wild and even more sleepy town of St. Petersburg, a city that never proved easy for either of my parents. For my father, it happened quickly. To bring in what a local job wasn't delivering, namely a decent weekly check, this prone-to-gambling father took off for the well-established St. Petersburg dog track, night after night, believing a good gamble won would lift the poverty from our early Florida migration. Eventually and sadly, he completely washed away all the money saved in that St. Petersburg bank which had been held in his name. Mama's tears fell easily at his loss, and by the look on his face coupled with empty pockets, he felt deeply the shame of it. No Syrian head of household had ever gambled away the support for his family. Despite a forgiving wife, Daddy blamed himself, promising Mama more than once he'd never gamble again without a backup to cover any loss. And he never did.

With a long goodbye kiss, my father sat behind the old steering wheel of the faded black pickup that had delivered us to this tropical world in these United States, and motored back on Highway 302 to Paterson. Luckily, he regained his silk-twisting job since the factory's foreman had declared my father one of the industry's best twisters. A twister is the person who takes a silk thread and twists it around a wooden pyramid. Daddy could flash those hands as if they were a machine, circling and circling, the fastest twister to earn more money for each pyramid he turned in. His weekly and substantial checks and green bills never failed to be forwarded to Mama who was still in Florida with me, believing now that she had his money in her hands, everything was fine. Sure, she had his money in her pocketbook but not everything was fine. Far from it. For my mother, money wasn't now the issue for the two of us living in that two-story old St. Petersburg stucco home out in a dense wooded area. We were on a dirt road used by very few cars, and far from any St. Petersburg city. What proved most troublesome and challenging were the southern lives of a semitropical Florida, its heat, and bugs, and long various colored rattlesnakes, animals whose aim, it seemed to bother the newly arrived human beings trying to make the wild land habitable.

Day in and day out, we were forced to endure unprecedented heat waves. The Florida sun could have no mercy. Far from city life, and the fact that no air conditioning existed in these early years of the forties. Yet, the most annoying Florida reality was its kindness to the abundant living of giant palmetto bugs that considered our stucco home theirs to enjoy. "Aneesa, we didn't have any bugs in Paterson. Why did your father bring us here? Didn't he realize that Florida was never going to be like Paterson? Our northern weather didn't welcome any kind of insects."

Oh, how often she whined even though I tried to cheer her up. But I didn't like them either and could scream when they ran across my bedroom floor. These big black palmettos roamed our home from every nook and cranny, scurrying across any zig-zag cracks they could find in our wooden floor. Mama would jump, stomp her feet, hoping to scare them back from where they came, but they seemed impervious to her approach. Sometimes she'd swat a couple with a handy dish towel, but usually her nervousness lost her the fight. She'd often and then go into the bedroom and cry. We lived in a hot, buggy house and that was that. The bugs never seemed discouraged. And Mama's favorite room, the kitchen proved their domain. These creatures unashamedly crawled along kitchen counters in open daylight, slept in corner cabinets, and delighted in eating whatever lay on any counter any time of day or night. You'd be crazy to come down for a midnight snack. They had already beat us to it.

The kitchen wasn't the only room these little fighters called home. We found them nesting in bedroom closets, dresser drawers, bathroom, every inhabited place. Mama cried shouting at the world through an open window: "Damn it, Charlie. Bugs are the enemy. We've got your money, but we are still prisoners of this insect city. God help us all."

At night, I'd often pray God, please send *Daddy back home. We need him to swat these bugs.*

But Mama's prayer? "Dear Lord, send me back to Paterson. I'm going crazy. Send my husband home!" Other times my sweet soft-spoken Mama shouted words I knew lived in the category of swear and doom. She was right to curse. Loud and clear one night I heard her from the bathtub. A daddy-long-legs spider had run along the walls close to the rim of the tub, God Himself must have heard her loud cry.

And yet, waiting for Daddy to come home, it was onward to more of wild Florida's challenges, this time it was Florida's reptiles. Everywhere in frontier land, a home existed for free-slithering and mostly unfriendly snakes. No developer's bulldozers existed then to destroy their habitats. No, these, yes beautiful colorful animals lived freely, able to roam where they chose. And our home, it seemed to Mama and me, was a perfect choice.

How often I had watched these fearless and scary animals slither in and out of our living room's open and unscreened windows, sometimes boldly perching and sleeping on the sill! One fell on Mama's head when she opened the front door, sending the frightened snake scurrying as well as causing Mama to scream for every neighbor to come rescue us both.

Despite her prayers, tears, and a neighbor's assurances that she'd be okay, Mama lived constantly terrified in that St. Pete home. Even though I wanted to protect her, I, too, ran when one circled the bathroom's toilet seat sending me screaming like my sweet Mama. I pulled down my panties and did my business by a hidden bush behind the house, a memory that still lives in me.

I don't exaggerate. Snakes defined our St. Petersburg's home and have left me with multiple scary reptile memories. Even recently, many years later, living in Maitland, Florida, I ran when a black snake appeared outside my greenhouse. He saw me, heard me, and slid into the swimming pool. I really panicked then, called my neighbor, but by the time he arrived, the black animal had slithered across the water, out the other side of the pool, and paraded his long body through Mrs. Crosby's yard. I knew we'd both have the story to pitch to each other.

Despite the challenges of bugs and snakes, something in my grown up self can't help but love Florida's tropical scenes. I often watch queen palms lifting their arms high to the tip of existing air, wind rustling my black curls as it rustled through their long branches. I often sit and listen to the warbling songbirds building their nests close by. Having a garden, I've discovered colorful blooms living with what many call uninvited wildflowers. Florida's natural look of the green landscape and above, giant bursts of the whitest swelling clouds filled its ardent blue skies and nestled deep into my heart. I became and have forever been a Florida girl. I've loved it here, glad that the religious community I would one day join was mainly blooming in Florida. My state wasn't complicated then, just full of wild nature.

In God's strange way of changing what couldn't be tolerated any longer, that tiny black creature that slept peacefully by Mama's pillow altered our Florida geography forever. A skinny black snake broke my mother's sense of competence and obedience to her loved husband. She pulled out paper and pen and wrote to my father the shortest stamped letter she'd ever penned. *Charlie, come home now or I'll take Aneesa and we'll hitchhike back to Paterson.*

As for this father of mine, he chose to remain in Florida despite the heat, snakes, and constant presence of bugs. He knew there were financial opportunities to be had in undeveloped Florida. He moved us to Orlando where some close Syrian friends lived and invited my parents to join them. For Daddy, he'd heard many Floridians speak that there was valuable land to be had in this tropical state, and piles of money to be made. When Disney announced a presence in Central Florida, he saw the state's constant rising of buildings, hotels, and soon theme parks, now that the invention of air conditioning had created numerous construction of neighborhoods. Two lane roads changed to four, vacant lands proved less and less vacant, and all sorts of encouraging commerce streamed and flourished. It seems that over the years, that old saying never proved truer: "Florida was for sale."

This man from Syria, my young father, saw Florida ripe for growth. His immigrant's vision never included an eight-hour shift of twisting strands of silk during the Great Depression in a drafty Paterson, New Jersey factory. No, no! Too easy! Too ordinary! When he had stepped off a New York ocean steamer at Ellis Island to leave Syria's poverty behind, he didn't have a clue how success could happen for him, but somehow and somewhere down deep brimmed a kind of upward mobility that included success. He was ready! The so-called American dream was alive with possibilities living in his soul.

The dream really began before the 17-92 Highway grocery, when my gambler father rented a small filling station on Orlando's Nebraska Avenue. We settled in the one back room that served as bedroom, kitchen, and bath. Serving up gas? My father? Never—but now, he'd learn about anything that would launch his own upward mobility.

For customers, he'd pitch that nozzle into a car's gas tank and serve up that liquid to any drive-in passenger. He'd take the money inside to Mama where she tended a kind of bread-and-milk grocery, a few canned goods, an early kind of convenience store. Everything was changing: a brother was born in that house on Nebraska. In that tiny store, Mama would pull out her breast, nurse baby brother and sister, cradle them to her chest and then quietly lay them back under the store's counter if a customer walked in. There was no stopping the process. A simple loaf of bread and a bottle of milk kept her busy.

In that little "convenience" store, profits built up along with high hopes, that hard work would really pay off.

In that time of the filling station business when it seemed every appliance was outside and despite their smoking habit, Mama watched closely over me. She had warned me not to get too close to that running washing machine and dryer. Somehow, I was engaged by the sounds made by the old-fashioned washing appliance running strong, watching the ringers turn and turn. I teased those ringers with my fingers when suddenly the plastic rollers teased me, caught my hand and my right arm between them. My arm continued to roll upward, the ringers pressing and squeezing it higher until I screamed as I was caught in its cycle: "Mama! Mama…" my scream attracted customers rushing to my rescue. But it was my mother's love and savviness that shut the machine, and just as quickly settled me and my broken arm into the passenger seat of our old brown Plymouth and drove us both north to an emergency doctor at a Florida Hospital. Never did I hear her loudly pray so passionately.

Dr. Johnson strapped a binding white cast on me with a reminder to be "grateful to God that I hadn't lost that arm." That right arm endured the cast and freed my hands to begin one day learning a piano's keyboard. Sometimes accidents are incomprehensible at first but reveal something else. A mother's love? A doctor's skill? A child's ability to heal? All part of every experience, more beautiful than any words can describe.

Years roll by, and that gas station/grocery became so popular that the filling station's beady-eyed landlord noted my father's success. Naturally, he desired the profit for himself and it wasn't long before my father got notice he was being evicted. *Not fair!* Mama cried again. But that reality of being kicked out of this place soon revealed another piece of my father's dream of the mythic American dream.

One night after the delivery of that note, Dad closed the store. My father, unable to sleep, jumped into the black pickup that had first brought us to Florida. He drove along Orlando's Highway 17-92, his dry eyes searching for something to take away the pain. The moon was high and bright, the street empty of cars, and my dad uttered childhood prayers as he drove asking God to direct him with a Divine plan.

And there it was! A tiny white sign staked in the ground capturing the light of the golden moon. That little sign was situated between giant orange groves on either side. On that glowing sign was the Divine message he'd been praying for and it said two heavenly words: "For Sale!"

That Divine message jerked his car to a full stop. He raced to it, got down on his knees in front of that sign. He told me later how he had looked up to God's moon with prayer bursting from his heart: "Oh God, send me this land and I will never fail to remember your goodness." Whether he kept that promise is not clear, but many times later, when I wore the black habit of the Sisters of St. Joseph, he'd send a check to the motherhouse in honor of that Orlando night when that white sign changed our life's direction.

In the morning, he petitioned the bank president of Orlando's First National Bank to give him the needed loan and whatever this five-foot-two, bald Syrian immigrant said to the bank's president, he got that money. Charles Haddad owned his first piece of Florida.

Soon the vacant lot felt that hard cement of four concrete walls rising upon it and a roof over its grassy plot on Highway17-92. Haddad's Market was born between rows of sweet-smelling blossoming orange trees, a fragrance that wafted into the completed store as the air inside was powered around by paddled ceiling fans.

Four glass grocery store doors opened in the forties, and our family lived for more years than I can remember in the four rooms my father built in the back of the store. The store behind which my mother had gone into the chicken coup and captured our first chicken dinner in months launch my parents into the American dream.

Since the Great Depression of the twenties had lingered in many parts of Florida, it fueled the custom of offering credit. Haddad's market was no exception. People promised to pay for the groceries at a later date. Mama kept a big red ledger under the counter to record every grocery debt. I remember Mrs. Murphy and also Mrs. Calhoun thanking my mom for her trust in them. They trusted my parents and my parents trusted them to eventually pay up. As my mother reported smiling, most of them did pay up and became the store's friends on a first-name basis.

Standing behind that counter hours and more hours, Mama said to me when I commented: "Don't look, honey." She hated the blue lines protruding on her legs attesting to those unrelenting hours on her feet behind that grocery counter or putting up stock on the rows of shelves. When I consider all the labor her body endured, I'm filled with loving warmth for this Syrian mother stacking vegetable cans onto grocery shelves, sweeping the cold stone floor, filling the empty wire bins from huge dusty sacks of potatoes, keeping the books for tax purposes, ordering shipments of wine and beer, and still forever able to joke with salesman. *How did you do it, Mama?*

Not only did she slave behind the counter, she'd walk to help customers. When the clock struck food time, she'd run upstairs afterward to prepare her Middle Eastern meals we couldn't get enough of, plus baking loaves of Syrian bread to last the week.

Then, late into the night, she'd sit at the old Singer sewing machine making our school clothes. Again, I wonder: *Where did you get that energy, Mama?*

One customer commented years later: "Aneesa, your mother was the unsung astronaut in your father's climb to the moon."

Here lies the final glory of my father's American Dream. Haddad's profits allowed him to buy various kinds of developing Orlando property. Gambling instincts had him laying down enough money to claim a small Clermont orange grove, part of Florida's giant citrus business which according to my mother, he knew nothing about. Yet this risk taker hit it big, sold his acre of fruitful trees and banked $8,000—more profit than he'd dreamed of pocketing.

With that success, a few years later, he picked up another empty plot on Orlando's trafficked highway, Colonial Drive, Florida's east-to-West highway. That six-acre purchase turned out to be my father's biggest gambling success. In 1956, his well-placed six acres magically sat across from what was destined to become the first 2,000-square-foot mall below the Mason Dixon Line. The construction of Colonial Plaza meant that my father had hit the big time, a kind of lottery win. Now, he was offered more piles of fortune. I'd never seen this Syrian father so buoyant, so jolly, so grateful. "Life" he beamed, "is now the reality I dreamed it could be!"

All joyous? Little did this entrepreneur father suspect that what lay ahead would be that his favorite daughter, who once sat on his knee reciting the Lord's prayer in Arabic for his Syrian friends, would choose to become a nun—a Florida Sister of St. Joseph—and break his heart. His twenty-one-year-old daughter would take a path away from his financial heart. He had beat many odds, but not the one he never even considered: his daughter would never be fashionably dressed and head of his company, but instead, a woman wearing only somber black and veil, opening a wound in him that never healed.

CHAPTER THREE

Trees and Streets, Back to Bars

-Andrew-

I order a cup of coffee, slip three packets of sugar into the cup's steaming brew, pour cream into it, stir the white plastic spoon around, lift the cup to sip slowly. Alone, so alone, as thoughts push through, run wild: Shall I, according to Kelly's advice, not tell the owner I'm just out of prison. Her words linger as I sit watching others enjoying a breakfast, chatting non-stop with companions. I wanted to be in that place, wanted to be just an ordinary guy having breakfast with friends. But I was an ex-con, alone, needing a job, without much hope getting one.

"Dad, a prison record isn't going to open any doors. Don't tell them." *Don't tell them? That ain't me, Kelly. I need to tell them if I'm going to work for them. Haven't I always been truthful about most things, even when the truth hurt?*

Finally, boss man sits down, a kindly looking old guy. Totally gray, eye half closed, big hand extends to shake mine before we exchange names, "So how can I help you, sir?"

Sir? He calls me sir?

"First, thanks for this opportunity to respond to that sign you have in the window. I'm not new at waiting tables. I waited tables to get me through college, pretty good at it too. I'd like to work for you here." The old man listened as I plunged ahead with my life, ignoring Kelly's warning. "You need to know sir, that I've spent some time in prison."

I watch his quick-changing expression, not sure what it might mean. He turns, talks to one of his waitresses, "Bring this guy another cup of coffee."

Somehow, I knew: *I'd lost my chance.*

There are things about every job that no one likes. I could tell by the sadness in his eyes that this guy didn't appreciate turning me away. "Son, you're a convicted felon. I've had three of your kind in here this past month. Maybe you're different. Even so, why would I have an MBA graduate waiting tables here. I'm sorry." He shakes my hand again as he gets up, leaves the table and the waitress brings me that second cup of coffee with a knowing smile making me want to crawl under the table.

A gust of wind whips around my face as I'm back on the street, feeling rotten, confused. Damned. It's quite clear, Kelly's on target. Restaurant bosses don't hire ex-felons. I find a phone, call her with my last nickels, give her the scoop.

"Dad, I tried to tell you. You're over-qualified. Okay, at the same time, you're under-protected. Who wants an ex-professor or ex-con working in their place? You gotta stop telling them your background!"

Kelly's advice was like that of Sister Dolores, a nun from St. Patrick's convent, who for years ministered to men and women coming out of prison. "Andy, you can't tell them about your prison time. Make up something. Tell them you've been in Europe. Anything. I wish it weren't so, but employers aren't trusting any guy who's been behind bars."

Okay, so what now? Back at my Fresh Start bedroom, I stare at the framed picture of a gray-bearded man with a message for the room's current occupant. I let him stare me down. I think of Sister Dolores: "The Lord has forgiven you, Andy you've got to forgive yourself."

Time finally runs out. Of course, I had to leave this place. No money in my pocket. No job on the horizon. And strangely enough, I didn't feel depressed. Somehow, I managed to enjoy my last Fresh Start night, all blessed and quiet time in that soft bed. But my time had been cooked.

That was the deal, wasn't it Andrew? I stare up again at those intense eyes of the beaded old man in that picture above my bed. He was…well, I don't know if he was applauding me or bemoaning my luck. I couldn't help but glance his way as I packed my few belongings. Suddenly, did I hear it? Did he say it? *Let it be. You can take it.* Something strong grabbed at me as I walked out that door for the last time not knowing what kind of future I could invent with God's help. Out the front door and my mind won't let me go.

You bet I can take it. I spent seven years in the joint. I endured stretched hikes up and down Florida following Gerta's blink and my breakdown, while total possession ruled. Oh yes, these soles and heels won't let me down. I can take anything.

Homeless! That's what they choose to call living on the street. I choose to call it urban camping, living outside at last, where trees soar to the sky and wildflowers serve up color to open eyes.

Truth is I never begged, or even found myself hungry on Orlando's streets. Soup, potato pancakes, meat loaf in blessed church hall, breakfast in Sally's cafeteria, sandwiches at the Coalition kept us going. Okay, maybe no regular roof over my head or mattress to welcome me at night. But when it came to hunger, whoever experiences that craving in benevolent Orlando must know the saying that travels along the well-heeled streets, a saying that carries plenty of weight. *Starving in Orlando's all about suicide. There's always enough food somewhere.*

What homelessness delivered was pure calamity, for nothing I did except getting out of the rain and into a church that one time when unexpected flashes of lightning blazed from every inch of a darkened sky. It was as if the devil was after my skin, that all the good behavior I'd exhibited since getting out of the joint was for naught. It proved the meanest shower that sent me tumbling.

I'd begun my morning stroll, when Orlando's downtown was suddenly taking it on the chin. Flooding rivers rushed through bricked streets like a speeding train. I pulled my threadbare jacket tighter, ran for cover in St. James Church by the post office where I attended daily Mass.

Soaking, but finally under the building's canopy, I noticed the church door slightly ajar. How well I remember my thought— *Why not enter?* Pews are empty, altar silent, sanctuary light casting shadows on St. Joseph's statue.

I wet my fingers from the holy water font, make the sign of the cross, genuflect, and dash up the marble back steps, two at a time, blessed to be out of the downpour. High up, I kneel at the rim of the choir loft, lower my head in thanksgiving, when suddenly a screaming siren fills the flung-open doors below. Church's ceiling bulbs flick bright light over the entire structure. Two yelping black Dobermans race up the stairs, slide to a stop at my elbow. Both fix a no-nonsense gaze on me. A uniformed cop in hot pursuit behind that barking dog is yelling, "Get him, doggies! Get him!" Dog closest pounces, attaching his jaws to my arm. Eyeball to eyeball we stare in a paralyzing moment. Dogs have always been my friends, having more pets than I can remember, loving each one, mourning the loss when one was either lost or had to be put down. This time, with this Doberman, I look directly into his eyes, we make a real connect. "Hey buddy, it's okay. I ain't going anywhere." This guy's considerably cooler than that yelling uniform making its way up the stairs, the muscled one frothing at the mouth.

"Who is it?"

A familiar voice calls from below. I recognize the shuffling feet slowly ascending the steps. I breathe a sigh of relief—Father McClean. Finally. *You tell 'em…*

"Father, it's me—Andrew. Church door was open. I got out of the storm." For some reason, he doesn't look my way. *But he knows me.*

I raise my voice: "Father, tell 'em. I'm the one who helps you after Mass." It isn't me but the voice of the piping cop to whom he's paying attention.

"Listen, Father, if you don't press charges, we can't keep running to the church every time we hear an alarm."

At that, my kindly old priest who'd so welcomed me to his church knowing I lived on the street, now gazed my way as if I were a stranger. *Can he be doing this?* Unbelievably he assigns my life back into the hands of the state: "Take him."

I'm handcuffed, shoved down the stairs, cop's hand on my head, pushes me into the police van. Motor starts up, sirens blaze, I'm hauled off to Orange County Jail. I don't speak a word. I know what's coming. They call my probation officer—Hardcastle. He too blames me with no trace of familiarity.

"The priest accuses you of stealing from the poor box."

"Steal? Me, the guy who puts coins there in whenever I can? Listen, Hardcastle, maybe I'm a crazed murderer, but I ain't no thief."

"Sure, sure. Tell it to the judge."

Kelly couldn't believe it. Sent back to Florida jail for who knew how long to await judge's hearing in Orlando? To be tossed in again with a roomful of babblers circling the cold cement floor, steel bars banging nonstop, the assault of MTV still blaring a decade following my first nightmare months of lockup.

Eighteen months later, yes eighteen months of non-stop crazy blabbering, the Judge dismisses the whole thing. And now, I sit under an oak, feeling lost all over again. Kelly's letter brings a smile. *Dad, I'm going after McClean. That's one dirty priest.*

Soon enough, I'm back walking the streets. My feet hurt, but no stopping the sidewalk trails. Under trees, I find park benches, take a load off the limbs, rest a while until a cop or a non-stop talker leads me to push away, push on, find someplace where my soul can walk in peace.

I ease myself into downtown Orlando's spacious library, once again letting books fill my days, my hours, my hope. I open mail from my post office box, glad to have squeezed enough cash from labor pool paychecks to invite mail into my world. Happily, this time, there's a letter from angel sister Sarah, who hadn't hesitated to offer her own counseling after this latest debacle.

"Get therapy, Andy. David Stewart is the best, no cardboard therapist. He just moved down from New York to Orlando. Bernard and I will foot the bill. I want my old brother back." He wasn't far—right down there near Orlando's Lake Eola where a geyser shoots up a stream of water a mile high.

I find his office, my left hand holding tight that pebble I retrieved from the ocean's edge. That little hidden stone had lived in my pocket all these past crazy months.

David Stewart opens his door with a smile that takes me in, his light blue shirt, maroon tie, dark pants, casually professional. I liked his grip and his offer of a cup of coffee.

In the weeks that follow, I script the autobiography of my life, each visit revealing stuff I hadn't thought possible to share with anyone. It was easy with David; his direction and warmth opens me up. Sarah was right on.

After a few sessions, he surprises me: "I've been thinking. Andy, you've got a story to tell. You may think you're alone out here, but you're a pioneer. You're a survivor. Survival is a subject that can't be told often enough. Everybody rejoices hearing a story about overcoming guilt." He walks around his desk, stands by the window. "In telling it, you'll be better able to identify just what went wrong."

"Tell my story, David? Tell it over again for others. How I killed a woman who certainly never even had it coming? How I found myself occupied by her just the same, swept up with powers I sure didn't want, didn't ask for? How I—my very self—disappeared in the process? How I tried to end my own life?" For the first time, my confusion wouldn't let go. Completely open to him, I wrestled with it all, my darkness, my questions, my losses wouldn't stop pouring out to this man who'd been a good counselor for me.

David moves closer to the wide window where Lake Eola's fountain continues to spray gallons into Orlando's beautiful blue sky. He remains there, and I'm grateful for the silence. Finally, he turns back to me:

"Yes, Andy, you must tell everything. You tell it, not just for others, either, but for yourself. For it's clear to me, dear man, that every one of us can be smashed to bits, boiled down to nothing, but there always exists the opportunity to bounce back, to learn, to grow, to become who you really can be." He didn't stop, and I gave him my full attention. No one, not even that prison psychologist who finally let me go seemed to care like David.

"Andrew. put your pen to paper. Write more poetry. What did you do with your poems? Go back there again. You know how it all started. Your pen will tell you."

At that, it begins to rain a hard rain. Outside, sheets of water pelt the glass. I feel the chill. David pours a second cup of coffee.

"God, David, nice pen idea but where do I start?"

He sits back behind his desk: "Start with your mother, Andy. You repeatedly speak of her. What about her letters? Why not start there?"

This is the letter that I found and read to David:

> *Andrew, in Belgium, 1938, you bounced into this world, yes bounced. You were a moving baby and I had to be alert to make sure you'd never fall. Mornings,*

I'd rock you on that back porch facing the Belgian blooming and always lively colorful forest. Years later, I'd sing Nat King Cole's lyrics to you. They sure came later at our place on America's Lake Rippawam. That was your song and I couldn't help but sing it to you:
There was a boy, a very strange enchanted boy.
They say he wandered very far, very far
Over land and sea...
And the greatest thing
You'll ever learn
Is to love and be loved in return.

"Good going, Andrew," David commented later. "I know that King Cole song. Yes, keep her going!"

"Oh, David! Mom had no idea how far I'd wander. Glad she wasn't alive to see my complete destruction." *Mom's letters? Sure, her writing was always key.*

"David, when I think about Mom, her life was up and down, moving from the States to Europe, then to the Congo, then back to the States, lugging her kids while her husband practiced civil engineering at global heights. It ain't no story; you're talking soap opera! Want to hear more?"

Andy, in 1939, after your first birthday, it was the Nazis who marched across Europe, aiming for Belgium. Jean Luc immediately took charge and shipped us out on the Normandy to America. I admit the tears, plenty of them as I had to let go things that had become so precious to me. Good-bye, Bonne Terre, our beautiful estate and Belgian forest. Good-bye colorful rocking chair that I was saving for your playtime. Bye-bye white-flowered crib, all family crystal, and precious old-world tapestries hanging in the back parlor. German Shepherd Misty knew we were leaving. That dog would sit in that corner looking at me and wouldn't come out. Perhaps I was too attached to secular possessions, but I didn't care. These were beautiful things of the earth and I'd grown to love them.

Yet, there was that bigger pain I carried with me. I hesitate to tell you, but always at home were tensions. From the beginning, your father, Jean Luc failed to sing your praises, rarely held you or rocked your cradle. I was at a loss about what to do. That coolness of my Luc toward my boy shoved a two-edged sword into my heart. My courage wasn't there. I couldn't discuss it with my husband. I knew he loved me, adored me, but sadly, very little love toward you.

"David, I don't have a word about where to start with my father."

David lay his hand on my shoulder, quick to reply: "Andrew, start with a happy memory. Let that be your cue to take you where life has led you."

"A happy memory? It's the Belgian Congo. Sure, I'll start with my never-to-be-forgotten friend, Moké."

CHAPTER FOUR

Choosing to Blossom

-Aneesa-

Years can never erase the image of Mama, a former beautician, who periodically sat me on the toilet top seat in our home's tiny bathroom to style my black and long naturally curly hair. She loved my locks, often grabbed her comb to groom them before rushing downstairs to open the grocery's front doors. Mama was a small woman, plump and totally motherly with a knack for treating customers to a sometimes-motherly experience when it came to grocery shopping.

She had been a graduate of one of Paterson's prestigious beauty schools. She especially loved naturally curly hair, and my hair was her delight. Usually, she just combed it, but if needed, she'd clip the long curls to shoulder length, her fingers twisting each ringlet around her finger. I think that's why I've always been so attached, maybe too attached, to my hair, wanting it to be just right before going out. You can imagine how I hated giving it up when I put on that religious headpiece and black serge gown.

"You're so lucky, honey to have naturally curly hair. Your father is bald and I had just plain straight locks." I loved being with her, loved the feel of her fingers pulling on my ringlets, shaping each strand. Afterward, when she'd let me stand behind the counter to ring up a total on our cash register, I thrilled hearing customers' compliments of my hair. Hair was a vital shared pleasure. Daddy's jealousy reflected that Mama and I had such a close relationship around my curls. He had lost whatever hair when only nineteen years old.

That's why I hated seeing those black curls scattered on the wooden floor of our St. Petersburg home when I was only about six years old. Looking through old photos, I found a picture of my curls, wisps strewn here and over there. I knew it had been me who had cleverly cut off those curls no longer hanging from my head. Those were the curls that Mama had loved. I stared long at that photo's unhappy memory.

I had to turn the page, not wanting to see what I had done, how I knew I'd hurt this mother deeply who saw my hair as a gift she considered from God Himself. I turned back the page, looked harder at the tragedy I had created, seeing the evidence at how a six-year-old had found her mother's scissors and chopped off all her black ringlets. Why? Did I even think about what Mama called, this gift of God? Probably not. Yet, why would I have done such a mean thing to a mother who had never hurt me in any way? I find no answers. As for the picture, I have no idea who snapped it. But more to the point, in that moment, I wanted her sweet presence back, her giving smile. I wanted to hug her, plead for forgiveness because I knew, even in those youthful years, I'd hurt her. I sit pensively and wonder if sometimes the heart, how even a child's heart, can fall into such a mean-spirited place.

The memory brings back the sound of the front door unlocking and Mama appearing. I was small enough to find a hiding place behind the two-seat sofa. I knew she'd see my curls all over the floor. I'd have to face her without ringlets hugging my head, without her artful and proud creation. I remember peeking from behind that tiny sofa to witness her startled eyes, her shock, and then her tears.

She began sobbing and stood still while focusing for the longest time on what I'd done.

I will finish the story but as I write these memories out on the back porch of our home in our old Florida town, I'm happily loving the beginning of a long-awaited autumn. I'd been waiting for the cool breezes that were now blowing over me and my computer. What richness can be felt when a memory, even a sad one, fails to dampen the present moment. No tears want to come, no blame surges forward, only the sweetness of recording what has been part of a past life, both the joys and the sorrows, the real life now never feeling punished by a former mean behavior. But no more. Back to story.

At seeing the work that I'd done, that mother of mine got on her knees, bending over to push her fingers gently, gathering every black strand. She scooped them together, cupped them tenderly onto a small side table by the window, all the while sobbing as if someone mean-spirited and hated had shaved off her own hair. I stood out, ready to take what she had discovered inside me, my flagrant disregard for her love of my hair. She saw me, could hardly speak, then cried even louder: "Aneesa, Aneesa. Why, oh why, why did you do that? Cut off your beautiful curls?"

The God in Heaven knew that was a question I'd often asked my students years later in a Catholic classroom when they, in a sense, "had committed disruptive misbehavior." They'd come back with that same answer I gave my mother: "Sister, I don't know" or in my case, "Mama, I don't know." I couldn't help but break into my own tears. It took only a minute but she tenderly took me into her arms and my tears mingled with her own. Together we sat on that sofa and let the grief of that hurtful issue wash over us and eventually out.

"It's okay, honey. Your curls will grow back."

Only after her death, did I find every strand pressed in the pages of her journal. Those strands of hair were still curly and black, unlike my gray head today. Still, finding those saved curls causes me to again wonder why I did that to her. No answers frame my mind and sometimes I believe even God has no answers to why we do some of these things.

Whatever the hidden reason, it gave me a story that floods back years later when I entered the Sisters of St. Joseph novitiate in Jensen Beach, Florida. Sure, I knew that like all nuns then, I'd lose my naturally curly hair. They'd take scissors and shave it away and I'd be almost bald like my father. In place of shaved hair, I'd be required to don a convent's black headpiece and veil that would always blow in the wind when I walked out there by the St. Lucie's river edge. I remember the day. I headed with the other postulants outside for our first haircut that initial week of entrance into convent life. I'd get a style never shaped by love, never trimmed by a loving Mama standing in a tiny bathroom clipping away the length of my black curls. No, this convent haircut would be performed outside unceremoniously on a spacious green lawn before the unknowing flowing St. Lucie River.

I sat in a straight-back walnut chair under a Florida sun, warm and infectious, shining calmly on both my haircutter, Sister Violetta, and myself. She had been appointed my "stylist." Thank goodness, I liked her, always seemed to possess a friendly smile. I sat still, feeling her long-handled scissors pruning away every strand of hair I'd treasured since forever, one chop after another, each ringlet descending until all God's gifts as Mama had taught me, lay on a white sheet below, black on white, a hint of death to the world that I had enjoyed. Something in me was happy that Mama living in Orlando, wasn't there to see "her" curls drop.

When Sister Violetta and all novices including Mother Mary had left the outdoor scene, I bent low, bundled the strands as mama had once done so long ago, held them close to my heart as if in an act of prayer. If my curls had been a gift from God as Mama always said, I wanted to be grateful for the years I'd enjoyed them.

I walked to the river's edge under that sun, stood before the waters a long while, and watched dolphins leaping in and out of the current. I had to swallow, filled with such confused emotion. After all, my hair, as with so many women, had been part of my identity, so many of my former high school and college friends labeling me lucky to enjoy the simplest of curly hairdos, never a perm or stylist needed.

Now, standing before that permanent horizon, loving the view of swelling white bouncing clouds moving with the tide, I felt God was holding these black remnants as well. I found strength in breathing, brought on by the sadness of saying goodbye to my black wavy treasure, and wondered if even a kind of anger was evident in Sister Violeta's convent scissors.

Suddenly, above the rippling current, in the clouds, there she was: Mama's smiling face on a quiet white one, colorful reassurance that all was well. "Oh, Mama," I shouted aloud to that image, "You forgave me that time, didn't you?"

I lifted my arms and tossed the bundle of God's black gifts into the river aware of passing on a vital piece of what had been my life.

Silly as it may sound, losing my hair proved a powerful moment then and a powerful moment now as I write these memories of my early convent days, bringing me back to a loving mother, to her smile, to ringlets, to the rivers of my new life, all evidence of a forgiveness unfelt until now in this telling of the hair story. Amen, God, Amen.

I want to include here a story about my father as well, and a memory that shaped my love for him even more. In the fourth grade at Orlando's Hillcrest Grammar School right off Highway 17-92, on weekdays I'd walk to school and home with a girlfriend whose name I can't remember. All I know is that she and I created a story that gave me a deeper love for my father.

On that day after school, both our two feet walked us home together under Florida's sun. I remember my sweater's arms tied around my waist as the afternoon heat beat down on us. As well as I can remember, no cars were stopped at the red light, at the corner where the Standard Oil filing station flashed its gas prices. We both caught sight of the candy bars stuffed in the giant rounded glass jars sitting on a shiny red Coca-Cola cooler. One of us suggested, and I can't remember who, that it would be easy to steal a couple of those appealing chocolate bars.

Now the truth must be obvious that my parents owned a grocery store. In that store were racks of candy bars and, if I asked my parents for one, I could easily enjoy a sweet taste of Hershey's or a Black Cow taffy bar. They rarely said "no" to me. So here, a mile away, on a Florida highway sidewalk, something in me, something I can't name, wanted this owner's candy bars and with this friend, was willing to steal them.

Our plan arranged for me to stand guard at the traffic corner while she'd run up to the containers on the red Coca-Cola machine in front of the station, grab two Black Cows and meet me back at the corner.

Yum—good. Taffy melted in our mouths as we strolled home, cars racing past, orange groves on both sides of the street were the only witnesses to our theft. For days, we sucked and chewed and enjoyed our after-school candy bars. I wonder now, didn't I never suspect we'd get caught?

Well, at the sight of my father at grocery store's front doors, I realized I was found out. Unlike his usual warmth welcoming me home, a wide scowl and his order, get into the car. That let me know our theft had been discovered.

Terror drove me in that passenger seat as my father pulled up to the candy gas station. The owner, a gray-haired man, dressed in blue dirty overalls, came out, stood at dad's window, looked over to see me huddled as far away from them both as possible. What was coming came gently with a force that simply slumped my dad hard behind that wheel. "Yes, sir," he said, as he pointed at me. "That's her. She's the one."

I'd never seen my father so low, so hunched, so unable to look at the owner directly. No friendly father now. This act by his disobedient thieving daughter was personal, a wound, Mama told me later, to his heart, a betrayal.

I stared out my window, unable to hold the pee escaping into my panties.

"Please sir," my father pleaded. "Don't send her to reform school."

Reform school? Did I hear right? Was that the punishment meted out for a ten-year-old who stole candy bars? Or was my father trying to scare me? If the truth be told, not reform school, but my Syrian father had been trained to believe physical punishment cured a child of any misbehavior. This time, I'd receive the spanking of my life, one I'd never forget.

Riding back home, the only sound in the car was the motor and my uncontrollable sobbing, not because I'd stolen candy, but because of the approaching spanking.

My father finally broke our silence in a voice that was shaking as if he too wanted to cry: "Aneesa, don't we have enough candy in the grocery? Don't I say yes when you ask if you can have a candy bar. Doesn't Mama say yes? Did you have to steal?"

Stealing to my father was the giant sin. He once told me what his own father in Syria had told him: "Son, no matter how hungry you are, no matter that no one's is around, never steal. You think nobody sees you but God sees you."

Finally, the brown 1943 Plymouth swerves into the store's driveway and Daddy turns off the motor. He says nothing more, leaves me, his eldest child paralyzed, out of control. I watch him as he drags his body back to the store's meat station where he daily stands on sawdust, cutting portions of meat, smiling to every customer he serves, a resolved business.

I stay for a long while in the car, my body shaking until I get out, climb up our back stairs, sit on the bed waiting, knowing daddy would come up the stairs, show me how angry he felt, that his religion of honesty had been blasphemed. His hard slaps would cure me from ever stealing again.

Time passed. I couldn't help the sobbing, fearful, terrorized, waiting, and waiting some more until I felt the truth of what was ahead, a sharp bolt of disbelief. My father wasn't climbing any stairs. He wasn't coming. He wasn't going to whip me. I would not be physically harmed and I didn't know what to do with my disbelief. All I did was sit and sit some more with that new awareness. And cried.

Mama found me upstairs: "You hurt your father because you stole more than candy. You stole his belief in himself, his ability to teach you the ethics of right from wrong. I know you'll never steal again."

Through the years, I hold deep in my heart the truth that I had wounded my father far more than he ever could have wounded me. We didn't speak of it again, although when I asked for a piece of candy, a chocolate bar, there was a knowing look in his eyes when he said "Okay." Some chapters in a family history we never forget. And maybe we're not supposed to forget…ever.

CHAPTER FIVE

Congo to Bingo

-Andrew-

In the Belgian Congo, a tall and very black Moké was our houseboy whose duties included sweeping the house, running errands for chef Butte, and always being on call for any member of the family. I was eight and never knew how old Moké might be but he was my best friend. We chatted a lot, all in French. So much so I was soon to forget all my English.

I loved that dark skin of Moké's that gleamed in the steaming sun as we walked different Congo paths together. His snow-white teeth would shine when he smiled! And he smiled more than anyone I knew, even more than Mom. He had brains and a ton of love to give us all. His mother even said so that time she brought Mom special herbs she'd grown for her recipes.

During the day, Moké and I would roam the wild Congo River's shores, taking in the musty riverbank's jungle odors. I loved the river's ability to send pungent whiffs crisscrossing into our nostrils. I'd pick up its jungle droppings and carry them to our chef for his newly planted greens. It was "our best fertilizer" Mom said. She scattered those droppings around her propped up tomatoes. And if I remember correctly, our tomatoes were the biggest, ripest, juiciest, better than any tomatoes sold in grocery stores.

Ours wasn't a big house in the Congo, yet a bundle of natives worked for my family. We seemed able to have all those black people tending to Mom and Dad's every need. Besides Moké and our chef, the yardman Kin kept the grounds. A host of others I can't even remember reported to my father. You can say that we were the colonials and the natives were there to serve us. At least that's what Dad thought and often said.

One day Moké heard my sisters Penny and Sarah screaming. He dashed to their room and soothed the jitters out of the wriggling snake dancing on their bed. "Petit *ami*, you want home?" The skinny Congo creature circled around Moké's stick as he lifted it, the snake's eyes watching the girls huddled in a corner. Moké laughingly aimed for the door: "I take him to happier hunting place."

I watched as he gently slid the creature down onto its grassy home, and as it did what snakes always do, wiggled away, happy to be where it belonged.

One day, out near the Congo's rapids, Moké held his homemade spear high like an Olympic athlete. I watched him waiting patiently for a fin to show in the gushing spray. Moké finally spots a Cichlid, one of the Congo's best known delicious fish. The fish spins toward me. Moké cries out: "Andrew, it takes two to catch one. Get your stick in water, shake hard, push the animal to me like he is a cow. I get him up here."

"Moké, are you sure he's gonna obey?"

"Hey man, he fish. You gotta think like fish."

I followed Moké's orders. I shook my stick and quick as a flash, *whack!* I barely saw Moké do it.

Hours later, the cichlid lay stiff and browned on our dinner table. As usual, Dad sliced the portions, while Mom, wanting praise for me and Moké from the head of the house, reminded my father: "Moké caught this fish. He is smart, Jean Luc. He caught that fish with his own carved spear. Let's register him in St. Michel with Andrew. With a good French education, he'll be a leader of his people."

Dad's frown was so big it forced his eyebrows to touch. "Please, Ellen. You know St. Michel's not for the natives. We need to provide an education for them, but certainly not in a Belgian school. I don't want to hear any more about this!" I was sure glad Moké wasn't there to hear this from the head of our house. As usual I held my tongue. But just as usual, sister Sarah took up the challenge: "That's so pompous of you, Dad. Look, Moké handles snakes, catches fish better than any white man. He could be taking us to school."

At that, Dad threw his napkin and stared Sarah down until she left the table. I continued to learn there was no way to get around that hard-boiled traditional stance my father held since coming to the Congo. White men considered themselves above the natives, smarter than them, able to teach them, no way to be taught anything by them.

That night, before my bedtime story, I asked, "Mom, why does Dad have to think like that about these people. What gives him the right to act so superior?"

"Andrew, I know it's hard. But after graduating from Louvain and MIT, your father followed your grandfather's footsteps to this Belgian colony. The King commissioned him to set up the Congo's textile mills. Now, hard as many colonials are on these natives, I am proud of your Dad. He generously cares for them in his own way."

I didn't say anything, just crawled under the covers. Speaking against anything Dad did was not *my* way.

Now we were back in America, in Manhattan, so unlike the land of my Congo. Here was the land of commerce, busy city sidewalks, and noisy traffic. Gone were the forests paths, the rivers pushing the water, the trees where I could pick a piece of fruit from a low hanging branch.

I was enrolled in a Catholic grade school and forced to learn English again. Eventually I soaked it up, but grateful for the French that Mom insisted we all speak at home.

The nuns ran the school and truth to tell, I hated all of them except Sister Agatha. Here was a nun I could like, a nun who giggled when anybody in the classroom did something funny. One day, this very plump nun stopped at my desk and picked up my written assignment. I waited while she read it silently. I was scared she'd find something wrong but suddenly, she alerted the class to stop what they were doing and began reading that short account of my Congo days aloud to them. I'd written that account in English, proud that I was learning Mom's native language again. Listening to the English words that had strangely tumbled out of me rather than my French, that long sickness of finding myself back in city-country suddenly turned okay. Maybe school wasn't so bad. That put Sister Agatha on my 'best-liked nuns' list.

Still, so often the Congo's bright shadow lingered in my memory. I missed my Moké, our hikes, our fishing, those swinging, fluid back-and-forth chats. What was worse here were the times my tongue would fail my questioning father, watching his long nose falling out of joint when not hearing my lips say anything, but simply bang up and down without a single word coming forth. I'd stand and feel his anger, see his arms folded tightly against his chest. But I couldn't utter a word, and he never understood that his oldest son could be so handicapped. He'd pass the minutes, eyes glaring waiting for an answer from his tongue-tied offspring perched on the hallowed old-school post of eldest son. Those were the times I wanted to die. Stuttering was like having a noose around my neck, choking the breath out of me, memories I wish I could forget.

The high school days really rocked hard on my soul. High school under Irish Christian Brothers nailed my mouth shut ever tighter, tongue failing to shape expected responses under pressure of a black-robed teacher. How well I remember Brother O'Neil strolling up and down classroom aisles, hands folded behind his back, demanding students reply to his Latin questions. Truth is, I loved that old language. But didn't care for it spoken aloud. Never did I clam up so fitfully as on that unforgotten day.

I stood by my desk trying to release the homework assignment I knew like my own name. Mom had heard me recite it aloud back home, twice in a row. But now, here in these four walls, with a Christian Brother staring me down, I had no voice.

"Mr. LeBoeuf...Mr. LeBoeuf...I'm waiting."

Fellow students turned to stare back at this red-faced dolt. If I could have died, I'd have been happy to climb into any coffin of his choice. The noise was deafening as Brother O'Neil's ruler continued to pound the desk in front of the class as a dire warning.

Tap, tap, tap. "Come on, Danny Boy, we haven't got all day!"

All day? All week won't deliver a sound out of my stuck lips.

"Le Boeuf, not doing your homework in my class, you know what's awaiting you. Okay, sonny! Outside."

Now his ruler taps hard on my hands in a series of lashes that have never moved far from my mind's recording the scene. My hands didn't bleed but the scar on my palm remains testimony to that day and other classroom days when my mouth wouldn't let the world know how well I knew Latin phrases.

As for that scar on my hand, I still own it. Sometimes I'm glad it's there as a reminder of something I endured.

CHAPTER SIX

Wonder-Life

~Aneesa~

I can't remember the word. I can't remember the joke, but one day after school, I came home to tell my Syrian father something I thought was funny, a pattern of words I'd heard from a student in my grade. That boy who told me the joke sat behind me in the seventh or eighth grade class.

What I do remember is the way my father blew up, a simple but thunderous streaming resolve to end my attendance at Public School located right off Highway 17-92. I used to walk there, down that Orlando highway nestled between blossoming orange groves.

The humor, or what I considered funny in those four or five words I said to my father, proved no humor to a parent who wanted not only his child's academic enrichment but a moral enrichment as well. I wish I could recall the exact words to know now what I was telling my concerned dad. Yet, whatever was said, words I spoke that day to my strict father were not acceptable.

Sure, the nuns were strict, he liked that, and he liked what a neighbor told him: "They are ahead of public school texts. Your kids are going to receive a great education." Now he happily drove us to school since St. James was too distant to walk. I admire his way and how Mama allowed what he thought was best.

It must be repeated that small events, seemingly insignificant happenings can determine one's life's directions. That lack of humor in a story naively shared, an attempt to induce laughter amid his constant work, altered my life's entire course. Catholicism entered my world and with it, a hidden God revealed beyond any God I had known.

St. James, a Catholic school still stands, one that still I drive by on my way to town. The child in me remembers fondly those early days sitting at my desk.

Moving us to another religiously different education proves how emotionally difficult it must have been for a faithful Greek Orthodox member to choose a Catholic school. Historically, Catholicism and the ancient Orthodox faith had been for centuries at odds. Plus, he had tuition to think about. A parochial school wasn't free as public education had been. But for this immigrant father somehow tuition money was worth the good morals his kids would be taught. Honesty, truthfulness and no off-color jokes would be around. (Oh, if he had only known.)

It didn't take long to be totally impressed by my black robed teachers in that Catholic classroom. Despite their unusual dress, and long beaded rosaries hanging by their sides, I was drawn to their way of life. I saw them as female creatures wrapped in God, an energized flock of women going from one desk to another, old and young voices lovingly sounding in my ears. I never before paid such close attention to my teachers, but here were such mystifying women scurrying up and down classroom aisles, showing only their faces. They didn't have a clue how their flowing robes brushing gently by me could lift me to such never-felt heights each time. When she leaned over to correct my spelling, Sister Rosetta easily caught my heart. It was hard to breathe.

Outside, when the rain fell, soft drops onto the classroom window, I remember this Sister stopped teaching and quieted the class. She allowed us to listen to the falling rain. In that moment, a deep silence fell as all our singular movements shut down. Water was dropping from clouds onto our rooftops and windowpanes as quiet rain only can. It might have been that wonderful raindrop moment that completely swept me into wanting their way of life. Could it have been so? I recall walking home singing that familiar Rogers and Hammerstein song: *Getting to know you, getting to know all about you. Getting to like you, getting to hope you like me.*

I can't explain why nuns had such a deep soulful impact on me. All I know is that after school I'd sneak into the back of their monastery-like wooden chapel feeling delivered to a heavenly place. I'd kneel and watch their bowed heads, listen to their singing in a language I couldn't grasp. The nun who played the tiny organ near me sounded the introduction, and they, as I now know, voiced the ancient up-and-down melodies of Gregorian chant, undulating lines that filled the chapel and my heart.

To that tender adolescent, these new creatures were the real thing. I never wanted to go home. And they were still the real thing when public school found me later sitting in classrooms having secular teachers. We had moved to an upscale Florida town called Winter Park. I attended Winter Park High School since in our new home, the Catholic high school was too distant.

I confess that I missed my flying-saucer ladies, missed their soft praying ways in that wooden chapel. I missed their kind of energy that made my soul sing along with them. In public school, life was always pulsing forward: biology, American history, English literature, all taught by different teachers. Yet, my teenage soul never forgot the black-robed Sisters' quiet ways, always rooted, as my father had believed, in the gospel values he had wanted for his kids.

Those nuns came to roost in my memory again on a never-forgotten Sunday afternoon, sitting alone at the dining room table, doing my senior class homework, rain softly pelting the window. When I searched the panes, Sister Rosita's direction to stop and praise the gifted rain floated back.

Suddenly, from our living room's large cabinet radio, I heard a deep male voice break the rain's song, an everlasting quote from the famous Prayer of St. Francis. The male voice delivered me even closer to Sister Rosetta's direction, to lay down my pen forever and simply allow all possibilities. I felt the force of St. Francis' poetic words. Sister Rosita would call this moment, 'mystical' I was sure. "You are a blank page and God is writing you." My heart listened with the strength living in me. I was afraid to look up, or around. Something or someone had entered the dining room as St. Francis's words drew me into its truths: *Lord, make me an instrument of your peace. Where there is hatred, let me bring your love, where there is injury, pardon, where there is doubt, faith...*

In that moment, I felt cradled, embraced, as if something deep was flowing in me like a river. In that split second, somehow as crazy as it might be to some, I knew that someday I'd surrender, dress in heavy black serge like my St. James mentors, and like them, teach others about God. I'd walk the aisles of my own classroom. I'd write on the blackboard the lessons that my students needed to learn, and I'd go back, now to live in a convent, get on my knees and always thank God that I'd been chosen to be one of "His" girls.

But before that decision to embrace a religious dress, and without telling him, I must share how my father saw a possible treasured experience for me. After a representative of the US Army had come to Winter Park High School asking for typists to work summers in their formidable five-sided building called The Pentagon, Dad agreed that I could go. "Really?"

Finishing my high school's junior year, my parents drove me to the train station to travel to Washington D.C. to work a job that would emotionally develop their daughter into the kind of leader my father wanted for me.

Oh, it proved a whole new world to sit behind an officer's desk. I was given typing jobs to get out military correspondence, letters with deep content about which I had no idea. Sometimes, the learning proved torture, getting every word right of a new vocabulary, its new directions, new conversations. But arguably, according to my dad, a great adventure. He, having been an immigrant, was proud to see his daughter in that esteemed, venerable piece of Americana, and could brag to his Syrian buddies about his eldest daughter.

In a sense, I began to feel proud of myself for working in Washington's military canvases. It was clear that my world grew so much bigger than I had ever imagined. I observed men and women working, giving additional meaning to the breadth of God's world. Their uniforms, their salutes, their humor at small things approached life on a grand scale. Weren't they also doing His work?

Despite the new role, the military uniforms, the salutes, still, the treasured memory of my engaging nuns never lived far. When I returned home after my Pentagon experience, those nuns returned to my mind, and in a sense, their presence haunted me. Despite that education in the best of military places, I'd be interrupted by a thought, a presence, a desire to leave, and prepare myself for the new life my heart ardently desired. I wanted to be a nun. I had to be a nun, wear another kind of uniform. I was lost and waiting for God to find me.

"A nun? You want to be a *nun*?" My father was shouting after I'd revealed my choice in life. It was noontime and we had just finished

one of Mama's best culinary treats. But the air played dark and heavy, shockingly disruptive, completely sunless. My poor father had been emotionally struck by my announcement. And that hit was heard in a voice that boomed throughout the house and even outside. Mr. Jenkins, who stood tending his garden next door looked up, stared suspiciously. I watched his listening and felt embarrassed by my father's yelling.

Poor Mama. She rushed to shut all open windows, turned the overhead fan on, and tugged on her husband's arm: "Charlie, calm down." Mama, ever the obedient wife, now stared intensely into his eyes. I knew she felt his pain as much as my own regret at hurting him.

I sat still, couldn't say anything after what I had announced. My thoughts were moving fast—about his pain, the difficulty I'd caused him. Could my father ever give up the illusion of controlling his offspring? Could he ever imagine his kids wouldn't always perform as he directed? Could he expect his bluster could or would change my choice?

Mama had once shared how he had completely planned my vocation. I'd be a businesswoman. Now, this choice was putting anathema to his plan.

Oh, Daddy. I'm sorry.

I watched his lower lip quiver, his right hand shake as he cried out softly to me, "I trained you to care for our business, but now you want nuns to train you, care for you? Feed you?"

My father had wanted nothing of any kind of dependence on others, one successful American Dream immigrant. He thought I could be like him, had banked on it. I'd be someone he could be proud of, a model for my brothers and sister, a leader to his Syrian friends. Now, his eldest was forcing him to surrender long-held plans. This time, unlike her Syrian habit of do-what-my-husband-tells-me, Mama threw this startling convent decision back on his shoulders. "Charlie, you're the one who sent her to Catholic school."

I couldn't be a nun without first being a Catholic. So, without anyone noticing, not even Mama, I'd gone out every Thursday night for ten weeks with my friend Angela who drove me to St. James rectory on Orange Avenue to receive Catholic instruction from tall and very handsome, Father Bremner—a real Clark Gable, but more, a priest who bore Christ's good news.

Taking Catholic instruction, I was a young openhearted teen falling in love with her priest, a crush my soul still remembers. In that small gathering of would-be Catholics, I'd grab a front seat, ask oodles of questions, write his answers, love any attention he bestowed on me until finally, he gave approval. Next, Catholic dogma called for a conditional baptism since I'd been baptized originally in the Greek Orthodox Church.

Yellow stars blinked in between white clouds against the black sky as we entered the sanctuary. The moon shone bright on St. James Church that Thursday night, in a sanctuary dark and empty. The year was 1953, the month in September, the day, the tenth when I stepped into a life-changing event. Only Angela, a good Catholic friend, stood witness. I bent over the font and felt its holy waters pour over my black curls as the priest sounded the ancient prayer: *In nominee Patris et Fílii et Spíritus Sancti*. I shook the wet drops loose and stood up in that moment to see a world completely changed.

I don't remember much from the weeks before I left for the Novitiate in Jensen Beach, Florida, the place where I would be trained to be a nun. Yet, I can't help but recall the heavy silence that ran our family house. Even my brothers and sisters clammed up, no talk of football scores, little conversation at the dining room table, even when Mama had prepared special Middle Eastern pastries.

My father's depression found him spending afternoons outside jerking weeds from our Winter Park front lawn. I watched him, saw his saddened face, but there was nothing I could do. I felt my deep vocation and couldn't back down.

Mama was caught in the middle, cried pools of tears out in yard hanging up our clothes.

Quietly, in my back bedroom, I packed my clothes for the Salvation Army: skirts and blouses, black-and-white loafers, shoulder-strap purses, my loved sleeveless rose-colored evening gown Daddy had bought me for that high school musical performance. I cried too as I filled my trunk.

Early morning, driving to Jensen Beach, nothing but bitter silence accompanied us. Not a word was offered. Sitting in the back, I could see how tightly Dad's fingers held onto the leather covered steering wheel. His tension was revealed in those fingers. My mind raced faster than the car as we sped down the state, past old haunts we'd once visited as a family. Obviously, this was the most difficult trip we'd ever taken. I kept back the tears, trying to know that we all do what we must.

Finally, the car rolled onto Jensen Beach's two-lane dirt road, a driveway completely lined with Florida's invasive melaleuca trees. They caught my eye waving silently in Jensen's sunny breezes far below the river nearby. *Invasive?* I bet my dad felt the depth of that word.

Then, "to our wondering eyes" appeared that spectacular two-story white mansion. It sat quietly on a hill, surrounded by majestic Florida breezy palms bordering on sunny St. Lucie River, a breathless *Gone with the Wind* manor. Who cannot compare the setting of this home to that classic movie?

Yet, at the magnificent sight, my father typically connected, not with the memory of the movie, but to the estate's financial worth. "Aneesa, is this the home where you're going to take a vow of poverty?"

As expected, on those beatific grounds, hugs would be brief, awkwardly a painful time for all of us. My father teared up so much he couldn't hug me, and stepped back into the car without even a goodbye. I searched the scene of him now behind the wheel. If I gave that scene credibility, he was feeling nothing but failure, never reaching his full potential as a disciplined father. And it only added pain to my own hurt. Mama got in. I watched their car disappear down the two lane dirt road.

A cold wind whisked through the landscape as I now stood alone. Clouds covered a superficial sunshine. I turned to a river rippling southward, suggesting all was well, that every prayer I'd ever prayed, every visit I'd made to an altar's sanctuary, every Bible verse I'd memorized had delivered me to this moment. I hoped to be okay with it all.

I walked up the hill back to the mansion's front door. I don't know why I stood so long before this Novitiate's giant mahogany door. Fear? Sadness? Hope? My hand was shaking. *Knock, knock.*

I pounded the door to begin a life that had finally arrived. All my dreams of being a nun were now opened. All memories held in that knock: my father's anger at a dirty joke, the classroom hours with Sister Rosita, Father Bremner's Catholic instruction and his philosophical quoting of his mentor, Joseph Campbell: *We must be willing to be rid of the life we planned so as to have the life that is waiting for us.*

CHAPTER SEVEN

Baby Face

-Andrew-

Summer before my third year at Georgetown University, everything in my life took a completely unexpected turn. It began on a moonlit Sunday, when I met baby-faced Anne at a camp in upstate New York. In the space of a minute, I fell for her infectious giggle, her long black hair. I loved the way she tucked her arm into mine, loved the way her blue-green eyes would take me in. But was it more about that curvy body, those upright tits teasing under a purple shirtwaist tucked into tight jeans? Oh God, I couldn't help thinking: will she be my first girl I find under my body? Lo and behold—it didn't take long. That night together. Who could ever forget it—*nine times!* Every night after that, I couldn't count the Divine connections.

Sure, we needed to keep our trysts under wraps for the sake of our camp counsellor jobs, and we did. But I was all out there, not caring who had noticed. I had to have her, somewhere, anywhere.

In a few weeks, I discovered more of this young partner's dreams, how she'd been planning to quit her too-parochial Alabama. I'd be her ticket out of there.

"I'm too smart for my little town, Andy. New York's where I'm headed."

For me, explosive first sex was all I could see. It was all so much, I had to take a walk down to the camp's lake. I stood firm above that calm, blue-green, bending over to see a chest and face reflected in that glassy mirror. Me! Was that the me doing all this with her? Things came up out of the deep. So now, are we hooked? Somehow does sex equal love? Can I...can anyone tell the difference?

On the night filled with shooting stars and a half-moon above, with camp bedded down, and my mind fixed on the shadows, Anne and I shot away in my dad's car, ignoring our signed contracts, violating all things merely reasonable. I was the son who never went where I wasn't supposed to.

Anne navigated every turn.

"Take that fork...don't bother about the speed limit...yeah, there goes the Mason Dixon!" All the time, her hand played a symphony on my thigh, squeezing it to bring out my high notes.

Hers was a small ranch style home on a narrow neighborhood street, two blooming gardenia bushes growing near the front door, white and upright, freshly soaked; some kind of new nature. Anne's enthusiasm knocked on that front door, arching her back until it opened. There stood a mother, fiercely checking out this guy standing alongside her child, holding her daughter's hand.

"Oh, Anne! who's this tall handsome hunk you're bringing home? My, my..."

"Mom, this is Andrew LeBoeuf, the camp's best counselor. We got to know each other really well."

Again, her mother's eyes rolled my way.

"Well, come on in! Andrew. A little hospitality's in order."

What a spread! Southern fried chicken, mashed potatoes spaced in lots of butter. Wow! My Yankee passport was up for grabs if Southern cooking all tastes like this. I looked over to Anne's dad. He hadn't said a word the whole meal. Did he suspect me? Could he be glad for his daughter's new beginning?

Suddenly, the strangeness of it all hit me. *What the hell am I doing here?* I put my fork down, looked at the cross hanging on the wall facing me. *Oh, Jesus!*

"Mom, I like Andrew a lot. I mean a whole lot—his smile, his unselfish ways. He's a real Christian, likes to read the Bible."

I almost choked. *What's up her ass?* I soon found out. It was all so quick. I found myself standing before a bearded Alabama justice of the peace, hearing familiar movie scene lines.

"You take this woman…"

"I do!" Stuttering now worked its way back. *I do?*

We hit the road. My mind wouldn't unravel. *I do! I said that? Who was that guy standing beside the oncoming trouble?* We stopped for lunch. It didn't take long. My stomach registered the scene. I leaned out the car's open door, released that Burger King and French fries I'd swallowed on the road, retched again until nothing else was there.

"What's wrong with you, honey?"

"Baby, do you have any idea what's ahead. College funds? Dad's horror? Mom's disbelief? My sisters? Get ready."

Miles later, we park in front of my New York home where life had been comfortable and routine-normal. We sit there in silence. I can't move, only checking out the blue-green cedar Dad and I planted years ago in the front yard. I keep staring as if it had some answers to this new arrangement. *God, how you've grown, standing like a giant overlord by the house.*

My mind is racing. I hold onto the wheel, trying to recapture myself. I play with introductions…*Dad, guess what? This is…Dad, I know you'll be upset…Mom, I'm sorry I've taken a detour…No, no, no Catholic ceremony.*

Up the brick path, I walk ahead of Anne. A squirrel dashes up the cedar as I prepare to knock. My knees do the knocking for me.

"Wait, Andy! Wait. Is my skirt too short?"

I take a long look at this suddenly flagrant innocence.

"It's too late now, kiddo. We're here and that's your introductory skirt."

I ring our doorbell several times. There are no words for what was going on with my knees, my stomach, my flooding armpits. Finally, there are the two people I've known since forever. They open the door together, staring wide-eyed at a son standing alongside a short-skirted stranger. This, their son, inhales, takes even a deeper breath, hoping he has a voice that can speak.

"Dad and Mom, this is my new wife, Anne."

CHAPTER EIGHT

Discovery

~Aneesa~

A plump, smiling Mistress of Novices leads me into a windowless dressing room holding my hand. Hers is soft, friendly, welcoming. I can tell a person by the way they hold a hand. I like her immediately.

In that dressing room stands a tall, young, dark-skinned Italian, white-veiled Sister Violetta whose name I learn when I enter. She's a novice, wears that white veil before she will take the three vows of poverty, chastity, and obedience and change to a black one. Her job now is to assist me as I remove my secular clothes, a frilly white blouse and mini-skirt, the kind of fashion I'd worn most of my life, the kind of fashion Mama loved to see me in.

I knew there was meaning to be found in letting every piece of stylish clothing go. I was now on a different path, allow my colorful attire to be replaced by a simple long black serge skirt, symbol of a convent sister, tribute to new life. Off came my favorite green skirt, a blouse given by Mama at that surprise birthday party, and finally, I hand Sister Violetta the pink nylon slip. Below, I slide into new granny shoes. All the clothing symbolized the breaking away of a so-called worldly life.

My waist was small then and I liked seeing myself in the mirror. The black attire gave me even a thinner look, right down to the granny tie-ups that caused me to smile, remembering how I'd lied to Raymond, a shoe salesman friend who asked why I, so young, would buy old-lady shoes: "I'm playing a witch in our senior play." He believed the story, and I? I remember being amazed at how easily I lied about becoming a nun.

So why did I have to lie? He was a friend. Wouldn't he understand? He was a Syrian and most of them weren't Catholic, didn't send their kids to Catholic schools, probably thought nuns were oddballs.

That lie told where I bought those granny shoes, caused me to always remember the encounter with Raymond, how he packed up the pair, how I handed him my twenty, and how he laughingly asked as he gave back my change: "A witch? You're always joyful. Why would you even want to play that part?"

Wearing those granny shoes now revealed in the Novitiate mirror, symbol of my new adventure into a future most outsiders wouldn't understand, especially Syrian families who weren't Catholic, many thinking dressing up in black is welcoming death. Perhaps, if I dwell on it, there is, in wearing black, a sense that one *is* dead to the things of the world.

Looking in that mirror, I try to smile, but am suddenly seized by a feeling of loss, sadness, confusion similar to my parents', of Mama and Daddy's tears about why I wanted to leave all that I'd known. Sister Violetta said nothing. I tried to wipe away every tear.

She leads me away as I let the flood of thoughts take over: *Isn't this what you wanted, Aneesa? What you were led to? Why the sadness?* Tears continued. Sister Violetta handed me a tissue and I blew my nose, awed by all my feelings. Wasn't I doing the right thing—leaving home, embracing a new way, a stricter way of life?

What I recount below is of early Novitiate days in the 1950s, before Vatican II. Roles and rules were tightly structured. Keeping the vow of obedience kept nuns well-enveloped in rules of the early Jesuits. (Although, I don't remember the virtue of charity preached as often as the virtue of obeying a Superior.)

Thankfully, convent life has been completely altered by Pope John's Council. He never stopped embracing the spiritual world and believed God continued to embrace it as well. He stood as the perfect and humble leader of all that was true of Catholicism. And I still love him.

Postulants were women mostly new to convent life. We wore a simple black veil over our hair. If I remember correctly, we could keep our hair any length until we entered the next role of Novice, the second step toward taking of vows.

At some point, Reverend Mother Anna Maria, the then head of Florida's Sisters of St. Joseph one day visited her new aspirants. Talk about short people. She proved the shortest but most bustling leader I'd ever seen. I loved watching her style of familiarity. She pitched her words from a deep spirituality and a considered joy: "Every day we are to bless God for everything given…for health, food, for clouds and sun, for all that you are meant to be, beautiful souls. I bless the amazing God for sending you here. With so many of you, we'll be able to staff Florida's new Catholic schools."

There was much to adapt to, starting in early morning. "At the sound of the bell, jump out of bed, Sisters. Dress and descend the stairs, and make for the chapel. Don't forget to use the holy water font, dab your fingers into it, and trace the sign of the cross across your breasts as you enter the chapel." Down on our knees we fell on the kneelers ready for daily Mass as the priest begins the Latin words: *Introibo ad altar Dei.*

Days passed and we followed the Novitiates' daily routine, developing in every new moment, active in every new lesson. Everything was to be as Reverend Mother had said, to find God in all things, small and big: taking a walk, cleaning up after meals, charging down to class to study the community rules, chapel prayers, letting God really do the directing. Routine, yes, but somehow, unlike some of the postulants, I was never bored with the repetition.

"Sisters! Understand me! Cleanliness is next to Godliness. I don't want to find any dust anywhere." Oh, if my father could have heard this Mistress of Novices enhancing our growth, I think he'd smile, be more inclined to think I had chosen well.

As I write this history of my Novitiate life, I'm reminded of Tevye, the Jewish star in the musical, *Fiddler on the Roof,* who sings about tradition, who honors it and loves it. He reminds the audience that tradition is a vital part of Jewish culture, and it is also a committed part of the convent life. Like Tevye, we were engaged in a sacred tradition of work and prayer, committed to live an orderly quiet life, knowing exactly what was always required of us in that ancient sacred kind of training. I never remember being unhappy about any of that training. Only with one Superior at my mission school did I begin to question the whole way of life.

In my free time, I run down to the dock that stretched far out over St. Lucie's waters, sitting on the edge, letting the natural world take me in, God's world, my Florida world. Puffy clouds, palm branches wave in quiet breezes, a Florida sun like nowhere else shining on its beloved planet. I feel as if my twenty-year-old soul dressed in a black singular apparel is floating on a magic carpet out under the bluest of skies. Oh, to be so in love with You and so definitely not alone.

I read Thomas Merton, my buddy in God's domain, a monk who fills me with delightful monkish laughing realities. Sometimes, I'd jot down thoughts that compelled me, thoughts on the miracle of just getting here, grateful that I could be on my knees in a small indoor chapel, pray with young sisters the Liturgy of the Latin Hours, sing and play numerous Gregorian hymns on the little convent organ. I vow that no matter what or how life will direct me and my white veil, I'll always aim to be happy here in this chosen world. I am given a vocation and I will never leave it. Little did I ever suspect it.

I was one lucky novice who could drive. Consequently, Mother appointed me to take the Novitiate station wagon to collect the mail from the community's post office down the dirt two-lane highway. I loved getting away, sitting behind the wheel where I shifted gears, another feeling of gratitude that Mama had taught me to drive. She was with me as I steered the Novitiate's "Cadillac" on Jensen Beach's narrow dirt road, there with her interminable patience, her sign of the cross when I drove into 17-92's left lane's speeding traffic, her quiet way of teaching me to parallel park, remembering her words: *"Don't jerk the car or press the gas pedal too quickly."*

It wasn't part of the trip to the post office but often I'd stop on the side of the road, allow myself to absorb again the picture perfect flowing St. Lucie. Nothing in that scene could prove more uplifting, and if I'm honest, no chapel prayer, no choral hymn, no recreation or treats could equal it. Mother Nature had my total attention. This was the Florida of my youth when St. Petersburg's tropics grabbed my heart as they still do.

Thank you, Daddy for settling in this tropical state.

Our Mistress of Novices, Mother Mary Louis, was always seated at the head dining room table. She'd grab every opportunity to spread her gospel values. "Sisters, you can learn to practice little mortifications. Drink your morning coffee black. Keep silent when eating. Spread no butter on your toast?" *Wait a minute! No butter on toast?*

This woman put a spiritual twist on everything: "Think of the less fortunate, the homeless who don't have coffee, much less a breakfast egg. God knows, some of us are given so much while others must beg for the little they receive. Be grateful you can give up even a little butter."

I'm often reminded of that special teaching of hers that happened around the dessert of a red apple. She had sliced her apple into two halves and then tapped the bell, a signal for us to "shut up" and listen. Our conversation dropped as her arms rose, holding high those two pieces of red fruit together: "Sisters, look at this beautiful apple, how appealing it is, good enough to eat, right?" Then, she separated them. "But look at what lay behind its red peel—a hopeless black core, completely rotten."

"So, sisters, you and I can look healthy, spiritually savvy, and appealing on the outside. Catholics see that outer black habit, our rosary dangling, and they think 'Oh, there go the good nuns.' But more vital than their opinion is God's opinion of us. The Divine sees the core, the inside, the soul, our soul. Make sure your outer life reflects an inner goodness. If not, you can deceive your parents and students but never can you deceive God."

The image of that Mother leader holding up that red apple still lives. I'm eternally grateful for the constant teachings she threw at us. I think in many ways they are continually renewed even now in my adult pathway to God.

Mother had heard somehow that I could play the piano. I loved that day she called me to her side, sat me down at the community's black grand piano, and randomly opened the St. Gregory Hymnal. Setting an open page in front of me, she smiled and asked: "Can your fingers play this hymn?"

No one was more surprised when my fingers, despite all the years I hadn't touched a keyboard, magically found and played the right keys in the right rhythm. I was making music and my heart leaped backward to my giving parents who had so often sacrificed their income to employ a piano teacher.

"When did you learn to play?" Mother asked. "Gosh, maybe in the sixth grade when my parents hired a Professor Nelson from Rollins college to teach me on an old upright."

She looked closely at me and what she said has never been forgotten: "Sister Aneesa, your parent's gift became a lasting gift also to our Sisters. I'm now putting you at the organ to accompany our sisters at Mass."

And accompany the novices, I did! I loved pounding out even

the difficult chords, making harmony, making sounds that created a sense that I was playing my notes in a huge auditorium. My fingers pressed the right black and white keys as my sisters, young and white-veiled sopranos and altos lifted their voices to fill the high ceiling chapel with their sounds, filling the outside landscapes, filling a flowing river, and a batch of white clouds dancing in the blue skies. My sisters were young and enjoyed their gifted voices as I hit the chapel's organ keys. I played like a woman in love with every sharp and flat, every harmonic chord, making sounds that I believed rendered the seal of my commitment to God. I determined to play for God forever wearing that black habit. Thank you, dear Mistress of Novices.

She proved a great leader, this Mistress of Novices, sometimes sneaking down to the river herself, with her own prayer book. Real, smooth, familiar, and smart, always this nun laid out little teachings that have been locked tightly into my aspiring soul.

"Sisters, behaviors build your nun's character. Don't hurry: walk calmly. Never slam a door. Always enter a room quietly without drawing attention to yourself, disturb no one. If someone enters a room where you're working, don't satisfy your curiosity but observe custody of the eyes. Focus your attention on your work, your books, your love of God. You want to be a saint? Remember a saintly soul is forged by anguish and renunciation."

Instructions from that saintly lady included making sure we turned off lights when leaving a room. Saving water when taking a shower, her teachings were nothing new to me; those directions flowed easily from my own frugal father. I drew in the notion that he'd approve of Mother's rule to save electricity, save water, and keep air conditioning at a minimum.

Thankfully, this nun wasn't all seriousness: "Sisters, recall that there are two kinds of nuns. One who gets up in the morning and cheerfully says, 'Good morning, God!' The other wakes up and says: *'Good God! Morning?"*

If I'm honest, there were some sisters who didn't find meaning in Mother's teachings. I felt that they wouldn't stay in the convent and sadly, or perhaps not so sadly they didn't fit and left for another pathway to God. But in the scheme of God's way, and in these many years later, many did leave when the church's tradition itself was being altered, filling up on a secular life that became sweet and living on an avenue more in keeping with who they were.

Love, peace, and happiness. It had all been there, as finally, my two years of training ended. I would join hundreds of other young teaching nuns in classrooms across the state of Florida. Oh, what joy! St. Juliana grade school would be my first chance to teach a roomful of kids.

As it turned out, in God's wonderful scheme of giving blessings, some of those special students of mine would become lifelong friends. I stand blessed by all the convent's and my own choices.

CHAPTER NINE

Onward and Downward

-Andrew-

If that scene at the front door had been videotaped, you would have enjoyed a good laugh watching wide-eyed parents greet their erstwhile son—almost cartoon-like, staring at a joke someone was playing on them.

My professional father, who could fill every room with his presence, who'd always led meetings, who without fail could figure out what stumped everyone else, now morphed into a speechless classroom dolt. His face grew beet red, beard and mouth quivered. I'd never seen him in such a bind, the first and probably the last time that I felt such sympathy for him.

"Jean Luc, maybe we can talk about this." Mom tries. Yet, in no time, Dad becomes Dad.

"Get your things, son. Millie will fix you supper. You've made your bed and, by God, you can curl up in it under another roof."

Off he goes, stomping to his home office. Mom shakes her head, looks at me as she pulls Anne into the house.

"Come in, Anne. Have a seat by the bay window. Andrew and I need to talk."

Darling Mom grabs my hand, leads me into my old bedroom, that traditional cozy refuge when things used to boil over, where my books were still on that shelf Dad had fashioned for me, where my stack of Boy's life still sat on the floor.

Now, standing with my back to Mom looking out my bay window, I cringe, remembering that's the ground where we buried my dog Charlie. I couldn't help but grieve the loss of him. And now, I grieve the loss of my simple life where so much was given. *Say goodbye to it all, Andrew.* I turned back to the woman I had so loved and who was mostly there for me.

"Son, I'll talk to your father, but honestly, sweet nature boy, you wandered very far this time."

I hold her tiny body close, run my face into her red hair, recalling memories of laughter at Charlie's antics. She loved that pup as much as I did. Suddenly, she breaks away.

"Honestly, Andrew, couldn't you have introduced her first? Given us a chance to get to know her?"

I wipe the wet from my own eyes.

"Geez, Mom. You and Dad would have jumped all over me. I must slog on. It's done now. We're married."

I take her hand in mine, look deep into her eyes.

"I'm sorry that I've hurt you, hate that I have. But Mom, I have to face the facts now. She's my wife."

"My God! Son, I thought I knew you!"

"No Mom, you didn't really know me!" I dropped her grasp to sit on the side of the bed, my head fell into my hands and I choked out. "It's never been more so."

Mom leaves the room and Anne enters. I pull out my new college suitcase, open drawers, pack whatever is there. Anne watches, says nothing. What could she say? What could I? I stare hard at her as I pack what fits into the suitcase. Suddenly, her own fury rises matching my own.

"Don't blame me, Andy. You said, 'I do,' too! You wanted me."

"Yeah, while your mother was glad to see you go? Why? *Why* was that, Anne?"

"Andrew, please don't take off like this. I'm ready to start life with you. We don't need my folks. We don't need yours. We'll make it on our own, with a lot of tomorrows."

I set my jaw, picked up my suitcase, took her hand, walked out that once friendly home, knowing that it, as well as Dad, would never invite me back.

Somehow, I managed to graduate. Dad, never one for surprises, but maybe because of his Louvain days, was big on military Jesuits. Including his turning around, I found my way to Georgetown university. For the most part, all my classes have vanished from memory except that fine hour with Paul Hume's glee club, singing my best base under his baton. We sang the three famous B's: Bach, Beethoven, and Brahms at colleges and universities. Even though I loved the sound of jazz, classical music and me always got along. And then my last senior year came and went with me, thanks to keeping our couplehood secret.

It was bound to happen. Anne comes out of the bathroom one morning, all sweet in her soft nightie to announce quietly: "Andrew, I hope you'll be pleased. I'm pregnant." *Oh, my God! A child on the way. What now?* I stared hard at this girl I'd allowed to change my entire life. *Be nice, Andrew, back away, find our one chair and let it support your shaking body.*

The draft was still on though no war was waging but the cold one. Probably I could have gotten a deferment. Friends suggested I go for a commission in the Navy, then apply for intelligence work. Well, that sounded okay to me, especially if my love of airplanes allowed it. I could pal with them. I'd always wanted to fly but that tyrant of tongue, my stuttering kept me fearful of applying.

As it turned out, Officer Candidate School in Newport, Rhode Island was waiting for me with much to learn. No problem with marching, but there was the rub. Taking my turn as the day's group leader taught me that failure could always be just around the corner. That it could be another Brother O'Neil day when I'd stand in class, unable to get a word out. My tongue was damn stubborn, wouldn't work. Because of that, I was sent to a special hearing committee to see if there was a place in the Navy for this peculiar stuttering candidate. Somehow and strangely enough, right words managed to tumble out at that limited hearing and I was sent back to class. Oh, life! How it could be up, then down, and sometimes up again. I was a yo-yo in the hands of strangers.

Another time we were formed in teams performing on the virtual fleet exercises, me as radio operator. Locked down once more, I stumbled my way through, mimicking static this time. That did it. Ensign bars were waiting for me at the end. *Oh, God, could it be? Could I fly now?*

Somehow, I did find my way close to airplanes working in air intelligence, the ones who tell pilots about their assigned mission, how to get there and back, what to expect in weather and if it so happens, enemy confrontation. That became my role. I was "briefing officer" and managed to keep briefing talks to a minimum while serving two tours, one mostly in a writing role, the last as diplomatic liaison. Then I was out. The question became: *Where to now?*

Both Anne and I had landed jobs in DC, before the Navy too, when completing my Georgetown years, Anne at Murphy's Bar and Grill, moi Chez Odette, the owner thrilled I could read his French menus.

"Formidable!" was the word he used to compliment me. As usual, I saw Mom's wisdom in making us speak only French at home.

Months passed. We paid the rent, never went hungry, watched a little TV on a nine-inch screen. Routine shattered the morning Anne came out of the bathroom, eyes misty, sheepishly announcing,

"Andrew, I'm pregnant…"

Oof! I found a quiet place to settle my nerves. How would it all turn out? I found paper, jotted words down, hoping the poem would tell me what I needed to know. The words didn't have the answers but line after line delivered peace. It felt so natural, I wanted to write more and more, yet…I kept thinking about the new child on the way. God help us both.

If nothing else, could Dad delight in his grandchild?

Rain poured itself gentle, one of those long cold gray days in our woods long ago. No way had first grandchild changed his made-up mind, as if held captive by that fixed-in-place heart. Sister Sarah's letter confirmed what I knew to be true.

"Dad was brutally (his word) hurt by your betrayal, Andy. His plans for you went awry. He couldn't brag about *my son the doctor… lawyer…* Truth is he's never even told anyone about your elopement."

Somehow, I can't remember, but I had learned, probably from Sarah, that he'd even offered to pay Anne's father off and buy her ticket home. Her dad bellowed! But what if he had agreed? How would my life have been then? That thought preyed on me. What if he'd agreed? No more shadows?

The reality was that now I had a wife and two sons and a daughter to support. Probably the most useful episode that led me right back to the bottom was learning to sell refrigerators as a Sears management trainee. I soaked up the training script.

Yes, Mrs. Jones, a bit costly this refrigerator, but say, when you do decide to buy, tell me, what color would you like?

Gosh, it worked! I was selling refrigerator after refrigerator. The family was being fed, but good heavens, that gnawing feeling! Is this what I needed to be doing? If I thought about it long enough, I'd cry up to the Catskill Mountains. *Hell no!*

Anne and I thought about the next role for my life. "You'd better start another step up the ladder, honey. Go for an advanced degree, return to school, and as long as you are at it, better not just apply for *any* degree."

Two years later, after much sweat, I had an MBA in hand from Columbia University. That degree propelled me up to Benton and Bowles, a top Madison Avenue agency. *Yes, yes, I can do this thing*, I kept telling myself. I became the assistant executive on a multi-million-dollar advertising account, then moved up to account exec with top consumer client Proctor and Gamble. I was commuting from our new house in Westchester just like old schooldays. Would this last? Would I finally settle down into a "job?"

Yet, like in the old days, there was no onward and upward here. It was again fall down time. They wanted me to deliver our new campaign to the major client. I'd stand up under pressure once more, and that kind of pressure couldn't work for me. Less than three years working there, hard working at account exec work, their pink slip finally finds me. I knew it as well as them: that work wasn't for me.

I tried substitute teaching in a local suburban school. I liked it. I liked the kids. They liked me. We had something going. When the kids wanted to know more about a subject, I'd study it, then we'd talk about it, like banking, or stocks and bonds. When they wanted to learn more about sex, I opened up about that subject not suspecting my ass was on the line. Parents didn't appreciate what I told their youngsters, how I allowed them to voice their funky ideas on that subject, write sexy words on the green board, giggle hard.

That afternoon, I found a dead mouse on my doorstep and another pink slip in my school mailbox.

This time, fortunately my resume paved the way to join the faculty of City University's Business College. In no time, I'm finally given creative time. I'd had it with business life, despite my MBA. The sun was brilliant that day. The mouse was gone. It was time to engage the guy who lived within me.

What lived in me was my abounding love of language and film and video projects. I transferred to that department and soon liberated the library's TV studio for the students' creative work. We produced shorts, documentaries, videos. The college kids loved working their creativity. I loved mentoring. We were hot. We produced a movie. We showed it on campus. Faculty stood to applaud. Anne was applauding too.

"Andy, you *better be working on your PhD, or you won't get past five years here.*"

Okay, I did it. I registered into interdisciplinary communications of my own design, right up to ABD—all-but-dissertation. I took night classes for NYU's Film Certificate, spending hours and creative energy defying emotional challenges in those classes. My family missed me, my boys, and daughter Kelly too. I thought it would all pay off.

Yet, five years of that kind of authentic engagement sadly took me no further than the dean's office. "Sure, you're doing a terrific job, Andy. Your work's original, and yes, the kids love you. But man, rules are rules, time's up without your doctorate in hand." Again, that old hitch, the same fall-down. I'm called into the department head's office.

But no matter! After five hardworking years, the department head bounces me because I didn't do the dissertation. I'm out the front door. Another *oomph*.

And of course, it didn't take long. That old sense of failure took over. I had no good news to bring home again, and soon began pacing the streets, out looking for another job.

Weeks passed. Sad to say, I had plenty of time to think. *Andy, the jobs you're always being paid for has little to do with your love of language. Why in hell all this time to keep hoping to recite the poems I'd written? Why always taking the wrong thing on? OK, never give up, job after job.*

I grab a beer from the fridge, sit by the tall window, look at my carpentry in the kitchen, work that didn't fail, work that came naturally, works learned from watching Dad in his garage, a slight feeling of accomplishment. I'd built blue and white cabinets at Anne's request, a butcher-block island that took me for a long ride, blue floor lines shaped in circular design. Anne's elation, her quick hug felt good. That time teaching college kids had been different, hadn't it? I was there for a creativity living in me as I'd never been before. I loved it, felt completely at home. The kids, the parents, the accolades had been thrown at me. Creativity was where I belonged.

One night, I watched the snow falling hard outside the bedroom window. It was next to impossible not to think of my time back home, when snow was covering everything green. Dad and Mom would never let a hard Sunday snow stop us. I felt inspired to recall those bouncy days we drove to church. At the kitchen table, out came my pen and from me came the surprise, my language straight from memory about that Sunday trip to church as my heart soared with desire to feel the sweetness of our family trip to that little chapel in the woods.

November morn in ordinary time

tap clap patter, spitter & splatter
tumbling silver notes tapclapping in the rafters
marking the moment infinite
transfixing us wide-eyed as if to see the symphony
here below in bundled burrows bunking
holding our breath against a cold gray dawn
it's just the way of things, nothing special so to speak
just another singing secret, freak of time
a hidden rhyme we call maquis

we snuggle for each other's warmth inside this steel austerity
merrily our bouncing jeep greets the weekly trek
"good rainy morning to you friend, rush pulsing, chill-ed stream!"
swing out, swing closed, swing in again, we're off to clear the woods
and mount by noble cedar row this meadow ridge,
bare maple crest, these playing fields on high
tiny picture postcard veering sharply by the left
coasting slope down meade aways to maybe catch a glimpse
and yes, her lonesome face full blessing treats
we greet her with a shout
"castle rock!" yes or no? heartily we 'fend the point
up mountain curves by cobbled drive to port of missing men
smooth sailing now to north-of-peace (am i dreaming this?)
another time it's golden's-bridge (did i miss it then?)
it's just the way of things, nothing special so to speak
just another singing secret, freak of time
a hidden rhyme we call maquis

little clapboard chapel fills
breathless silence in attendance

gentle rain, angelic choir
word made flesh and dwells among us
a dozen fresh hard-rolls
and twenty-five pounds of the new york times at penny-a-pound
sputtering fire come crackle to blaze
mom's fresh glow everywhere hovering
cold plates and jam and animated banter and the smell of wet oak
tap clap patter, spitter & splatter
yup, just the way of things
nothing special so to speak
just another singing secret
a freak of time
a hidden rhyme
we call
maquis

Time passes. I sit in that kitchen, read my lines over and over, deeply feeling the truth of those young days. Will a day ever come when I publish the thing, when someone else wants to include it in a collection—gosh, maybe publish a collection of my own? All I know is I've got to go somewhere—again!

CHAPTER TEN

New Window

-Aneesa-

The night before I entered St. Juliana's assigned fourth grade classroom, I had to take the pill Sister Michelle offered me. Anxiety was running wildly up and down my back, in and out of my stomach. I couldn't find my rosary, then it was my black stockings, and even the granny shoes. Sure, I was present, ready to take up my professional life, but mentally pushed to unknowing the *how* of it all. I'd never taught school before. Inner questions persisted: *Can you perform as well as your community expects you to perform? Teaching? Kids? Me the boss? Dear God, where the heck are You?*

Mother Mary Louis had tried to give me the needed confidence: "You will teach as a professional, Sister Aneesa. Your black habit and dangling rosary at your side will identify you as a Sister of St. Joseph. The kids will know you're the boss. And your music skills are a huge plus."

Despite ever-present butterflies howling in my stomach, I finally stepped into that classroom. And there they were. Baby faces, God's blessed offspring, all forty-five tykes dart my way, and in one grand standing, they cry out that traditional greeting to any nun entering a classroom: "Good *morning*, Sister," the music of that greeting still rings in my head.

To my delight, checking them out, row after row, they were beautiful children, harmless enough, and reminded me of Father Bremner's counsel: "Realize, Aneesa, if you wear a black habit, you'll never bear children of your own. Yet, you'll be mother to more children than you ever could physically bear."

It didn't take long to recognize Father Bremner's sweet warning about "bear children" meant bear with high-spirited leprechauns upending my Novitiate's rule of silence. Oh, I was nowhere. What happened, Mother, to the boss role I was supposed to play. I had no control, not an ounce. Not one child was listening to me.

I never forgot the sight and sound. Giggling boys banged their textbooks to the floor, thrashing them down. I try to pick up a few when they raced down the aisle. *Oh God, have I lost my vocation?* Was I really trying to be the teacher Mother Mary Louis said I could be?

"Come back here." I tried to raise my voice above the din. My teaching days became a losing drama. One, the littlest girls, yes, a girl, raised her hand in the air and whizzed a paper plane past me.

I sat behind my desk. I was the bystander, they were the players. I was the intruder, they were the hosts. I sat and looked at what I'd inherited. My stomach felt the noise, the angst, the confusion. If you're reading this, by now you've got the picture. I'm complete toast. *Mama! Mama, help.*

"You can always quit, Aneesa," Mama said, "come back, wear colorful skirts and blouses and help Daddy in the business!" Her voice at the other end was light. Did she even understand what I was enduring?

What else was I to do except leave the class, get away from those kids, rush to the principal's office and knock as the tears wouldn't stop: "Oh, Sister, they pay no attention to my voice."

"Sister Aneesa, I've watched you. Your voice is too soft, too gentle. Speak up, dear. Show them who is boss."

I blinked in total confusion. "But, Sister, I was taught not to raise my voice. Nuns don't raise their voices. Now you're telling me to raise it?"

"Sister Aneesa, no healthy child can resist running around those desks even if protocol says children remain in their seats. Remember, your students are children. You're the adult. Act like one!"

Dazed, I walked back. I wished. I prayed: *Dear God, I'm the enemy, and I'm completely losing the war.* I found the payphone and called Mama again.

"My kids won't shut up."

"Want to come home?"

"Oh, Mama, it's not an option. I want to be their teacher, want to take control."

"Well, what do think will work with your kids?"

"I've got to find a way to teach them."

There was a long silence. Then like her wonderful show of belief that life always turns out okay, Mama stepped to the high ground: "Honey, remember in the deep part of us, we're really all the same. They may be kids, but they want what you want. Try to see them that way. If things get too rough, like I've always said, 'Pray like hell.' It might take God to shut them up."

"Pray like hell." Mama wasn't kidding when she instructed me to pray like hell. It was her way. When my baby brother was still in diapers, he accidentally swallowed a nickel. After two days of intense poop-checking, plus hours of petitionary prayer, this mother finally, gratefully pulled that doo-doo-covered nickel from his loaded diaper, practically kissing it before she washed it to a shine.

And so, I prayed...*hard!* And another voice weeks later came to my release. Our Palm Beach Sisters had been invited to a lecture in Miami by an older well-seasoned nun/teacher. This eldering nun wore her own old and tattered black habit. She proved very short, very plump, but employed the wisdom God sent my way. I grabbed a front row seat, pulled out a pad, and hoped I'd learn how I could handle that class of angels—in my book, fallen angels.

This old nun, known throughout our order, sat up on a dais, and spoke to us in a voice that rang soft with true authority. I took in every syllable. She was a survivor who had learned from her own early days how to really teach the kids God had sent. This little fat nun began to teach lessons I needed to hear if I were ever to be the teacher my students needed.

"Sisters, too many of you were taught by school principals never to smile, to be stern with students until around Christmas. Only then can you relax. Their message was meant to show the class who was boss. Hold a ruler in your hands, they said, as you walk the aisles, back and forth. Discipline, they said, makes a good teacher. Well, dear Sisters," and at that point, she stood to her full stature. Her voice became a strong command: "Maybe that worked for some teachers but it never worked for me. I believed God sent those children to me, and that my job, like God's job, was to love them, yes, simply to love them in a way they recognized that love. I learned if I did that, if I always called them by name, shared a compliment, they would in the end learn everything I wanted them to learn because of that love."

*Gloria In Excelsis Deo...*I took in every word. My heart was ready.

By the following week, that nun's teaching and Mom's dictum to pray like hell either changed my kids or softened me. I packed away negativity, packed away my need for silence, raised my voice to accompany a broad smile, and saw my kids as needy, wanting to learn more about everything, wanting to please me as much as I wanted to please them. Suddenly, they bloomed in my presence, grew dearer and dearer to my heart, and I found myself loving them, one by one, getting to know each, to compliment them whenever I got the chance. I came alive with love.

Oh Mama, nearer my God to Thee!

Compliments were magic. *"Ooh!* I like the way Michael is sitting up straight." Immediately, all of them adjust their positions, their backs upright, hands folded on their desktops, and a wide-eyed look of hope came my way. All that behavior blanketed a new confidence in me, a fresh way of teaching, obviously, a more human connection.

Oh, there were still times they challenged. But in a good way, that left a quotable memory, like Donald, one of my favorite students, who raised his hand after I'd told them we were going to church to make a visit. "Sister, you told us that God was everywhere. Why do we have to go to the chapel?"

And I can never forget when my little boy, Steven, sitting in the front desk was disturbing the girl behind him. As I rushed to his seat to correct him, he put his hands in front of his face for protection. Oh, that sad feeling: "Steven, I'm not going to touch you."

And the truth is, I never touched the kids for any kind of punishment. I'm proud of that and sadly, not all nuns can swear to that truth.

Then there was little and very blond, Merry Francis who followed me everywhere after school. I never fail to smile when I think of her.

And when my students gave a piano recital, and I seemed to be forcing sweet Susan to play her piece, she cried so hard her father had to come to her rescue.

Oh dear God, my classroom memories...how they linger.

Somehow, these many years later, I still feel close, as if not only having taught them but mothered them as well. I slowly trusted that nun's direction to love my kids, willingly and able to welcome their sometimes-abrupt spontaneity. Oh, maybe I can say that best of all, I could never get enough of that musical greeting as I walked into my classroom: "Good *morning,* Sister." Sometimes, I mimicked them. "And good *morning,* children."

Oh, Mama, finally, I grew my own way to practice this profession called teaching.

Along the teaching role, living with sister nuns meant involvement in a variety of after school hours. Some loved Shakespeare and played parts, some pulled out Scrabble games before bells rang for supper. Others picked up new recipes, cooked them, and our sweet tooth consumed them eagerly. One smarty nun tossed riddles and laughed delightfully if we couldn't solve their mysteries. One older, wrinkled-faced Irish nun rang the bell most days at four o'clock to taste/eat her newly baked scones, butter, and jelly treats.

But it was my Superior Sister Francis de Sales, who loved houseplants and who led me to grow and love a garden, a daily nourishment to my soul. It all began on an unexpected day after school when she called me to her side:

"Sister Aneesa, I don't have time to tend our houseplants and the garden outside. I'd like you to handle them."

What? Is she kidding?

Gently, I tried to explain. "Sister, I'm a Florida native, a grocery store owner's daughter, familiar with stacking and restocking shelves. I love teaching my kids. You've helped me there. But plants? Please ask someone else."

"Ask someone else?" She stared at my answer as if checking a disobedient puppy. *Am I really arguing with my Superior? You know better.*

"Aneesa, listen. I know you want to live a spiritual life as well as a professional one. So, let me tell you about God's spiritual gift that's found in gardening." And with that, she related what was living in her heart before dragging me to the outside wooden bench. What she revealed in that garden moment has never died in memory.

"God nudges us to see holy dimensions in the most mundane blooms. Look at that rosebush. I believe a new bloom on a rose is a glimpse of God at work. Gardening, dear sister, is spiritual revelation. Often, on a hot day when my veil feels hard, pressed on my skin, I'm ready to give in to sweat and exhaustion, but suddenly I'm comforted by a refreshing breeze. I stand, look up, watch the wind flow through the palm branches, feel that same breeze refreshes my skin, cooling my body," she said as she pressed her palm to her heart. "Plus my soul. I have had so many of these sacred moments in this garden. I feel the presence of God here as much as in the Blessed Sacrament."

As she spoke, I watched the way she tenderly touched the leaves on the fichus. "So, Sister Aneesa, something has been hidden in you. Go and find it. Go and look deeply at a purple African violet. Something is waiting for you."

If Sister de Sales says so, maybe I can learn to love green things too? She was another nun I trusted completely.

In the end, her love of a garden, plus my vow of obedience trumped all protests. After school, I'd clean off my desk, pin my habit's skirt behind my back the way we did when cleaning, walk outside to the convent's back garden, and under a sunny sky, grow immersed in a green world, learning each plant by name. I had discovered a new twist of talent. I became finely tuned to a plant's drooping leaves, to know when thirsty, to prune dead leaves, to feed the kind of food that charged not only its outside but its soul.

Life was full and I was full of new life for I'd rush home after school, hoping for a new bloom on some of freshly potted geraniums, loving how a Florida sun could light up a red rose and how my soul took in that sun's beauty as well. I couldn't help but sometimes sing as my fingers played in that soil. What often came back were the lyrics of that old Protestant hymn I'd sung as a child in Sunday school before becoming Catholic: *I come to the garden alone, while the dew is still on the roses, and the voice I'd hear, falling on my ear, the Son of God discloses...*

My Superior wasn't finished. And for this gift she kindly gave me, I was and would always be in her debt. That next year, this time, a

musical challenge. I knew not to argue, that somehow, I'd come out on top. And blessedly did.

"Aneesa, you sing, you play the piano. Let's make your talent work for our kids and the whole community."

Could I ever be grateful enough to this nun who believed in what I could do and lead in ways I'd never dreamed possible. Is that the Divine way? The talent of a good superior? To believe in others and what lies inside them that is still to be discovered?

And so, it was. There I stood, baton in hand and below me my students, their mouths open wide, their most beautiful sounds filling the auditoriums where we performed. I suppose the kids themselves never dreamed they could make such angelic sounds. But there we were! I directed and my St. Juliana's kids performed like accomplished artists. They executed lyrics and moved in sync to words as if they born to the stage.

Our first production—Gilbert and Sullivan's *Mikado*—was sold out. In full costume, grade school youngsters lined the stage and belted out the show's first and quite famous lyric: *If you want to know who we are, we are gentlemen of Japan. On many a vase and jar, on many a screen and fan...*

My three little Mikado maids, straight from heaven, cutest little girls that elicited a wide smile from any observer watching and listening: the famous characters called Yum-Yum, Peep-Bo and Pitti-Sing. These three fourth graders dressed in bright silks, held colorful Japanese fans, and had painted faces wearing Japanese style makeup. I marveled at how they memorized, delivered, and spirited a three-part harmony of that famous ditty: *Three little maids from school are we. Pert as a school girl well can be, filled to the brim with girlish glee—eee. Three little maids from school.* They never forgot to twirl their corrugated fans, pirouette in provocative circles, and enjoyed every minute of their presentation. Little Pooh-Bah was followed by the emperor and then tenor, Nanki-Po. These kids successfully captured the audience's heart, every character taking in a standing ovation at each performance. Parents advertised the show, pulled in huge ticket sales, and the entire St. Joseph Motherhouse watched our convent bank accounts swell.

Our next show stopper was Victor Herbert's operetta *Babes in Toyland*, which introduced me to a former Rockette who volunteered to choreograph the school's third and fourth grade soldier boys dressed in red high hats to bow in sync for that well-known number, "March of the Tin Soldiers."

"Broadway, here we come!" laughed Mrs. Gilbert and we moved to Palm Beach's Royal Poinciana Playhouse to perform our last musical, Humperdinck's *Hansel and Gretel*.

Many a night, on my knees at bedside: *Oh, Mama, I'd been delivered to places I'd never dreamed, the kind of surprises that you said can only come from God.*

And then, that memory day, when a little boy's gift raised my heart straight up to where God lives. October third, the Feast of the Little Flower, a moment of blessing that's never left my heart…

He walks in late to class and says: "Sister Aneesa, Mama wanted you to have these." My little fourth grader was holding one dozen red roses in his tiny hand and delivered on this feast of St. Theresa, known for her promise to send roses down to earth. *Oh God, Are you for Real?*

I drew a deep breath, carefully pulled the bouquet from his fingers and held the dewy roses high before the class, like an Olympic torch, as one student said. I had their fullest attention: "Kids," I almost shouted, "we've been talking about miracles? Look what the Little Flower just did!"

Little could that tiny Bobby Myers who had arrived late on the Feast of the Little Flower clutching twelve red roses or his mother have known the why of my visceral reaction. I'd read St. Theresa's autobiography, *Story of a Soul* and it became my bible. I'd read, and reread it out on the dock, let her soul coach me. We merged into one out there. Her small acts of kindness to other sisters were done with big intentions. I wanted to imitate that small way and gave myself credit when I remembered to do so.

I pressed those twelve roses in some book on my shelf, a reminder of that time when a darling boy with black hair, now almost in his sixties, handed me a mystical and yes, I believe Heavenly message. I remain astonished at that surprising gift from, not only a little fourth-grader, but truly, from another invisible source.

Little did I ever suspect what a glorious time I'd enjoy at that St. Juliana school. Hard at first, yet the children sent to that institution taught me more than I ever would or could teach them. They helped unearth the talents I'd never known were part of me. They taught me about love for kids that I never suspected could be living in me. They helped me use those talents with laughter and fun. The many musicals we presented to the world have never left most of our memories

In truth, by teaching, I became a mother, and a woman as well. Learning fueled life, not only about matters at hand, but about finding myself through talents discovered as I went along. Not all kids gave me their total trust. But most faces lit up when I walked into their world, and nothing has ever thrilled me as much as my classroom and the musical plays we produced. So many of the students who passed through my world shaped the world I now live in these many decades later, a world filled with gratitude for that first St. Juliana assignment.

CHAPTER ELEVEN

Who Am I?

-Andrew-

Years fly by. I live for my kids, enduring the long commute down the Hudson River to boring slots filling in the kind of work any male or female could do. But it couldn't go on, not now, not any more. Not when, for the first time, brand-new channeling they call 'poems' begins to find its way into my ear, onto the page, and, "whadoyaknow" I discover a fluid tongue. I put the word out.

The questions wouldn't stop rolling in as I walked home into my wife's daily disappointment.

"Not this again! Another ending? No job again?"

The thinning wallet? 'Freddie Fuck-up' was my title according to her. "The place poetry's leading you won't put dinner on the table."

My Kelly disagreed. When her class held a poetry night, she had me come to share my latest sample about my lack of a highly paying job:

the color of my parachute

what color is my parachute?
why bright blue of course!
steely courage blue
deep imagination blue

first class achievement blue
gift wrapped faith blue
monochrome gender blue
beloved sea & sky blue
penetrating eye blue
sensually rich blue
sensitively sharp blue
fiercely independent blue
persevering steadfast blue
empathetically true blue
emphatically light optimistic blue
but parenthetically downcast blues blue
for alas with shattered careers long lost thereunder
not in earthly descent o'er all these places together we flew
me and my parachute of lofty soaring dreams blue

My sister Sarah offered me a stay at her farm in Vermont for the summer. Why not? Anne was wrapping up her own master's degree, the kids were off to camp. Truth sat on the table: nobody would miss me. If anyone needed to find *me*, I sure did. In Sarah's barn loft, I rigged up a corner room and sound system, played Bach organ concertos, lay back, listened, let go of the blame. In no time two very clear voices took up places inside me. They couldn't have sounded more apart. Skitz and Skatz were their names, right out of central casting…

Skitz (speaking authoritatively, low-voiced): "Monsieur LeBoeuf this is not where you belong. I suggest you get your feet back on the ground."

Skatz (in quiet, fluid tones): "Hey man, cool it. You're doin' right. Keep it up. Take it straight from here. You got it!"

I listened for days to these two go back and forth. "These guys need to be taped!" Before long it became clear who was in the lead. Down came the order that took me through the rest of my life...

"Look, Mister Manager, I can't fire you but you're not in charge anymore. It's true, you do have something to contribute. But from now on you work for me, not the other way around!"

Back home after that summer, it was clear where reality was lit. Michael at twelve, Daniel, ten and now young Kelly—all the fires of my life! Nighttime pages, Saturday cartoons, sunfish-sailing on the Hudson, biking in summer, skiing in winter. Our little ancient-looking split-level on the ridge, big Mike on the top floor, front-to-back room of his own, bubbling over with connections to living things, the latest being his salt-water aquarium. Dan in his second-floor room next to ours, desk built outdoors' under a big hemlock. Another tree appeared on his walls, his creativity blossoming everywhere. Feline buddy Charcoal couldn't get any closer to him. They were truly a pair of lovers. But even here, all wasn't exactly golden. Kelly's dragging limp tore me up, too often bringing her home in tears.

"Daddy, that Freddy always makes fun of me. Can't the doctor give me a longer left leg?"

Dan began disappearing into our neighbor's church and not just on Sundays. Each Wednesday evening for Bible study, then weekend retreats and overnights. I was losing my son to another family whose only son had long befriended him. I quit looking for another job that summer and drove my boy to his first Christian camp. Sitting beside him in that steel chair, I sang the fervent denomination's hymns, prayed their petitionary prayers, even as what couldn't escape my convictions of this kind of cardboard religion never entered my own heart. Nonetheless, when the minister put it to us, *"Anyone desiring to*

turn their life over to Christ?" I did amble my way up the wide aisle. Who wouldn't want to reclaim their boy?

"Son, you are saved in the name of the Lord Jesus Christ!"

The audience clapped as if I'd won a Divine lottery. I walked back to a grinning Daniel. *My God, I'd been baptized in a beautiful Belgian cathedral, not in a tent, not in a religion that had little history.*

Reverend, I'm here because I want my son back.

Michael had a bad summer that year too. His own best friend, the guy more connected than any other to date, was killed on his bike. Big Mike, always so full of spirit, energy, and joy didn't know where to start, never fully could find his way back to the Mike we always knew.

It rained all week, muddy milky rain. Time was running out, so was money, and so was Anne's patience. I needed help and dialed Rick Murphy. The drive was long but my therapist-priest-friend was worth the gas. In his waiting room, I sat on a wooden chair observing a schefflera wilt before my eyes. Finally, the door opened and Rick's smile accompanied him as he extended his hand.

"Glad to see you, Andy."

A short guy, he wears casual black, usually checking his wristwatch when a session's time has run out. This time, I didn't notice that habit of his and felt good about it. He sits down, pushes a glass of water to the side, throws his feet up on his desk.

"Andy, it's been a while. What's up?"

His plenty tired eyes focus on my own. I sta-ti, sta-tu…stutter again, am completely shipwrecked.

"Take your time, brother. Let's have a cup of coffee. Sally just made a fresh pot." I try again; nothing! He takes his feet off the desk, leans forward.

"Andy, stop. It's okay."

I hear his kindly tone. I relax.

Sally ushers in a tray of coffee and sweet rolls. Rick delves in, pours me a cup.

"Drink up, man. Take a few more deep breaths, Andy. I'm putting my watch away. We've got all the time we need."

The quiet in the room feels like freedom to say nothing, just to sip, get my bearings. I hope to be okay with my bungling in front of this giving soul. I start up again.

"You said once that I live in an iron gray world. God, Rick, I'd say it's a journey into gross blackness. Everything's locked down, tight. Meaning's dropped out. I don't sleep, got the shakes like an alcoholic without a drink. Truth to tell I'm only existing. Time to time a poem still comes, but not a clue where it may take me."

Rick swings his feet up onto his desk, leans back in his black leather swivel. I ride on, in a more confident tone.

"Yesterday, I dropped Dan off at college. We didn't say much. He kept gazing out the window. I thought that I was losing him again."

"Is that what happened?"

"Yup, but here's the thing. After we hugged goodbye, he turned back, came up close, shocked the hell out of me."

"'Dad' he said, 'don't let Mom stand between you and what you want to do. If it's your poetry then for sure, do it. If it's listening to Prokofiev...just be the you I for one know you to be.' *Goddamn it,* Rick, *be the you I know you to be?* My son was back, closer than ever, son turned about-face-father."

Rick fell forward in that swivel clapping his hands high above his head, his long hair falling.

"For sure! Listen up, Andy, I was thinking about you before you called. Play poker if you can with this deck of cards I'm dealing and remember that line from Rilke: *For here there is no place that does not see you. You must change your life.* Yes, dear man, you, Andrew, must change your life. It's a rule for all of us at one time or another. It means taking the high, the different, but difficult road. In all my marriage counseling, I've never told anyone this directly, but Andy, this marriage of yours is not helpful to you as far as I can see."

My hand began to shake.

"That's no news to you, is it?"

Rick checks out my twirling thumbs. They begin to wobble even more.

"Well, last night Anne screamed about her empty wallet. '*Freddie Fuck-up! That's who you are.*' I took it in, she was right after all. But not cheerleader Kelly who ran into the room.

"'You're the Freddie Fuck-up, Mom. You're the one who's always putting Dad down. You can't do this, you can't do that. I know he's having problems, but stop doing that to Dad.'"

"Must have been some show."

"Rick, this wife is a good woman, loves her kids, is good to them, dinner every night on the table, takes Kelly shopping, surprises Mike with a new phone for his room, is closest to Dan. She's put up with my failures. God almighty, of course, a woman needs security and I can't seem to give her that. How's she to depend on me? Doesn't take rocket science to know I'm losing it, her, and the rest."

"You're right Andy, Anne is a good woman, a very good woman. And you are one good man, no matter the trials. Your hardest work will be to believe that, to love yourself. Who can forget gospel's second-most quote after loving our God. 'Love your neighbor as yourself.' Damn, doesn't that make yourself close to number one? Damn tough commandment, this loving self."

I rubbed my hands over my face, the smell of coffee everywhere. I had to get away.

Two weeks later, the final turnaround came, the phone call to change my life.

"Mr. LeBoeuf, a friend of yours from CUNY was down here on holiday, suggested you might be our man. This is Don Beattie,

Director of our South Florida Community College's New Programs. We need a teacher with a good grasp of what video can do in and out of the classroom to design curriculum and classroom for our students. Everything tells us this new medium is about to become one of our students' treasured learning tools. Would you be interested in talking to us?"

Sudden confidence rang in my response: "Would I! That's me, sir!"

After exchanging more, where I'd learned video, something about the college kids I'd taught at CUNY, we set the date for a local interview. I hung up, howled loud enough for Anne to come screaming from the kitchen, a giant spoon in her hand ready to pounce wherever it was needed.

"What the hell's wrong?"

"What's wrong? *What's right!* Finally, no busting my balls for any dumb ass to hire me."

I swooped Anne into my arms, danced her stiff body back into the kitchen.

"Yeah, Annie. Someone wants me—in South Florida of all places!"

"Oh, No! That far?"

"Honey, you bet! That's the job. Especially down there. Just think, I get to do something I love, start to finish, my poems, my video."

Was this really me talking, chest swelling, blood rushing, fists clenching? Not one God-damn stutter.

Sorry kids, I gotta go!

CHAPTER TWELVE

Bye-Bye Black

~Aneesa~

The wondrous time of the 1960s glued nuns to the television set watching history-making unfold. Our fingers were crossed listening to spirited speeches from Catholic candidate, John F. Kennedy. Handsome, debonair, rich! We giggled, hoped and prayed on our knees in chapel that the miracle could happen, that America would recognize Catholics as equal to any candidate wanting to be President. And his wife, gorgeous and smart, proved equipped to speak different languages to the huge crowds. We sisters joined our hands together with the on-screen applause. We laughed at Kennedy's jokes, imagined a Catholic sitting for the first time in the Oval Office. And finally, what do you know! By the slimmest of chances, an election affirmed that anyone born in the U.S. could be President. An Irish Catholic took center stage and his wife became our First Lady. Our Superior at the time, Sister Francis de Sales popped the cork, and wine flowed into our glassware and we stood around the community room table, happy to the point of tipsy, toasting a fresh and brilliant White House resident and his adorable fashionable sexy partner. Americans were living in a new political era.

Following that, the famous sixties also focused us on Selma's marches led by Martin Luther King, Jr., police and barking dogs waiting to attack black people holding signs for their cause. Civil rights were up-close-and-personal and torture rampant as brave black teens were dragged off the sidewalks by the hair, men and women pummeled with wooden sticks and firehoses. I had to close my eyes; it proved too hard to watch. Very hard. But we were happy to read Thomas Merton's timely praise for television's contribution. Everybody in America, especially in the South, had to see what was going on. Bad as African American people's suffering pounded at us, undoubtedly television had a huge and good influence on civil rights, letting everyone in on the terror.

During those sixties, I added a new decade to my years as I turned thirty and the community decided to transfer me from St. Juliana school to Jacksonville's Kenny High, a hard change at first. I missed my grade school life, the musicals, the convent's backyard garden. But with God's grace, and my determination to fit into my new assignment, I began to love the school's older teens sitting in larger desks, the boy's legs stretched out before me. Their challenges were cool and inviting and friendly, teens old enough as Steve Jobs once said, to think differently, to read daily newspapers, to drive their own cars to class and to write essays good enough for publication, to own legs hearty enough to race up the two stories to my choral class while even chanting the Beatles' response to the Vietnam war, "All we are saying, is give peace a chance."

Catholic high school truthfully was wild and admittedly, older Catholic kids were teaching me things I probably needed to know. They were early activists, enjoying the widest of social justice issues I'd never indulged in, raising the level of class discussions to hot and heavy, questioning me on church's religious issues. I was opened to a world beyond Gilbert and Sullivan operettas, even taught more religion than I had ever passed on to my young lives, a life different and beyond my Novitiate/grade school world. More than my concerned dogma, these teens were widening my eyes to abandon the pray-and-obey of my convent life. A daily newspaper lay on my desk, and the highly complicated world of business and historic news was being presented to me. God had certainly taken me into a new, extended way of looking at the meanings that had been bundled up inside me.

What proved not so pleasant in that two-story convent was the fact that I saw plump Sister Melana sneaking behind the chapel wall to pull out a cigarette, lighting it and furiously puffing on it. I should have moved on but watching her was a mixture of fascination and horror. A smoking Nun? *Dear God! Is she really smoking?* I couldn't tear my eyes away. Finally, she saw me, covered her face and defended her behavior: "Aneesa, you have to understand. Smoking calms me down. Really! I need this cigarette."

Truth to tell, I've never forgotten that sweet nun puffing on a cigarette even though something in me knew I shouldn't have watched and surely not judged her behavior. Something in me knew I was totally rude to embarrass her like that. Even so, as weeks turned into months, the constant lack of disconnect I felt with my dinner companions stirred concrete feelings of isolation. Long walks along the convent's back yards of wild life helped easy breathing, fostered more prayer: *Please, God, do something!* Perhaps I realized there was no separation except in my own mind. I had to work hard to get really centered and back to where I belonged.

One day, Sister Martha, my kind principal called me into her office and offered me a giant breakthrough. "Sister Aneesa, Vatican II has been born, and I want to send you to New York's Manhattanville college in Purchase, New York to study music. You'll get a professional degree in Music Education. I'm proud of the choral work you're leading around here." I literally jumped up, gave her a hug and my soul sailed out of her office.

I felt down to earth lucky to be sent away, thrilled to study piano, theory, and composition in a different environment. But the change was not just about studying music. Lunch and dinner time brought the onslaught of studying young nuns and their vibrant conversations about what was taking place in the church. I loved hearing their excitement about Vatican II's teachings, as if making way for a convent future that wasn't written in the rule book. Their table conversations kept me thinking: *Dear God, What's so important about being a nun?*

Manhattanville proved a breaking point. I was pulled into the church's new theology and doctrine as well as learning details of piano composition and new keyboard skills in preparation for my exams. I was challenged, renewed, and uplifted daily. Mother Morgan, the head of the music school, sailed in professors and scholars who lectured in Manhattanville's beautiful auditorium. Invited guests, famous writers and professors increased my excitement at being part of a new church. I simply couldn't get enough. I discovered an insatiable mind, a mind that kept seizing every opportunity to capture another new slant on a nun's life well-lived. One lecturing priest, Adrian Van Kaam left me telling myself: *Aneesa, life is not a problem to be solved, but a mystery to be lived!*

In those piano rooms, I spent hours practicing that keyboard, while sounds from the next room I could hear sopranos and contraltos voices practicing their opera roles. It was a world of music, of Gregorian Chant, of orchestral chorus. My heart soared at hearing violins and trumpets sending melodies into my ears.

But what filled my soul even more were the thoughtful, smart-thinking young nuns, the inspiring back and forth questions that I hadn't experienced back home, the kind of questions that excitedly re-evaluated our role in post Vatican II. These nun friends voiced language which proved why scores of nuns and priests were leaving the church's outdated rules. Some were marrying, some were creating original kinds of mission life. Vatican II had inspired a whole new change of how to joyfully get in touch with a joyful God.

Returning to Bishop Moore at the end of my final summer, Sister Martha—the kindest and a most loving Superior—met me at the back door, took my suitcase from my hand, shared her winning smile but welcomed me with a question I completely found difficult to answer: "Are you glad to be home, Sister Aneesa?"

Dear God, I loved this nun but totally felt unable to say my truth: *No, dear Sister Martha, I'm not at all glad to be back! This isn't home anymore!*

Home? The truth was I did love the classroom antics of my kids, their joy, loved the chapel hymns the sisters belted out at prayer time to my organ accompaniment. Yet something about community life, especially after Manhattanville's summers had grounded me elsewhere. I did wonder if I belonged in this community anymore. In that Vatican II era, not every nun reflected changing her life the way I was doing. Not anybody's fault. Not mine either.

On an ordinary afternoon, how well I remembered plopping myself out in the garden on a bench, loving the breeze that cooled Florida's heat when suddenly, I heard animated female and male voices flowing over the backyard fence. I peeked over that fence: young couple from next door was tending their rose garden, digging, planting, and laughing together. Whatever it was, whatever the work they were completing, hearing and seeing that loving relationship beaming my way, I felt caught in their sweet net of joy. *Am I longing for something like that?* Something beyond living with convent sisters? Could I find that kind of simple sweet joy anywhere in one of my religious houses?

I was not supposed to forget why I came here, why I had searched for more of God. Something was going on, and honestly, I didn't like that something. I charged back to my cell, got on my knees by the side of the bed. *God, where are you? Have you left me too?*

Only my Irish seventy-year-old Sister Brendan could cut through convent irritation. Conversations with her, silly jokes, her ability to dwell on things that mattered never failed to lift my spirit. I loved her. In all the time I lived with her, sitting beside her at table, or in the community room, this old nun never allowed any convent challenges to defeat her. The smile came through. Classroom kids loved her and she easily befriended them—lauded and laughed at their foolishness. Her Latin classes' desks were never empty.

Always full of surprises, I found a package in my mailbox one day, pulled it out and discovered a newly printed Jerusalem Bible. It had arrived without a sender's name. I asked around, but had to call the publishing company to learn the giver. And how she chuckled when I tagged my benefactor. That was Brendan, a real joy of generous sunlight.

I also loved how accomplished and well-read she was. When I asked her why she read *Time* magazine's back pages first she chuckled: "Aneesa, decent news is found on the last pages."

On that last day of classes at Bishop Kenny, I suffered the worst of my teaching days, worse than dinners with complaining nuns, worse than finding my blooming orchids scorched by a Florida sun. I had to find my Brendan. There she was, sitting in the community room, an open book hiding her face. I slumped down beside her, feeling victimized, angry, and mean, fired because my high school principal had come to my classroom's back door and with the strongest of voices, yelled at me in front of my senior boys. She had found them sitting quietly, just reading newspapers or magazines because I'd given them permission to do so. It was the last day of school. My grades were in, so what else?

"Were they noisy?"

"No, no! Good boys. They were just all still."

"Okay, so what was the problem?"

"Well, the problem was prissy Sister Susie, principal. She marches by, screams as if these young men had been sucking blood. She stands at the back door, uses her best scolding, loud enough for the whole school to hear her push her fire at me: 'Sister Aneesa, get these boys back to work or I'll give them something to do.' I stare at her, and felt a damn anger hook me. If I'd had a knife, I might have aimed it for her heart. How could she embarrass me like that?" I felt tears just telling Brendan.

Brendan placed her hand on my knee. I needed that assurance that I wasn't crazy. The warmth of noon sun poured through the window across from us, creating blessed sharing of truth contradicting the cold air-conditioning in my soul. I felt happy tattling on the principal. Everyone knew Brendan never tolerated any nun yelling at kids, much less a principal yelling at a class's teacher.

"Oh, Lord! Poor kids. But listen, graduation's only a few days away. Your boys weren't going to do anything to jeopardize that." Brendan leaned close, wiped my tears.

"How can I ever work under her next year?"

Brendan leaned back in her chair holding my hand. "Aneesa, it's the last day of school. She's a wreck. Probably the bishop is on her case. Parents won't let her alone. You'll be okay. I suppose she'll even apologize."

"I'll never forgive her embarrassing me in front of my kids like that." We both sit quietly as sun poured through the wide floor to ceiling windows.

*Oh, The times are a changing…*Bob Dylan's truthful words come roaring as this older nun and I sat side by side in our community room. Everything was changing, coming down hard and apart. Little could both of us ever suspect that our beloved Catholic President Kennedy was about to be assassinated that year, that the entire country would fall into mourning, and that eventually, I'd finally leave the convent after sixteen years of teaching and wearing black robed serge covering every hair on my head!

"Brendan?" I interrupt her reading. "Are you ever sorry you didn't marry that doctor back in Ireland?"

Her red cheeks bobbed like a little kid enjoying a joke. "Not at all dear one. This life I chose, chose me. Now stop stewing and let's go and find out what's for lunch."

In the next school year, the air was wine and the Florida maples were a tapestry of rich airy colors. I rested on an outside back cement step, alone, wanting nature to heal me, save me from myself for what might lie ahead. A few sycamores held tight flaming leaves, some falling. I picked one up, fondled its darkening self.

Leaf, you've endured sun, wind, rain, and now you are to give your body back to the earth. Did you agree to turn brown, and fall? It's about death, isn't it? Death, that event still awaiting me. Still teaching me? Yet, maybe, in God's wide reality, a death to all I've ever believed in will finally huddle up close. Will I ever be happy again?

CHAPTER THIRTEEN

Soul Doctor

~Andrew~

Sitting in an airplane by a window, something inside me always harkens to language when I'm in the air, to a happy mood for writing, to lofty beginnings. I hoped this new adventure would prove that to be true. That ride down to this city of last resort was no different. Out came a poem I titled "**on the wing**".

> *soaring misty blue warms me*
> *making time atop cottony puffs*
> *heaven-bent my life now takes me*
> *feet no longer dragging*
> *powering now nacelle-like*
> *swept back with god-speed on rakish wing*
> *i was numb this morning*
> *numb to goodbye with best-friend-&-foe*
> *numb to the hauling and the schedules*
> *(tho i dropped nothing. i wasn't late)*
> *numb to a teary gray bleary gray goodbye*
> *of wet waking city brick*
> *and shiny weeping asphalt*
> *silently on yom kippur i crept out of the old*

of all childhood partings and farewells
there on westside's steamy quayside
or filled with thrill midst idlewild's swaying reeds
no one, not one now
beneath me here and left behind
tho beckoning still in powder eiderdown
a past no longer containing
childhood no longer expectant
from sparkling perch, here at thirty-five thousand feet
my lord releases me
to fly free again

The lumbering DC-3 pulls up to South Florida International's terminal. Arched over the entrance, shouting in black letters: *Welcome to the Last Resort.* Hurrahs with oops attached. I find my way across town to the little motel that awaited per setup by FKCC. The contract was for two years and I couldn't wait to get started. But first to catch my breath on my new isle of creativity, far from everything burdensomely familiar, truly sparkling like a fairytale come true.

Oh boy, am I in for it! (And just how so I hadn't a clue!)

Next morning, I take a cab to the campus, find my way to Don Beattie's simple office. Nice guy; a welcome change. After a short chat, he leads me to my office down the hall, a wide window and I went right to it. Yes, you could just make out the bay there in the corner past spreading coconut fronds.

The job ahead was configured in three steps, none would take very long. First, design the new off-studio classroom, so they could get started on it. Second, generate a syllabus for teaching video and film, another for giving them a start with the new portable ¾-inch porta-pak. Finally, once those schemes were submitted and approved, I could specify the equipment to be ordered.

I can already well sense my students' thrill; a brand-new world is being born, yes for them but for me too, finally a new world born in my soul.

Almighty God, I bend my knees to You.

That next week, I am invited to join the City's Poetry Guild, poets delivering poems aloud, sometimes under the stars, sometimes for audiences, all one real *wow* for me. Things were finally up at last! My muse was pitching words I couldn't scribble fast enough, and all became a matter of simply writing down, rarely composing. Most surprising of all, my muse was voicing words in a fluid flow. Who'd ever guess? Is this possible, far from alone, this band of folk here similarly charged! One guy creates vocal lines on the spot, no writing in between. Also, our most moving speaker, lead organizer too, was a crusty fisherman-poet Jessie. Oh, the soaring I did in that guild. Art and nature, works of words, a perfect layering of peace had never turned up in a stutterer's paychecks.

As for Anne, a beginning feeling of overtime discomfort.

Dear Sweetheart,

It's been three months. I miss the kids. A gnawing grows in me. You and I knew I landed this job for the paycheck, for camera work, but especially for me, my creative take-off. I know it's crazy in your book. To write poetry baffled you, never could bring in the dough. I'm sorry for that. Yet, in all honesty, Anne, I've never been so together, so smooth around my video work but more, around this brightness of writing verse. Small and long lines flow easily, never felt so rooted.

Can you ever understand that I miss you but have never been sorry to have left?

Andy

One night, there she was, a simple blond sitting in back, rapt and wearing a catchy smile as I danced over my signature lines. We were in Jessie's girlfriend Alice's art store on Collier street, where we did our public readings. After the last one, it didn't take long for us to find each other in the crowd. Her name was Gerta.

CHAPTER 14

TRYSTS

~Aneesa~

In the sixties, Vatican II had roared in under Pope John's vision, Catholic teaching broadened, and old-fashioned rules completely shifted. Priests and nuns stepped into new ministerial worlds. Some set up residence near homeless shelters, some embraced prison leadership, others marched to protest America's Vietnam war. Some fell in love, promised to take each other in sickness and in health until death would part them. Everything was now crushing that once granite and immoveable church. On such a scale of change I was being torched into by reflective flames, Vatican II's heat burning inside me as it had done to nuns leaving their vows behind. *Leave the convent? Could I? Would I?*

It took my observant and truthful brother to shift me to where I would go. When my assignment trusted me to live in a newly built red brick two-story convent home that almost resembled some Park Avenue Mansion, I felt the answer I'd been looking for. Located on the shores of a Lake called Fairview, the building proved quite opulent, a wide dining room, glass windows with a view of the lake, a structure with second story Sisters' balconies overlooking the water. And as I walked my brother around that building the sense of living simply had been broken. He sensed it as I did too.

"My God, Aneesa, it's lavish, rich. You take your meals in an imposing dining area with wide, glass windows overlooking a wide lake, you enjoy a private bedroom having a personal balcony, all beautiful, all costly if you ask me. But didn't you take a vow of poverty? What's the difference being a millionaire or living like one?"

My dear brother had come to visit. It didn't take a long look for his shock to set in at my convent home's enormity, its grandeur. As we toured, his unleashed comments embraced the silent reserve I'd felt when I first saw it. I looked into his eyes, loved him for his honesty, revealing what I had too long denied. The home was certainly not a sign of our poverty virtue, and that long hug of his at the end of our tour accurately predicted I wouldn't be praying in this structure by the lake much longer.

Soon transferred to Coral Gables in Miami, St. Theresa Convent, I was happy Sister Brendan had been transferred to this same convent a few years back. She greeted me with warm hugs and her jolly laugh: "Imagine that now we're living together again!"

The question of leaving-or-staying puzzled me still. The nuns I was living with weren't as complaining as my high school sisters. But—and maybe life has a way of making sure it gets its way—the answers to my quest became clear on my thirty-eighth birthday in the month of May. Why then, I couldn't say, but I felt nothing but the urge to leave on that day. Brendan listened as I spoke up my doubts, soon lovingly gave the sweetest permission to leave the life of black.

Scared and confused, on an early Thursday morning, I donned a pair of old Levis, a white sleeveless top, and a pair of brown sandals.

I walked down St. Theresa Convent's long hallway to say goodbye to the most blessed of friends, the saddest of goodbyes.

"Look at you," Brendan cried. We hugged long and hard. My eyes flooded. We sat on the edge of her bed, arms around each shoulder, bonded by convent memories, words she used to liberate me from guilt. She took my hand firmly and her final words caught my leaving into sharp and confident focus. "Darling Aneesa, whatever job we do we can make it a work of the heart. You don't have to change the work God committed you to. Continue that good labor for Him. All of it, whatever you set out to do is part of God's noble design. Not wearing a habit doesn't mean you don't sweat for His sake. And who knows? You may sweat even more."

"Brendan, I'll never forget you. Will you write?"

Brendan did write, up until the day she could no longer hold a pen. This noble nun lived into her nineties, always flashing that smile when I visited her, always welcoming.

The warning of philosopher Ralph Waldo Emerson haunted me as I pulled open the large mahogany front door: *There are the voices which we hear in solitude, but they grow faint and inaudible as we enter the world.*

Outside into God's fresh air, I descended the high cement steps, scared silly seeing a whole new world: racing cars, rushing pedestrians, a dog barking. Thoughts ran every which way. *You're leaving a familiar world where you've been nurtured and educated and loved.*

Church bells rang out over the city. Loud, joyous, celebratory clanging, as if a wedding on this Thursday had just taken place or a priest had been ordained. I needed the sound of those bells, a joyous sound. I needed someone besides my Brendan to tell me it's all okay, that I'm safe and will adjust after these mostly happy sixteen years of convent life. Am I really doing this? Leaving the life I had been called to? I remembered how years ago, I'd paused before that Novitiate door in Jensen Beach. And now another pause, another step toward God?

As my friend drove me to my parent's condo, a line from Charles Dickens' came roaring in: "One forgets a place once they leave it behind." *No, no, Mr. Dickens! You can take the nun out of the convent but you can't the convent out of the nun.* No, again, Mr. Dickens. I will never fail to reminisce about dear Frances de Sales, slipping me a bottle of wine to help me boycott a sleepless night after so many intense musical rehearsals. And, how this nun loved God's green Earth, taught me to see all plant life as God's planting, to rejoice with every bloom.

How could I ever forget days of recollection when I found silence pure gift, when I listened to Jesuit retreat masters inspire me to do more, be more, love more? For the convent's money spent for a Manhattanville College education, when I studied music and was privileged to hear inspiring theology lectures? When Mother

Morgan called me over to meet Bishop Somebody, as if I, a little studious nun, had been somebody? And of course, Mr. Dickens, how could I forget the kids I taught? The bright and noisy leprechauns. Oh no, again, no, no, Mr. Dickens. My memories of convent life live in my brain's scrapbook. And by God, always will.

CHAPTER FIFTEEN

New Life with Shadows

-Andrew-

From the top, Gerta you were poor Glys, the mermaid to me. I never did finish the film.

How charming! No make-up, nothing beyond pure you, ready smile, and that hint of a European accent. Who could be more natural, complete with your authentic caring? What could be more like home? We were hanging out with new poet friends at your little rented abode. Then, how you loved the water. How many times we'd duck in the bright side of sunset, on my days off. Once in the sea you did become one of its familiar, graceful creatures- deep-diving, up-soaring, arms raised to the sky, utterly selfless, fluid departures, one after the other. Truthfully, it all did feel magical to me, something I never did proclaim out loud because somehow I did know that wasn't exactly the word. Something very much bigger. Come to think of it, I do believe it was your own great fear that you kept hidden, one grand power taking you so inside another. Sure did take me awhile. But that's getting way ahead; time to see you here live on-screen.

introduction to the sea called ra
for feature-length animated musical

Many tides ago in the blue-green Sea Called Ra there lived happily a princess dolphin named Glys --or Gleese however you please. Anyway that's what it sometimes rhymes with, and Princess Glys really couldn't be anyone else. Ever.

In a family of a reef-ring of a sea of HIS JOYNESS HIGH, Glys performed her duties so well everyone she touched knew it, and smiled it, in about that order. She lived happily in a little pink corner of fan coral she took to be her castle. And it was from there that every morning, when the sun was just high enough to warm the tips of your toes, or the tip of your flipper as was her case, why then every morning princess Glys could be seen setting out for her work.

Now you knew she knew her work well. In Ra that means when the sun first smiles at you, you smile back. And not because you have to, either. It just sort of happens that way . . . if you work at it.

To be fair hers weren't the hardest chores in the land --uh, sea. You see Glys was the princess in charge of helping all the young female dolphins in Ra to become princesses. It's not that she was called anything fancy. You could just sort of tell. If you wanted to be a princess dolphin, Glys was the girl to see in this sea. She was the happiest a princess dolphin could be, alone.

Now before I go on with my story, there are some things you should know about the Sea Called Ra and the folk that inhabit it.

(Oh big deal. another fish story!)

Well then perhaps I better tell you about me first, just so you know I'm not making all this up.

Name's Jeremy . . . (sings)

sometimes i'm a butterfly
sometimes i'm a tree
sometimes i'm a breath of wind
and sometimes i'm a (me) . . . thank you!

but mostly i'm a bunch of words
and thoughts you just can't touch
and so i live in inky tubes
and places no one cares for very (much) . . . thank you!

but if you set me free to be
the me you see as jeremy
i'll be for you the same way too
and say things true for you
. . . for YOU !

CHAPTER SIXTEEN

Longing

~Aneesa~

"Daddy, I've left the convent." I whispered into the payphone near their condo. I heard his deep breathing, hoped he could easily recognize his daughter's voice, it had been a long time. I waited and waited some more. Would he hang up? Would I, on the man who loved me from baby time?

"Aneesa," his voice choked but finally I heard a voice more elderly than I remembered: "You gave those nuns your best years. Why did you leave now?"

There he stood at the open condo door, his brown eyes wet, my mother standing behind him, more wrinkles on both. He folded me into extended arms, a long heartfelt hug. Mama came forward and hugged hard as well. Her dear whisper sailed into my heart: "Honey, I've prayed for this moment."

In their dining room stood a wide table laden with the Syrian way of displaying hospitality: each dish a work of love: *kibbe, malfoof, salata,*

108

and of course, traditional freshly baked bread, Mama's specialty, bread she used to bake in our old house upstairs above the store, beads of sweat accompanying. How well I recall the baking of Syrian bread that kept her running to the kitchen, pulling out the hot loaves, pouring butter between their folded circles and passing each loaf around the table onto us kids. "Oh, Mama, I've missed your Syrian homemade. Thank you!"

I couldn't help the tears at that familiar, Middle Eastern food! Never had any convent table been so laden, my culture setting out platters brimming with long hours of creating food claiming best and healthiest of dining cuisines. I sat with relish and Mama began filling my plate.

At this, my first meal home, seconds were in as I watched Daddy cut up a giant onion to top another steaming bowl of lentil/spinach soup, liquid possessing lots of lemon. They knew it had been my favorite soup. "Mama, I have missed eating this kind of food in every convent I was assigned. Roast beef, baked potatoes, and green beans are satisfying American cuisine but nothing beats *kibbe* and your kind of *salata*." At that, my father got up to load even more "seconds" on my plate.

"Daddy, enough!"

I toured the new condo, totally decorated Middle Eastern style. How both parents loved sitting on their second-story porch watching young children swim up and down the length of the condo's backyard pool. I was home, especially when Mama brought out her nail polish to do my nails. Red nails? It was truly a new beginning.

That week, I wandered Orlando's new neighborhoods, hardly recognizing the city I'd left behind. Daddy's business life flourished as Florida became a tourist mecca, a city made upscale by Disney's presence, theme parks, innovations delivering visitors from all over the world. But me? If I thought long about it, I missed my warm, sleepy old Orlando.

As if on a pilgrimage, I meandered down Robinson Avenue, taking in many of its changes. Lake Eola now was host to a giant green fountain, brimming water into the city's whitest of clouds. I stood before it, gazed at a bit of nature doing its thing, then wandered down to Eola Park where tourists strolled its cement paths.

Over to my left, St. James School remained a beacon, the place where I had first been introduced to Catholicism. I stood, taking in that fierce presence that had brought my body and soul into a black habit like the nuns who taught there. That school proved evidence of how I'd first fallen in love with strange looking St. Joseph's nuns. I pondered the reality, and how amazingly, the school has remained alive, still a vibrant educational facility, still an old Catholic establishment, but now with few if any nuns teaching there.

Looking at that playground, I could see again how my shy father had approached the pastor, Monsignor John Bishop standing outside amid several parents. He nervously asked him about tuition required for his non-Catholic kids. This Irish prelate gave him a smile above all smiles, and an answer that he couldn't help but relate to Syrian friends and practically every customer who entered our store, so impressed by this compassionate cleric. "Mr. Hadad," Monsignor answered, "Pay what you can."

In a much earlier time when I was about seven or eight, sitting in the front seat of our old brown '43 Plymouth close to Daddy we were driving on that same Robinson Highway. Suddenly, out my front window, they appeared, the first I'd ever seen: two completely strange creatures dressed in black, arms up their long open sleeves, scurrying along Lake Eola's sidewalks. I jumped up on the seat and pointed.

"Daddy, Daddy, look! What funny people they are. What are they?"

Something of that image touched deep into my baby soul, and even now as I type that memory, I see them from that car window, still sense the oddness of their dress and the stark awe I felt. I'd like to think, they unknowingly cast some kind spell on me.

At breakfast, the next day, laughingly, my father threw a little of his pocket change on the table.

"Think there's enough for your new Toyota?"

That new Toyota drove me south where I commenced work as a music director and religious educator. I'd been hired by a lovable Irish priest, Father Mike. I'd met him when studying theology at Miami's Barry College and as the group worked together, Father Mike's presence burst alive wonderful feelings in me, like I'd never experienced. Little did I suspect, I'd fall for this man like many women do, both single and still married who fall hard for their pastor.

At the church's pulpit, it was his preaching more than his charm. Like me, Father Mike's listeners absorbed his Vatican II sermons, his emphasis on family life and what really mattered. Often, they would question him after Mass, focusing on his personal few lines.

This priest proved so down-to-earth, so beautifully understanding of his parishioners' woes and anxieties, of their challenges as parents, it made some them wonder how he could know of such things. Undoubtedly, a well-rounded priest. I wanted some of him for myself.

I tried to keep my mind on what I was hired for, to train teachers for catechetical work and to lead a parish choir. But from my religious education office, I couldn't help peeking out the window to see my boss, Father Mike, on Fridays atop his rumbling John Deere tractor, trimming the parish grounds before Sunday Mass. Some would say that Father Mike was a kid with a new toy, a tractor toy. I liked that about him. That attraction to him morphed into the closest companionship. He called on me too as I helped plan his sermons. Soon, we were composing youth liturgies, attending home Masses in parishioners' living rooms, and reaping a scrumptious home-cooked dinner afterward.

It seemed so natural. I became a woman in love with her priest. Had the bishop known, Mike would have been booted out of the parish. That's the way it was in those Catholic days. All dinners and movies had to be secret. I had to stop journaling about our close companionship.

My days nurtured a happiness I'd never known. Love came so naturally, and never did I feel guilty but confident that in our changing Vatican II Church, the vow of celibacy would go down in history and my title in the parish would become Mrs. Mike. Even more, little did I suspect it was not to be.

Our summer vacations were spent in various foreign countries where I could publicly be Mrs. Mike. The Virgin Islands, Ireland, Canada, we even visited communist Poland. Walking treed sidewalks with him, we celebrated love in the open. Passersby smiled and I could smile back. Vacations spelled freedom to sit close at dinner, to sleep in the same hotel room. Hearing the news of a newly elected pope who took the name of Pope John Paul, we thought this Pontiff who'd suffered a communist regime would surely abolish the celibacy rule. How wrong we were.

Time passed, and at some point, I recognized a budding hateful truth: no church change on celibacy was forthcoming. Even if it did someday come, Mike was never going to leave the priesthood, so in love with his work.

It soon became apparent I was paying a heavy price for a secret love affair, fighting an institutional church, fighting the loss of the dream. The struggle was tearful. I cried more than laughed, spent time more alone than together, and all my former joy had become a pained time of woe. I traveled to my parents' condo home, sobbed on Mama's shoulder. I'd lost the only love my life had even known.

"Aneesa, darling, you have to protect yourself. Start something new, just for yourself. You'll see what you're made of when on your own." Coupled with Mama's counsel, the brother who had called the shots on poverty about that giant red brick convent, now called the shots on this failing relationship. "You've got to get out, go on your own. This relationship isn't going anywhere but down. He's sweeping the floor with you. Why are you letting yourself be treated like this?"

That night, on my knees beside my bed, more tears wet my clean pillowcase: *But God, can I leave the only love I'd ever known? Even if it's failing? Is twelve years of drinking from the same church cup and working to lead parishioners to a deeper spiritual life, all over?*

And yet, all proved clear. Mama and Roland too. Loneliness is not to be tolerated. I'm too socially needy.

Finally, I found an escape. A good friend, a former nun had moved to Charlotte, North Carolina to take care of her dying mother. After I attended the funeral she invited me to come visit her, stay a while. *Connie, here I come.*

Under a sky so blue, so big as I looked out the car window, my packed suitcase jostled on the back seat. I drove north and was heartily welcomed. Her note had read:

> *Thank you for your sweet comforting. Thanks too for coming to mom's service. She and I planned it several years ago. I have a deep sense of peace now, a gentle closing and opening to another of life's chapters. But what about you? Your stressful priest relationship? Why don't you come up here, get another job, stay*

> *with me, use the second bedroom? And bring your*
> *Company Cat.*

A cold winter traveled me and Company cat that perched lightly on my driver's lap. With open arms and an icebox filled to the brim, Connie brought me into her home and heart, as if I were part of her family. We settled in and time spent with this friend meant living on fertile ground where I could sob, let out my anger, play melancholy tunes on her own piano, and try to sink less into apathy. Her open heart slowly lifted my soul.

"Don't stop crying because of me. Mom and I emptied a lot of tears in this place before she passed." On Connie's own Yamaha, we blended perfectly with what I call my holy hymn, a popular classic called "The Rose", written by Amanda McBroom: *Some say love, it is a river, that drowns the tender reed…a razor that leaves the soul to bleed…*I played and played that hymn some more, shed the tears that had to come to release the pressure pushing down on my heart. I loved Mike and probably always would.

Connie's love proved a bright light: "Something good will come out because of all your tears. I think that's the way God works."

Mike called a couple of times but we both knew it was over, he more than me. Yet, that hope to be with him hooked me to a long and hard unwinding.

One morning, Connie proposed a healing recipe: "Aneesa, let's ride up to one of Asheville's famous storytelling workshops." And so, we did. North Carolina summer's proved panacea.

We sat outside on green wooden benches under moving puffy white clouds listening to one professional storyteller after another. Everyone's eyes and ears were opened, nourished by tales that spoke truths and myths, profound messages soared, stretching feelings of loss in me to hints of acceptance.

It has been said many times. Story telling possesses an amazing ability to heal every problem. Both Connie and I were lifted anew in that audience. I heard one story, a well-known tale called "The Rabbi's Gift" on that mountaintop. I found a version in M. Scott Peck's bestseller, *The Road Less Traveled*. I include it here loosely translated:

Once upon a time, a great monastic order far away from the city was now in decay, only five old monks were left praying in the chapel. The Abbot agonized over the monastery's imminent death. Finally, he determined to ask advice from the Rabbi who lived in the woods. The Rabbi opened his door, knowing what the Abbot needed. They sat together at table without any words and soon both began to cry. No words, simple sobbing as if finding and excavating some deep truth. Finally, the abbot asks: "Tell me something to save my dying order."

The Rabbi pauses, then says: "The only thing I can tell you is that the Messiah is among you." At that saying from the Rabbi, they both stand and hug each other one long time. The Abbot then returns to the monastery. The monks greet their Abbot, "What did the Rabbi say?"

"The only thing he said was that the Messiah is among us."

In the months that followed, the monks pondered and wondered the significance of the Rabbi's words: The Messiah is among us?

Did he mean the Messiah is one of us monks? Did he mean Father Abbot? Father O'Brian? Certainly not crotchety Brother Alfred! Of course, the rabbi didn't mean me. I'm just an ordinary person. Yet, suppose

I am the Messiah? The five contemplated who the Messiah might be, and began to treat each other and themselves with extraordinary respect.

People came to visit the beautiful forest and the monastery and soon, visitors sensed a powerful aura in that place of prayer. They sensed the extraordinary respect that now filled the monastery. They came to the monastery to picnic, to play, and to pray, bringing friends, and friends brought friends.

Some of the younger men who came to visit the monastery started talking more with the older monks. One asked if he could join them. Then, another and another if they could join the abbot and older monks. Within a few years, the monastery once again became a thriving order, a vibrant center of light and spirituality.

Sitting at the piano, hitting the keys to sound major chords, I felt the rabbi's words would heal me, alleviate my pain, return me to a sense of worthiness, of an ability to be help to others, to pray without the constant stream of tears.

I stayed in North Carolina. Working at a women's college located near Belmont Abby, as the dean of students, I counseled young women, helping eager young ladies find answers to their problems, somehow uncovering a few personal solutions to my own problems. God knew what He was doing, sending me to young women. Little did they know how much I needed *them*.

Longing for Mike slowly fell away. I didn't think about him as much, enjoyed more ice cream cones with Connie, played Scrabble, never could top her score, but at the piano, my fingers hit the right keys, and my heart danced with those keys. We sang tunes from *The Sound of Music*, "Do, a deer, a female deer. Ray a drop of golden sun..."

My soul found a slant of sunshine again in that North Carolina state, and counseling young women was, in a way, another mother role. *God, you're writing on my page again.*

I fell back into keeping a journal, as if composing prayers, line by line, grace on each page. I guess you'd call that a bit of healing. Happy again? Not totally, but on the way to that place every human soul wants to find itself living.

Mom had become ill and needed me. Connie and I cried at my leaving as she waved to me from the front door. Company Cat nestled against me, now freed from Florida's fleas after living in Connie's freezing air conditioning temperatures. We aimed the Cadillac back to Orlando on Interstate 95, wind blowing everywhere around its speeding tires.

As for me, I was a much resolved and hopeful woman. It takes a heap of change to make things different. My cat and I were both ready for Florida sunshine.

Home in Orlando, many of Mama's Syrian friends hosted parties for me. They loved Mama and that love spilled onto me. Gratitude abounded in this new beginning. Where would it lead? I had no idea. Like most journeys, it took me to the place I unknowingly wanted to go, to a healing place where I hoped I would find the soulful prize: another soulmate, not a priest, but a lover. It was a prayer uttered that God answered in His own and challenging way.

I didn't have to wait long. But what appeared left me to wonder at the green work of God.

CHAPTER SEVENTEEN

Tie One On

-Andrew-

How to put it all together? A jumble, this little list I'm working off laying itself out across three and half decades, one rare looking-back. Still here does it live and loom.

The blink, the fall, the powers, the trials, tests, triumphs, torrents. Those seven trips up and down the peninsula, walking away from her, back down then up. That final return; final for sure, no return to speak of. Plenty of shrinks before and after, exorcist or two. All my doing. Where'd it go wrong? Where, oh where did we?

I don't remember ever arguing with you Gerta. Whatever was the problem? Weren't we living the story of mermaid Glys, in pure magic those days? Somehow it all had to do with that quiet of yours. Something was bothering you from deep inside. You didn't want me to know. The more you hid whatever it was, the more I wanted to find it out. After all, you were my princess.

There was that café down the street I was arranging for our poets in The Guild, a new setting, me in charge. You never complained. The final after-all when all was truly over, there was that one word that never stopped knocking around in my head. *Hubris!* What I will never forget too was mid-morning moment together at the kitchen table. Where'd it come from? What'd I do? *The Blink.* Wow, no wonder so much hidden quaking about what you were sitting on. No wonder that one craved memory you did divulge about having once been sensually whipped in place. *Blink!* That's all it took to usher me out. Yes, some power of yours, and your family's too, now that I recall our late visit up to Canada. No, who can ever put a finger exactly on what I'm talking about?

So then, what? I was gone, starting with the loss of pen-on-paper along with these new fluid orations, and all those friends' connecting voices. In their place, stranger things were surfacing. I made myself understood in another's head in total silence, heard thoughts of theirs the same way. I left where my feet were standing and found myself someplace else altogether. I could move things without putting a hand on them. Pointless energies drifted through, headed to no place at all. I'll never forget the first rub. Someone had pulled up outside our house. Something got to me, maybe his loud radio. I could see the black car from our upstairs bedroom. My mind spoke him away in no uncertain terms, amazed at how fast he left. You would have nothing to do with any of it. Who could blame you? I had to leave, find my real self again.

While I'm at it, better put these new things to the test, find out what's going on. First trip out you did supply a used road bike—what got me no more than two islands before I ditched it, maybe to better tap my own resources. Then those immigrant farm workers…*maybe I can join them for a while.* Wish I had. I kept walking. Over the months seven trips out and back remains a merged jumble, each one stretching higher up the peninsula, brimming with things entirely out-of-life. Sometimes my thumb was out, something new for this exec-trained hand. Made-up travel van picked me up early on, the guy offering much kind advice. Another in a convertible supplied the opposite, returning me to the pavement in short order. Never a word spoken. My head wrapped in a loose scarf against a cooking sun, cops stopping me once for nothing more, hauling me in, depositing me in a large cell full of blazing hard creatures and a blaring TV. In no time, without a word, I was in control of that room through the screen. Someone called the guards, I was removed to solitary. Then in little time ushered from courtroom back out to the streets. One night in the same neighborhood, beneath an obvious broadcast tower, I let loose over the air an angry statement about the place's security forces so-called, as usual short of anything outward sounding. Another time I found myself on the beach. Oh, what a pretty girl. I tapped into her mind. She fled to her cabana. Beach cop approached, advised me in language undeniably audible: *Get lost!* Each time out for as long as weeks on end I'd reach the place where I had to go back. Running out of money? Maybe, though never had any to start with. Somehow that final place always told me those swirling doubts no longer added up, that I belonged to her, that it's time to go home. On one trip—I think Fort Lauderdale—I brought all my poems to the beach, tossed the whole bunch in the ocean—binders and all. Somewhere in the back of my head an odd hope swirling around that *someone will find them, will look for me. And all this will be over.*

I ventured over to my deceased mom's old church friend from growing-up days outside New York, a Monseigneur who had a parish of his own nearby. There he was, these decades later, opening his rectory door. *For God's sake, free me from this possession!* "No, I won't. Come to our service tomorrow instead." So, I did, and there, straight from his pulpit, did he publicly admonish this raggedy guy from the past. *For sure. But God, what'd I do again to deserve this?* On an earlier trip were cops under the bridge in their car. I tried to contact them, testing my mind-speak. They mind-spoke right back. "Okay, so you can hear us. What's going on?" Too complicated, I couldn't say. "Well, you got a long way to go. Better get back to learning life, boy."

On a longer trip out I made it up to somewhere in mid-state. Exhausted, I checked into a barn. There were horses inside. Was it okay to spend the night? "Sure thing, try the empty stable over there. We feel bad for you." I'll never forget them, still feel close to the family whenever I see one. Next day I made it to a restaurant's back door. Owner invited me in, brought me to the main room, offered me breakfast, kind as the horses. Told me about his place and his family, asked me about myself. In no time, I was helping him repair his roof—all out loud. He let me stay across the street in his ice-house, invited me to join his family at church on Sunday. I was touched to the core. Innocent teenage daughter got things going furiously inside. No, not this after all your Dad's done for me. I took off the next day without a word. There was the time I tried to get myself admitted to a Miami hospital. They wouldn't take me. I did somehow land in the biggest jail of all in Miami, don't know how, the place loaded with other mind-speakers. One inmate took me on, kindly heard me out, offered me much guidance on what went on there. In no time, I awoke in some type of asylum, addressed like a child. Gerta had Baker-Acted me, Florida's method to get troubled family members out of the way.

So on and so forth, the jumble never letting up, plenty more crazy moments than I can remember now while never at the time literally tabbing myself with such a condition. I do remember testing these strange powers on my own in every way. *What was going on?* The last trip took me all the way north to Jacksonville, where, as a kid right out of OCS, I'd been intelligence trained by the Navy. Surely, they need to know of this national security threat emanating from South Florida. I made it to the air station's intelligence office, where in no time I was politely escorted off the base. I called Gerta from Jacksonville's Greyhound station. On arrival there was another woman, couldn't recognize the very face I'd married. She took me to another house where she'd moved in with a girlfriend. We spent the night together but there was nothing left. She said it as directly as she could. "We're done. The only way you're going to get rid of me now is kill me."

Oh, my God, Save me!

CHAPTER EIGHTEEN

Longing Never Ends

~Aneesa~

"Jill, I'm home." I spoke and felt my voice shaking. I was definitely nervous. Would that best friend forgive me for waiting so long to call? We had been so close. I had loved that closeness at college—how we had roomed together, studied, exchanged blouses and skirts. This friend, another Catholic.

I wasn't sure why I hadn't connected earlier, maybe because of my secret affair with a priest. Would she have approved?

The Jill I had once known squealed happily into that mouthpiece, bringing my nervousness to a quick end. "You're out of the convent? Oh, thank God, Aneesa! Ring the church bells and come. Come to dinner. I can't wait."

Little had I ever realized what lay ahead for me; how this friend would become a close partner in my journey toward finding my real love, this friend who had played with me on the college's outside swings when we were young; how we'd carved words in trees close to the dorm, how everything then seemed possible. She had been wonderfully understanding about everything, was filled with imagination about the things of life, a woman who cared and was willing to give time to whomever she considered in need. She'd bring the food I loved to the dorm, Syrian baklava along with peanut butter cookies, and who hated the day I decided to don a black veil. Except for Sister Brendan, Jill Stone was the female bonding I'd sorely missed to share about my priest lover. And now, here she stood at her own front door, back in my life again, that familiar smile. We embraced in a long overdue hug.

Then, there was Todd: "I've heard so much about you, Aneesa." Jill's husband's hand felt warm. A twinkle in his eyes told me my life would be richer knowing him as well. This doctor took me right in.

"Did I ever thank you enough for loaning me your yellow striped dress when I gave that speech to my history class?" Jill laughed that infectious giggle I remembered.

"Yes, you thanked me and I think I gave that dress to you."

"You did, sweetie, you did."

Jill cooked dinner herself, proved to be her old special chicken and rice menu. The chatting never ceased. They shared proud details about their kids, Suzanne, three, and son Richard, five, both away at camp. So much had changed for Jill since we first roomed together. She'd left her Catholicism, honored Todd's mother to convert to Judaism, and that night and if I'm correct, sitting opposite of Todd was my first time meeting a Jew.

Little did I know how much Jewish life would influence my future, would deliver me to a world of religious faith so foreign to this former Catholic nun. I couldn't have dreamed how many Jews would eventually enter and enhance my adult world, teach me newer ways to know the Jewish Jesus, to love God in all His diversity.

Jill and I carried our cups of peppermint tea to her lighted back porch to watch a brilliant moon ride across the dark Orlando sky to the east while we caught up personal histories.

"Jill, I fell for him."

"What? Who? Tell me."

"A priest!"

"No, no! A priest?"

"No, no! We weren't doing anything wrong. We were headed for marriage when it all came apart. He was switched to a huge parish and it took his time and his love, in that move, diminished his love for me. I was crying more than laughing, loneliness sucking me dead almost daily. Sorrow became the norm."

"Oh, honey, why didn't you call me? I'd have been there for you, you know that."

"I guess I was ashamed." She handed me a tissue and I blew again. "I finally headed home to Mom, traveled up to North Carolina, lived with Connie, I don't think you ever met her. She was a blessing. Jill, it was pure grief, crying and that emotional feeling of homelessness. I didn't know where I belonged anymore. Parish life was over."

"Aneesa, all I can say right now is again, why didn't you call me? I would have been there. You always said I owned a barrel of understanding for another's troubles."

"Don't ask me why. I can't really say. God, I didn't know I still had more tears over it! I'm sorry to be bawling like this." I blew my nose, I hoped, for the last time.

"But, Jill, here's the story that really tells how that door to Mike finally closed."

Understandably, Jill looked confused. "Say what you're talking about?"

I wasn't sure I should share my dog story. It was such a make-believe unbelievable fairy tale.

"Honey, guess a part of Mike still lives in me. Evidently, I can't shake him completely."

She handed me another tissue, got up to pour me another cup of tea.

"Aneesa, take your time. Want another piece of cake?"

"No, no, just let me tell you what I've never told anybody,

except Mama." I dried my eyes, took a sip of her warm tea, and felt comfortable, safe being able to share my tale of Mike's rejection.

"One early morning when I was completely in grief, I took my cup of coffee to sit and watch the sunrise on the lake. I leaned on the tall cement wall that faced the lake. In that constant feeling of emptiness, I needed the warmth of a Florida sunshine, needed it to work heat over my shaking and always cold body."

Jill smiled easily, "Of course. Any breakup wires a brain almost crooked. It damn well hurts and continues to hurt. My first boyfriend did that to me, whatever. Make no mistake, Aneesa. It happens."

An owl sounded in the distance and I rested my voice and breathing a bit before going on. The moon began ducking behind another cloud. More darkness. I waited. Jill laid her hand gently on my arm: "Okay, Aneesa calm down, sip your tea. Go slow, okay?"

I blew my nose one more time. "I cried a lot more out there before the lake, as I sipped my coffee. Suddenly, I noticed this rippling in the middle of the water, something bobbing up and down, a movement of the most questioning kind."

I took another deep breath. Should I even be telling Jill this kind of crazy part? "It was, yes, a dog, and when his body reached the shore, his fur glistened as if holding onto diamonds. This animal, he, or she, who cares his gender, was a dachshund, the kind that Mike had owned and that I had loved. This animal seemed so alive, so purely dachshund. Mike had a tan and black dachshund. I couldn't believe what I was seeing. A dog? Coming out of the water? Had he known my condo was here? But hey, I sure asked God if I were seeing things. Maybe my tears had blinded me to reality?

"This animal like all dogs, shook off the drops clinging to his back. And then, slowly, honestly, this tiny four-legged creature began loping toward me, staring, coming closer until he stopped in front of me. I didn't move, just stared at him as he stared back. I didn't trust my belief or my disbelief, how his eyes dug deep into me. Was this animal for real? Then, without a bark, and me without a word, he bent his front legs, plopped down beside me still catching my stare. It was like this animal was not an animal but human. He knew me. He knew something.

"Jill, I can't say how long this dog and I sat together, in that kind of fixation, or how long my goose bumps were charged. I wasn't afraid but wondered if this was any kind of reality. Questions soared through me: *Where in the world had this animal come from? Why so close to me? Why a dog? Why, why?*"

"Yes, yes, yes—sounds crazy, but if you say so, Aneesa, it happened. Don't stop. Go on."

I looked hard at my friend, extremely grateful, hoping I hadn't gone over the top with her, this crazy kind of story, all this past stuff thrown at her on our first night together? We must have been good friends in those early days that I would trust her like that.

"Well, the dog stood up again, shook off more water, and as he did for the third time, I finally got it! I got the reason of his shaking, the message this dog was delivering. *Shake Mike off, shake off every memory, shake every missed dinner, every broken movie date, every stolen glance at another woman.* A shake so clear, it was impossible not to get it."

Jill found my hand and said in the sweetest tone: "I think I know where this is leading."

"Right, Jill, that shake taught me what I had to do."

Jill stood, came close and I stood as well. She hugged me hard and long, and I felt her love, her friendship deep and lasting. "Aneesa, this is downright mystical. Saint Theresa of Avila couldn't have caught that sign from God any better." She paused, moonlight fractiling our shadows.

"Your story has been, well,… like an alleluia. You finally got out, Aneesa, right?" She stood back, looked deeply into my eyes. "Honey: we're still close. I'm feeling your goose bumps, glad you shared all that with me." And then she held out her hand: "Look, my hand is shaking almost as much as yours."

At the door, we stood still with a last parting hug: "So now, Aneesa, I know what's ahead. I really know!" That was Jill, always a woman with sensibilities. She knew my truth before I said it.

"You're not looking for a job, because you have one. You're not hoping to find a friend, because you've got one, me, but a guy, the right guy, the really right guy that dog knew was waiting for you."

Two weeks later, breakfast at her suggestion, a dear little restaurant called, Good Hope. She affirmed it was the best eating place to get everyone's deep wishes realized.

We ordered. Eggs and bacon arrived and Jill got down to the dream. "Got your list?"

I pull out a small notebook where I'd written a list describing that partner God is supposed to send me. "It's short, Jill, but I think I covered every piece of what I'd like in a man."

"You want to start with his bank account, right?"

"Right, sound selfish?"

"Of course not."

"He doesn't have to own a Ferrari, but at least, not depend totally on my resources."

"Here, give me that list and let me read it. "Okay, like Todd, you want someone who can make you laugh. That's what a man is for."

She giggles that old infectious, still-familiar giggle, then continues to read my instructions to God.

"So, he can be bald like your dad and brothers? And yes, he should be educated, spiritual, and after that, well…are you open to whatever God sends?"

"Well, of course." *I was trying to really be truthful, that I WAS open to whatever or whoever You'd send.*

After breakfast, Jill stuffs my list into her purse and says: "Aneesa, that's a short list, and shouldn't be hard to find that kind of guy knocking on your front door. But let's do what scripture tells us to do, okay?" She closes her eyes and utters that Bible verse familiar to us both. *"Ask, and it shall be given to you, seek and you shall find…"* I join her, *"Knock and it shall be opened unto you."*

"Jill, think we could ask that he come really soon? I'm so ready!"

On a Tuesday and Thursday, Jill and I drive to St. Margaret's chapel, kneel, light two candles.

I whisper: "Jill, it seems so simple. Suppose God has other plans for me."

"Aneesa, making a list for a possible lover is not uncommon. I've heard how women list their preferences. Sometimes it happens just the way they petitioned it."

"Yeah, but sometimes God has the last laugh and women end up with a completely disgusting partner who drinks or womanizes."

She whispers in my ear: "Don't be so darn pessimistic. We'll do the best praying we can."

During our chapel visits, Jill knew I'd been ready to purchase my first home. A place I could call my own with a backyard for gardening, an extra bedroom to entertain friends. A place with a little taste, and certainly in the final analysis, no more rent money. I'd rented a place ever since leaving the convent. I was ready to own. I told her my other story about how the house forced me too.

I drove my real estate brother to the house that I'd seen and thought would work. We walked through its lovely rooms, happy for a convenient split-level design and a huge back porch. I stood at the back porch and dreamed of owning it, so awed at the beautiful landscaped backyard where a giant swath of land is protected. No one can ever build anything there. I'll always be able to just see pure wild Florida. *Oh, dear God, I want this home, and thanks to my father and mother and You of course, I've got inheritance money to buy it.*

Getting back into the car, and driving down the front of the street, we're both ready to talk about making an offer. But suddenly, both shocked, we stop the car. Across the street from the house of my dreams are two flying pigtails on Black children playing on the front lawn of their house. Stunned, I admitted I hated the feelings that came roaring through me. *Oh God, help. I'm not supposed to feel this way.*

By the look on my brother's face, he too was feeling the shock enough to say: "Aneesa, you can't live here."

His words signified what even my father would have probably said, even though this brother knew I'd been doing prejudice workshops. "You can't live near a Black family. This is a mixed racial neighborhood." His comment reflected how we'd both grown up in a racist Orlando. Black faces meant separate restrooms, separate water fountains, and certainly no white face living in the same neighborhood occupied by black people. Florida had been and still is a racist society. Neighborhoods are still segregated. One of my workshop participants had clearly stated that the most obvious reflection of separation happens on a Sunday morning when we're all in church, the blacks in theirs, whites only even in Catholic churches.

My feelings were closing me down. My brother and I were part of that awful racist attitude. Not only that, but the rule of economics played in this decision. I'd probably lose money on my investment.

I stared over at those two playing children with brown faces. At some point, my mind and heart finally took charge. *Aneesa, when you taught school, hadn't you stood for something else? Didn't you teach religion at Bishop Moore, teaching kids virtues that defined Catholic beliefs, my church's beliefs that said every man is your brother or sister? Didn't you teach your Catholic kids about prejudice?*

How well I remembered! When the civil rights battle was taking place in the sixties, I'd hung a picture of a white woman refusing to be railroaded out of her home because blacks were moving in. She'd put up a sign that read in big letters: *This house is not for sale.* Standing against a racist culture. Now it was my turn to put my religion on the line, hear my own words, print my own sign that would read: House is sold!

Weeks later, I met my Black neighbors at a gathering. I shook their hands, knowing I'd never touched a Black person before. I loved their smiles, soft and friendly, brilliant white teeth. It was such a first for me. For all my racial, political, religious, and cultural convictions, of speaking out against all profiling, this was an original moment given me. A black hand didn't feel any different from a white one. *In truth, I knew God was holding both of us in His hands.*

"So that's it, Jill, that's it!"

CHAPTER NINETEEN

Blink One, Seven Outs

-Andrew-

That decision to come back to Gerta never should have happened. She sure was moving on to somewhere else. I was possessed more than ever.

That last morning broke with sunshine and soft balmy breezes, everyone headed to today's work & play. I looked up at the sky feeling only dread. Coming tragedy. Loss of spirit out of body. We headed to the dock, early morning's steak knife firmly in my pocket.

Just as we got there, a guy was chartering sailboats from the dock. I tried to change everything, asked him if he needed help. He must have seen it all inside me. "I don't need your help!"

We were end-of-pier for our planned swim out to the offshore dock. Gerta dove right in, swam out, pulled her way up. I looked around. No sailboats. No other swimmers. Nothing but us. Large white bird at pier end's gave me last hello & goodbye.

This is it now, Andrew. Do make it happen what she asked you for.

I got to the dock, climbed up, went right for her. Her face was naked. She didn't pull back. I acted harder than I'll ever remember, went for her throat more than once, next plunged into mine. Sobbing, I dropped the knife, and took her into my arms.

Her cries not loud were last given to me, then to others nearby.

And to others nearby. Soon men in uniform were up there with us in no time, pulled her from me, slapping me with cuffs. They dumped me into their boat. I blacked out.

Waking up that night in dark single cell to jailer announcing it deep in my ear: "Man, your wife is dead."

Why not me?

CHAPTER TWENTY

Arab and Jew

-Aneesa-

The moon rose so beautifully in the black sky that I stopped what I was doing and where I was going just to sit and watch its rays cover my front lawn. Oh, you beautiful gift, all ablaze with heartfelt glory. That very night, I was on my way to a Thursday meeting of Arabs and Jews and Catholics, which has never proved anything but a powerful learning experience widening my world around its varied religions. Sometimes when wanting to make some kind of impression, if a person asks me my religion, I smile and give them this answer: I'm Catholic, Buddhist, Jew, Sikh, and even sometimes I'm bold enough to exclaim, I'm an atheist.

Because of Jill and Todd guiding me in a few Jewish practices, I had watched how, on their Sabbath no money was to be exchanged. I learned how the feast of Yum Kipper directed Jews to apologize to anyone offended. But what I loved best: fun and seriousness of Friday night Shabbat dinners. Learning Jewish songs, learning the blessings over the bread, learning rituals that sailed me back to attendance at my own Holy Mass, I soon realized how much our Catholic faith had been born from Jewish friends' traditional rituals.

Talk about being linked. We are so connected. God's little or not so little religious serving.

And oh, the Jewish weddings were thrilling to behold and attend! How the couple is married under the chuppah, a canopy, and how the bride and I think the groom as well, walks in a circle under the veil. And then, that sounding ritual of the groom stamping on and breaking the glass to pieces after the offering their vows. Oh, I swear, there are no other weddings so alive like Jewish weddings! And then bursts forth the thunderous music signalling the vibrant dancing. Whether wind howls or heavy rain pelts the roof, the dancing goes on!

I have watched the movie *Fiddler on the Roof* numerous times, demonstrating Jewish family life, the ancient homespun customs exercised again and again, and at the weddings that exciting dancing. Whenever I receive an invitation to a Jewish wedding, I might go out and buy a dress like no other. Someone at one of those weddings asked if I might have been a Jew in a former life. I swear it could be true.

Many times, driving home after one of those marrigaes, I easily often reflect on God's special secret about me, that in some former life, I was a Jew. And that my Arab father's tirades about Jews mean less and less, don't count in me anymore.

One year, I signed up for an interfaith New Year's celebration at Canterbury Retreat Center in Oviedo, Florida, led by Jesuit John Zogby and Zalman Schachter. They were a popular and beloved teacher duo in a New York community, and modeled their devotion to loving their neighbor no matter the religion.

At the start, Father Zogby instructed us to "Find a comfortable symbol that represents the biases you've particularly known and perhaps have suffered? It might be the prejudiced material in a book, the lyrics in a song, a news clipping, or something you have felt expresses that kind of bias following you through life."

A long silence dominated the group. It was an open question, hard to admit what names or attitudes followed our beings. But, Michael Jackowitz, a lawyer who sat at the end of the circle, was the man to answer with difficult honesty. He raised his hand and began with a quote from Robert Frost: "Before I built a wall I'd ask to know/What I was walling in or walling out…"

He paused, then reached into his pocket and pulled out a white handkerchief, waved it over his head like a signaling truth. He stood and everyone waited. "This handkerchief is about the plentiful tears that have been dropped onto the society because of prejudice. I am a Jew. Christians repeatedly try to convert me and my people. They want to pour the waters of baptism over our heads. We're only second best. To be a Christian is where we need to be. They claim that Jesus said, *I am the way, the truth, and the life.* I'd like to ask you Christians to quote Jesus rather saying: 'I am *a* way, not *the* way?'

Silence, that kind of sad quiet but thoughtful silence followed, the kind that can fill a room. Michael's comment was so real, to the point, and reflected what most of us had known since forever. I thought of my gay friend who'd suffered at the hands of Christians to the point of considering suicide. Of course, as I look back on Michael's bravery and wisdom for saying what he addressed aloud, obviously anyone with a sense of history knows how Jews suffered European pogroms. How even our Pius the twelfth pope hadn't spoken out against that horrific kind of prejudice, while as a child I'd also heard my Arab father angrily roar as he chopped onions for his Arab dishes, how Jews had taken Palestinian land for the establishment of Israel. He even went so far as to disparage his own beloved America for its obvious role in the establishment of Israel.

Oh God, when are we going to learn to be the Jesus that we say we adore?

Father Zogby quoted a line from Mahatma Gandhi: "I call him religious who understands the suffering of others." I thought of Jill's conversion, how happy she grew to share Todd's faith, how both were teaching me to know and respect Jewish life and all its traditions.

That New Year's retreat demonstrated only a beginning in my journey to bridge religious differences. When a conference on prejudice reduction caught my attention, I flew to Boston to study under Cherie Brown, a leader in the field of reducing prejudice. Cherie filled the board with truths we had harbored: "You are black, I am the lucky white. You are gay, I am normal. My roots are from across this American state. I get what I need, you don't deserve my caring."

I shared my father's neighborhood and prejudicial strike on his own immigrant status. I said aloud: "When this financially independent Syrian tried to buy a house in an upscale section of Orlando, neighbors thwarted that purchase. The realtor Jones reported to my dad some of their comments, but basically, they thought they were protecting their neighborhood: "No 'foreigner' is going to live on our block."

At that Boston workshop, I watched Cherie Brown demonstrate helping a Native American overcome some of the hurt he had endured: "Tell us what happened to you, Sun Man." Cherie directed the giant of a man standing beside her. He had volunteered to speak out! Sun Man's rigid face told of past hurts. In a hardly audible voice, he described a schoolyard wound born from jeering classmates. "They laughed at my long hair. Tugged at it. Every day!"

Composed and confident, Cherie holds his shaking hand inside both of hers, moves an inch closer to this tall American still suffering from that hurt.

"What would you want to say to them now, Sun Man?"

"I'd tell them to stop."

"So, tell them."

In the room's unbelievably dramatic scene, our eyes are focused on the two in front, our minds curious how this would go. We wait for him to speak. After a gentle prod from her, he whispers, "Stop."

Cherie orders,

"Sun Man, say it louder."

"Stop!"

She pushes even more. "Louder."

He finally screams: "For God's sake, get off my back."

My eyes are wet as we furiously applaud his authentic cry of pain.

A black man sitting next to me shouts: "Sun Man, nobody will ever pull on your hair again."

I chew on that scene much of the night. Sun Man, Cherie, her hug, the laughter, the clapping. When the two-day workshop ended, my soul had been present to every incident. Somehow all hurts and name calling and walls built against the human beings present, turned me more to the world's needs. We can't keep building walls.

I slept a wonderful sleep as if prayer had been alive in me all that day. Maybe those details were a prayer offered for each one's growth.

In the morning, before my flight back home, I sipped hot chocolate served by a brown Latino. Something new about God's presence was changing inside me because I saw this waiter differently, not just as a service provider but somehow as a brother, a Christ figure, maybe according to "The Rabbi's Gift", as perhaps another Messiah? His smile, in a real way seemed not strange, and I offered him my best smile in return.

Waiting for a taxi, I see a hawk flying. Oh, what a beautiful bird! He flies over the building's canopy and then perches high over my head. We lock eyes. Poet Rilke's lines I'd read only that morning in my hotel room came roaring back in memory.

I live my life in widening circles
that reach out across the world.
I may not complete this last one
but I give myself to it.

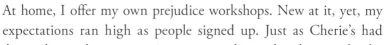

At home, I offer my own prejudice workshops. New at it, yet, my expectations ran high as people signed up. Just as Cherie's had directed us to share our stories, my group listened to the group's tales of hard encounters, of times when chips were down, and somehow, even *my* own group found a way to offer a participant's tough issues some tender thoughts.

One old Irish guy took us back to that time in history when businesses propped signs in their windows: *No Irish need apply.* Then of course, *it could easily be in the south: White Only wanted.*

In my own teenage experience riding Orlando's city buses, I didn't like how many blacks walked past me to the back of the bus. There they would sit for the ride to town. It is totally easy to thank God for Rosa Parks, the woman who refused to give up her whites-only seat.

Now, in this time of high calamity for Arabs, I certainly let it be known to the groups how my own people were constantly being labeled terrorists by some reporters and politicians. I wonder with the group if prejudice has been around since Adam and Eve.

In one unforgettable Christian/Jewish workshop, picture the scene when two Christian fundamentalists were sitting in the front seats. One, a gray haired outspoken man and his wife. They had just finished spouting the goodness of their faith in Christ. It was too much. That speech of theirs prompted a woman sitting in the back to shoot up and forward. Standing in front of the black and white group, brave lady that she was, she faced the group sitting in steel chairs and practically shouted: "Look! I am a Jew. I have heard your spiel, a spiel I've heard throughout my life. Look at my head. Do I have horns as some of you believe and even might have said I have? Have you thought about that history that has followed me, yes, me all my life?" Her shaken voice revealed how visibly nervous this Jewish woman was in her declaration, as if all her life she had wanted to shout that defense to any accusers.

When she sat back down, I was simply struck dumb. Could I or should I have commented on her truth? Somehow, I merely thanked her for speaking up. I asked the group to ponder deeply what she had given us. This Jewish lady had openly knocked down that cruel and blatant and anti-Semitic history that might have been living in those perhaps innocent Christians present in this workshop. After a long silence, one woman raised her hand to say: "It honestly takes a long time to let go of our stupid beliefs."

Working around prejudicial issues wasn't the only topic that filled my mind as participants filed through the open door and signed the registration sheet. Often, I'd look up from the sign-in pad longing to see a possibility, a fantasy of that perfect someone emerging from my soulmate list.

Would it be asking too much, Jesus, for him to show up, sit in front, look fondly at me, ask for a date, and well, eventually slip a ring on my finger?

CHAPTER TWENTY-ONE

We're Done

-Andrew-

Days pass. My eyes blur most of the time, my body slow, dormant, grown skinny. I'm allowed fresh air, drag myself outside, walk the yard, find a bench, see a small jagged rock, pick it up, rub it. Rocks know things, know life. Tell me, I ask it, why am I still here?

Sarah's soft eyes, her closeness helps peel away some isolation. She hugs me, a genuine long loving. "Of course, Andy, I had to come."

We sit in silence. She holds my hand, squeezes it occasionally. A guard walks by to check on us. She turns: "Andy, you gotta know that wasn't you who killed her. The brother I know would never harm a mosquito. Something went dreadfully wrong."

We both tear up. That eternal question pounds me to shreds. Why, God why? Why her and I'm still here?

words fail me—words fail me—words fail
me words fail—me words fail—me words fail—me words
fail me words—fail me words—fail me words

CHAPTER TWENTY-TWO

Speaking Out

~Aneesa~

Michael's comment about Jesus's A way, not *The* way, so transformed me that I grew more involved with neighborhood Jews. I rang the doorbell of the married couple, the Middle-Eastern group leaders, Erica and Omar Schliefer who just happened, (probably a God-ordained coincidence) to live close.

Like another Cherie, Erica proved fearless and confident, reminding the Orlando leadership board of our purpose: "We work to bridge the separation between Jews and Arabs here in Orlando, locally to spread our work globally."

I loved her smile, her ability to laugh when the discussions got serious and often painful. Flare-ups easily happened. After all, we weren't talking about the best pizza recipes in town. We were Jew to Arab up close, sitting side by side in our meeting, navigating each other to understand better our differences that a long history had perpetuated.

Erica was clear: "Don't expect to know where your own hostility comes from. It's never clear, so in our Middle Eastern workshops, we simply follow the program's attempt to listen, to understand and try the best we can, to build bridges."

At one of our workshops, sunshine poured through the large

windows as Jews spoke of their take on our separateness. The room often got too warm and quite heated when Arabs heard speeches like this: "You Arabs don't want to make peace. No! Arabs want to push us into the sea."

Was it the way he said it, this wizened Jew who pointed his finger at a senior Arab-American woman, holding back nothing. His buddies in the corner clapped but that didn't stop her ability to stand up and shout back: "Listen, Mr. Weinstock. You Jews took our land. All your accusations are part of the problem. Israelis are pushing us from our homes, bulldozing the places we've lived in for generations. Please! We have been as rejected as you."

Tempers ran amok. I don't know how she did it but Erica could always take control, mirror both sides, echoing what each said as if to honor any personal beliefs no matter if she herself owned a different view. That was her strategy, always to affirm comments.

I was steeped in the subtleties and sensibilities coming from this woman leader. I grew to know that it wasn't about right or wrong. It was about bridging hurtful gaps that exist, always being about trying to make peace, and always honoring participant differences. A fresh pot of coffee and home-baked apple pie helped.

In my estimation, Erica proved a Christ model. I was learning so much from her way, her genuine caring even for those who might have vocally held anti-Semitic views. Feeling her warmth for each board member, I couldn't help but call it out as we got into her car one morning: "Erica, you're more a Christ figure than some of my Christian friends." Without a blink, as she started the motor she uttered: "Why not, Aneesa? He's one of our boys." I have shared that quip with many Catholic friends who think in terms of Jesus as a Christian and need to be reminded that Jesus was a Jew.

Even in her funny way, this Jewish woman owned a precious manner of speaking lovingly of God. My Christianity couldn't help but honor her, and I value her close friendship to this day.

What follows here is how I was totally gifted a freedom to work with these Jews free from a hidden Christian shame. Admittedly, a quiet shame followed me for all the abuse we Christians had imposed upon Jews.

That freedom happened one Thursday night as I was getting dressed for our board meeting. On my dresser sat Mama's gold cross—a cross she'd given me from the Holy Land. I loved that engraved piece of gold and usually wore it, but always kept it hidden in the presence of any Jewish friends.

Did I hear it? Did it really speak to me? That cross, that Thursday night?

"Wear me!" *What?* I stared at its gold. "Wear me openly and be proud!" My stomach turned knots. *No…no…I can't wear that relic in the presence of a Jew. You know it reminds them of ghetto life, forced baptisms, yellow stars sewed on their jackets.*

But that night, here it was, hanging openly from my neck. My Jewish friends sat close and could notice that relic hanging in the open. Not only was it revealed outwardly but suddenly, something in me had to express the fear, the unease I'd carried all past months in the presence of these close friends. I raised my hand high before the break.

"What's up?" Erica asked from the front of the room. I made my way to her, turned and faced those seated friends. Erica took my cold hand in hers. I felt its warmth and softness. I reminded myself I'm in the presence of friends, close friends, and surely, they won't throw stones just because I wore a gold cross.

What bubbles out of me was obviously a leap of faith, a trust that the words I hadn't planned could be spoken, a surprise to myself. But there they were, words that still wrap themselves around my heart these many years later: "You Jews need to know that Christ is the light of my life."

For a moment, silence. Nothing is said. The room is dead with stubborn silence. Had I really said that? But in a moment, Erica's marvelous ability to bridge any gaps at a meeting enters the scene. She drops my hand and charges this little Arab Catholic to do the impossible. She points to all those watching: "Okay, go, look each Jew in the eye and tell them just what you have said. Say it to each one."

It was direct order.

Timidly but with an inner instinct that all would be okay, I circle the room, bend down to each Jew, not blink as I look directly into their eyes, and in a voice no longer my own, repeat my faith:

"Omar, Christ is the light of my life!"

"Louise, Christ is the light of my life!"

"David, Christ is the light of my life!"

Years later, when I reflect on that pivotal night declaring my fidelity to Christianity in the face of each Jew, I not only voiced my own liberation but also voiced an inner liberation for the Jews that were present that night. I supposed they'd never heard a Christian declaring her religious belief publicly without any malice, a Christian who wasn't about converting anyone except to the possibility of creating a world community, a world of tolerance, a world where it was okay to be who we were in the presence of someone who is not the same.

Driving me home that night, Louise stated plainly: "Aneesa, I don't mind if you Christians try to convert us. It's when you kill us because we don't convert that I have a problem."

I felt the truth of her words as I got out of the car. "Oh, Louise! So right on." She called me the next day. "Aneesa, we profited from Erica's order to you as well. Ask Pastor Walsh if you and Erica can present our work to his Sunday congregation?"

Father Walsh was quick to respond. "Sure, but only for five minutes."

That next Sunday we stood before my parish's pulpit. We were Arab and Jew, before St. Margaret Mary's thousand worshippers, promising Father Walsh not to waste a minute of given time. Quick-witted Erica grabs my hand, holds my arm high, and declares in pulpit voice, "Aneesa represents my double enemy. She's a Catholic. Growing up in Belgium, I ran from Catholics. They threw stones at me calling me dirty Jew." Her words, bold and eloquent, summed the rampant anti-Semitism she had known.

Still holding my arm, she takes a deep breath to declare: "Aneesa represents another enemy, an Arab. My people and hers have yet to make peace."

With knees shaking, I held tight the microphone to confess: "My Arab father distanced himself from Jews, often voicing his political complaint: 'The Yahood (Arabic for Jew) control everything.' That line I heard more than once and it had probably created a subtle anti-Semitism in my own heart, an anti-Semitism that simmered until I met and fell in love with this Jewish woman and my other Jewish allies, moving me beyond that not-so-subtle mindful separation."

I had planned to stop there, yet, in a church so amazingly quiet, not even a cough, I felt pushed to speak as I looked at my friend: "Erica, you are no longer the Jew to me but a believer as much in communion with me as those sitting here in Catholic pews."

At that, the silence burst into endless clapping. We stood before a standing ovation at each of the Sunday's five Masses. We welcomed their smiles, their affirmation. Father Walsh threw me a delicious wink as we stepped away from the altar. I had been standing on a heavenly cloud taking in a vibrant gift of cheers and clapping.

Still, it must be told that as we stood outside taking in warm comments, wearing a wide-brimmed hat a senior lady approached Erica and me. Not shy a bit, she hit her with a stare and that demeaning ancient accusation. "But why do you refuse baptism?"

Erica turned to me, grabbed my arm and we found our car and let it drive us home. The lady's comment wasn't worth a response. *Oh God, when will they ever learn? When will they ever...learn?*

CHAPTER TWENTY-THREE

Anytime Now, God

-Andrew-

One day I find in the prison library's pages, the story of Clarence Earl Gideon, a poor Florida cracker boy to whom I owe my new life, if that's what it can be called. He is credited with the law that says the state must provide an attorney to defend him of any charge. He's called a public defender. On June 3, 1961 Gideon was arrested and charged with stealing $50 plus bottles of beer from a Bay Harbor poolroom. Pleading not-guilty he was denied a lawyer. "But our US Constitution says I have the right to defend myself," he told the judge, who ignored him and went ahead with his conviction and sentencing.

In the final passages of that book that I'd been reading, our once Attorney General, Robert Kennedy, brother of John F. Kennedy, wrote:

> *If an obscure Florida convict named Clarence Earl Gideon had not sat down in his prison cell with a pencil and paper to write a letter to the Supreme Court, and if the Court had not taken the trouble to look for merit in that one crude petition among all the bundles of mail it must receive every day, the*

vast machinery of American law would have gone on functioning undisturbed. But Gideon did write that letter, the Court did look into his case; he was retried with the help of competent counsel, found not guilty, and released from prison after two years of punishment for a crime he did not commit. It changed the whole course of American legal history.

Big thanks, Gideon. You, of course were way ahead of me; no question of my own guilt. But thanks too for my fine public defender, Paul, who found me wilting in my jail cell, who determined to form a plan to bring me back to life.

"First, Andrew, let's get you mentally checked out." His action led to the following statement that he informed me a week later, unbelievable news:

"Andrew, the psychiatrists' investigations leave little doubt: three shrinks have found you insane when you committed that crime. Our next step will be asking the court to know that you're correctable. We'll get you to the department's clinic for some longer term chemical treatment and analysis. When that works out, I'll appeal for a jury-free plea-bargain sentencing. Finally, if all works like it should, we'll appeal for prison sentencing, not state asylum, because there's never any leaving that worst horror."

Often, I sat pondering if this Court Appointed Attorney named *Paul, might have seen something in me worth saving? You're young, totally on your own every bit on your own, never a chance to air any of it with blanked out killer-client. By God's design, I live now because of you.*

Andy, did you get that copy of the Divine Office I sent? You always did love those prayers. Maybe they'll help keep things together. Here are a few New Yorker

cartoons between the pages. Enjoy a laugh or two between your sacred chats.

~ Sarah

I'm aiming to move closer, Dad, visit you regularly. This last time that horrible female guard strip searched every inch of my body. Gosh Dad, I didn't like your dry skin, blood shot eyes. Are you sleeping? You must be in constant danger, the place is so full of shanks, drugs, and killings. Tell me Dad, what's prison really like?

~ Kelly

God, Kelly, what a question.

What could I ever tell you? I can't say what it's really like after all these years. I don't want you to know it's no state institution; convicted bullies run the place. Privacy's long gone, always a busybody poking over your shoulder, even in the john. And how about the non-stop, tortuous language I have to listen to "mother fucker" this, "mother fucker" that. That's the worst. Or maybe not: all this black and white stuff at the same time. We're now the minority, at the receiving end of so much long-hauled black rage. Whenever it's all done, will I someday write about any of it? None of it's for you now, Kelly. Besides, truly bigger things are happening here, Kelly, believe me. Now this is what I'll write you...

Kelly, darling, rest assured, I'm not going to be here much longer; the present does become amazingly clear. I owe it to this monastery routine and voluntary quiet. Wrapped around early Merton writing, it didn't take long for me to button my own mouth. Besides, if that young guy in the next dorm over does silence for who-knows-why (they think he's crazy), surely with this monastic model in hand, I can claim my own silence.

Honey, here's what happens at countdown. When the whistle blows, we line up, morning, noon, and evening for headcount. Taking off from Benedict's Rule, that whistle becomes an abbreviated bell's call to prayer—Lauds, Sext, and Vespers.

Meantime, there's the prison factory plant. My hands are occupied, mind at ease, I'm helping make office furniture. Ora et Labora! Our young team head is one fine leader, comes out with "Ain't no thing!" when something's off. I owe lots too to a fiery minister named Shamus who comes to visit me after hours, brings cookies, helping me see how these bars matter less and less. So, you see, more and more life is becoming an inner one for me. So, for heaven's sake, Kelly, don't take that new job to come down here. Don't move away from your Ron. I'm going to see you again soon enough.

- love, Dad

Because I don't answer when questioned, the guards all become convinced I've gone over the edge. Or worse: I'm challenging with fierce resistance all my own. I call my silence a "word fast." Even my good boss at the furniture plant won't stand up for me because of my continued silence. So, as a result, I'm now on a bus to The Rock,

Florida's high-security prison in Stark where the state's own killings take place. Damn, life's now really ending, a final payout for Gerta's life.

For a long while, everything is routine until one day they escort me to the prison shrink's office. *Okay, about to get worked over.* I sit in silence, watching him scan me from behind his desk. He gets up, surprises me by gently removing my handcuffs. "Call me Chuck." He offers me a cigarette. There goes any resistance. I grab the weed without guilt; sure beats smoking butts off the prison yard.

"Would you like a pack?"

Oh, I know where this is going. Old good guy/bad guy routine. Anyone with a speck of military intelligence knows.

"Andrew, you coached that young inmate, Guy, in French! Good work!"

Chuck leans back in his chair, taking another long look at me. I say nothing. "Listen, you've been silent for too long now." He returns to scanning the folder on his desk. "What's going on?"

I'm in no hurry, friend.

Now it comes to me straight out.

"This much I can tell you, Mr. LeBoeuf. The state can't release you while you're in this whirlwind of dysfunction. You're worse now than when we admitted you. So, to get free…well…listen, how about you and me talk this time every week? Go back to your cell, have a hard look at how much longer you intend to keep this up. I do assume you're wanting to leave this place."

Well, of course! It's been three years of this silence, ten all told behind bars. By God, if all it takes is talking my way out of here, I'm game.

Our third connect does it. "Okay, doc, have it your way. But let me start by saying this. My purpose never was to attack you guys with this silence. Sure, I understand how authority can take it that way. But I'm simply following a spiritual regimen that helps me through."

Out came the words without stutter, a voice I'd almost forgotten now mercifully let loose. Chuck sat back with a smile, exuding victory. Still not convinced of proffered con-mind health versus lying prison authority. Then suddenly, Chuck surprises me without the unexpected immediate dismissal to Step Two. Ever freer conversations continue in our weekly meetings, gaining my trust. There's something authentically warm and friendly about this Chuck, something very misplaced here in starky-Rock. We're covering much ground.

Thursday afternoon during a heavy rainstorm there it is, the final conversation. "Andrew, you've come to the end. I'm signing your release. You've got a life out there waiting for you. Go to it!"

My insides run at a gallop. Nature here I come, out there big where rain itself so freely falls...*I'm free!*

CHAPTER TWENTY-FOUR

Jill's Promises

~Aneesa~

Jill follows me to the kitchen:

"Todd and I love your hosting these Shabbat meals, hearing the different sounds of Hebrew, Christian, Muslim prayers across the table. That African woman here for the first time. Big thanks for including us."

My faith-filled friend stands at the sink washing dinner plates, rinsing, and stacking them into the dish holder. I stand near, grab a towel, and start to dry. As usual, we're a team. And as usual, I start my litany of complaints.

"Oh, God, Jill, I'd give you the world if I could. Sure, having all this diversity at my monk's table seems like what I've been called to do since leaving the convent, leaving Mike. I'm to bring the world around my dinner table, share what's vital. But Jill, seeing all these couples sitting and sharing, I think God's on Sabbatical; *where's my man?*" She looks hard at me. "Yes, I'm whining again."

Jill pulls the towel from my hands, grabs both hands and pulls me to the back porch. I love how her love can easily lead me around.

"Girl, hear me. For sixteen years, you and God were a couple. If any man ever thought to go after you, he'd face a Catholic firing squad. Now you're out, you show your gorgeous black curls, your slimmed down figure, your infectious laugh. You're inviting. And you've got your family's inheritance so no one has to take care of you. You've got it all. What you don't have, it seems to me, is a lot of trust."

I stand mute. She looks out the screen's porch door at her beloved Todd walking the garden's paths under the light of the full moon. She turns back.

"Maybe, Aneesa, you have to wrestle with God a little before you meet God's successor."

That night, I drove to Mama's condo, found her in bed. I looked long and hard at this face that had been such a close comfort, mentor, totally hard worker for my father. I launched into expressing my joy at how she'd been for me:

"Oh, Mama, how you tended to my needs. Every time I needed your comfort, you were there, cried with me when Mike chose another: sponsored my plane ride to Boston to learn the techniques to reduce prejudice. You taught me to look at life's accidents as God's sharp pruning for inner growth. And you taught me how to smile."

She pats the bed. I sit down beside her, knowing her time was coming, maybe almost now? *And now, Mama, is it your time for more inner growth? Will you also teach me how to face death, the hardest facing of all?*

She opens her eyes wider, turns to face me.

"Aneesa, I know you want me to stay, but for what? Another lunch or dinner with a friend? Another phone call to contribute to something? Cook another meal? I've had enough of all that. If it doesn't sound too corny, honey, I'd rather have lunch with God."

In the following weeks, brother and me sat long hours by her bedside. Often, the stories of our lives are repeated: how this mother had left everything familiar in Paterson for Daddy, then pregnant with my brother to accompany my father to Florida, that tearful goodbye to her own mother like saying goodbye to herself; how Grandma had waved a surrendering white handkerchief as the pickup truck rolled down the narrow street aimed for some Florida road, soon out of sight.

Then, weeks later, that terrifying accident! A car hit Grandma and she fell into the snow—helpless. She lay there for no one knows how long. No one saw this woman; and so no one came. She died in another of Paterson's blizzards.

Mama's sorrow was indescribable. She lay days in bed, not getting out to work behind the counter. Daddy had to wait on customers as well serve their packages of meat.

"No, I can't let you go to the funeral," he shouted loud enough for the whole neighborhood to hear him. It's a hard story to tell. We both cried even in the retelling.

For days, I looked longingly at Mama sleeping more and more, a sleep so unlike her.

Images of her vibrant and happy tore at my heart: Times we had sat outside on the back porch as she loved painting her fingernails bright red. I sat as witness to her pride in well-manicured hands.

I referred once to how often she'd tolerated Daddy's selfishness, only slipping her a lonely twenty as she and her buddies drove to Florida's malls for weekly Thursday outing, shopping, lunch, and whatever older women find interesting. A twenty probably wouldn't even buy a pair of stockings.

We laughed remembering that poor snake that landed on her head in St. Pete when Daddy was away.

"I wish I hadn't been so afraid," she said. "Those animals were doing what snakes naturally do, climbing into warm snug places to sleep like I'm doing now."

"Mama, actually, when I drive past acres of Florida's undeveloped woods, I'm happy to think of them free, no bulldozers scaring the hell out of them....maybe St. Pete was our growing time."

"But now those bulldozes are ruining Florida. always tearing up places animals call home. I declare that Florida has become a state for sale."

The next day, I fixed her an egg salad sandwich! She bites only a few bites. I watch as her eyes close.

Oh God, is she on her way out? I wanted to keep a conversation going instead of letting her drop away.

"Mama, do you miss having lunch with your buddies?

Now I could say what I had wanted for so many times after Daddy died. "Mama, did you always have to pay for their lunch. Your buddies said after Daddy died, you'd never let them pay."

"Listen, Aneesa, it was the first time in my life that I could throw money at friends. I could come and I could go. I didn't take orders anymore, free of a grocery counter, of standing for hours, of keeping that smile burned on my face. What did I know then of clothes, perfume, and jewelry?"

The day was quiet. The window reflected a setting sun's beams pushing on the tile floor.

I watched the lines beginning to separate from her earthly life. On those last nights alone, I held her hands, checked her brightly painted nails. I got into her bed, lay close, rubbed her arm, her side, the happiest I'd been in so long. I found love living in me that I had never before felt so deeply for a mother who never abandoned me. Maybe in her passing away time I become or became aware at just how precious a mother/daughter bond can be.

Finally, the sun hovered over the earth on that morning, All Souls Day, November 2, 1983. Mama breathed her last. I wondered if my loss was too deep to cry. I stole over to the piano and played hymns, one after another while waiting for the ambulance to come.

Mama followed my father in death. He had died because he'd hit his head when exercising at the YMCA on Mills street. The operation on his skull proved successful but again like my father to do his own thing, against doctor's order, got up out of bed when he came home from the hospital. Down he fell in the kitchen, trying to cook up some authentic Syrian meal. Mama came running but she couldn't lift him. An ambulance delivered him to the hospital and this talkative father, who'd directed many a Syrian in the ways of making money, never spoke another word.

Our Greek Orthodox priest and friend, Father Diab, led the funeral service and often I visited Daddy's grave where he was buried in an Orlando Cemetery. Mama now lay beside him in that plot she had arranged for herself after daddy's passing seven years ago.

Little did I dream that in a few years, I'd stand beside their graves holding the hand of a man I would one day marry, the man I believed my mother brought from her angelic post, the man whom God had directed to stand at my side, be the soulmate my friends and I had prayed for.

At her funeral, friends jammed the church, shared memories of Mama's maturity, her legendary generosity of donating sets of colorful dishes to the Syrian-American club, mailing checks to St. Jude's children's hospital, donating furniture to Lebanese immigrants. An old friendly salesman to our grocery store stood up to offer a side of the Mama few knew, except perhaps my father. He shared how "Your mama could tell the best off-color jokes. She had all of us salesmen laughing."

After the day of her burial, I knelt on the side of my bed, feeling so connected, sending me back to close memories, to that time when she didn't sit me on our old toilet seat top as she usually did to cut and comb my curls, but to tell her eight-year-old daughter the facts of life.

"Aneesa, you're eight years old now and you need to know what happens to all girls around your age."

Picture the scene of this aproned mama lifting her skirt to reveal what all women know and yes, yes, endure: inside her white panties, a stuffed rag was soaked with blood. I can still see that rag full of her blood.

"Oh, Mama, are you hurt?" I remember crying.

"No, no, not hurt. Look closely. I want you to know that one day you'll see blood on your own panties too. No, no, honey, be assured. I'm not hurt. For us, that flowing blood is precious, totally normal. It happens to me every month. Someday, it will happen to you."

"Why would I bleed down there? Hurt myself to make it bleed?" At that question, she bent down close, cupped my face in her sweet hands, turned my head toward hers, and looked closely into my eyes.

"It's okay, Aneesa, to be startled. But it's how women give birth to babies, how I knew the joy of having you. Blood will help you have your own babies when it's time. Don't be afraid. It will appear."

"Don't tell me anymore." And she didn't. She would save the other news, she said, until a special night when Daddy wasn't home, a story about how babies were created.

On July 9, my wide eyes saw those red spots she had predicted would appear on my own panties. I had gone to pee in Aunt Beckie's green-tiled bathroom and there as I pulled up my panties, I saw my obvious maturing, red circles, all in a row. I was an excited kid as if I'd won the lottery, running out to tell her the news: "Mama, I saw the blood you told me would come."

Many friends have honestly said they never learned how menstruation comes to a girl from a mother's telling. They either find out from girlfriends, sorority sisters, or yes, a boyfriend which makes me wonder how do boys know what so many girls have yet to learn.

I stand proud of my mother, of her self-confidence which allowed her to speak intimately and openly with her firstborn about something so naturally real.

"When you are older, Aneesa, I'll tell you more." And as she promised, this mentor took me to her bed one night when my father was away to explain how all of us come into this world. She didn't mention the pain it takes on the mother. I listened but didn't want to hear, made her repeat that it was a loving act.

"Really, Mama? Really?" I thought it over for a while. "So, that's how I was harnessed to you and Daddy?"

Tears flooded the bed as I knelt, recalling her kindness to her eldest daughter, wishing I could tell her how on the day she died, we were bonded even more completely for somehow, I completely stopped bleeding on that day she had taken her last breath. I never endured another monthly period, never bought another tampon, and forever have remembered the mother who shared vital rituals with her daughter. That night, I couldn't sleep, got out of bed, walked the garden outside under a kind moon.

We become orphans, losing both parents, suffering the reality that had always been promised. I don't like that reality that must happen but life's plan always wins. I try hard not to be bitter. But sometimes in the silence of the night, I hope to become my best self—my real self. I sit up in bed, raise my hands, fashion them like praying hands under my chin. With eyes closed, I deliver my spirit to the place where God lives in me. I accept my state in life as it is, the death of my parents, the single life I lead, the gift of so many close friends, and the possible truth that a man may never come into my world? It's a moment of awakening to life as it wants to be, as God wants it to be, of deep trust that despite all the losses and longings, all is still well, and that all shall be well, and that a soulmate may and can still be possible, and just might eventually show up on my heart.

Jill says it will happen. I try to believe her

Many weeks later, at breakfast in our favorite hang out, out pops Jill's sixty-four-thousand-dollar question: "Anybody answer my classified ad?" She smiles between bites. This close confidant had placed a personal ad in the couples' section of a Florida newspaper with my reluctant permission. Could a simple printed call bring on that soulmate? Our friend Louise had found her soulmate that way. Maybe it could happen. But to her question, I had this to report to my Jill.

"Yes, Jill, it did catch a hit but didn't strike gold. In fact, that meeting was pure joke. And I'll tell you why.

Lunch with him last Tuesday. The guy's name was Gene and he really sounded okay on the phone, identified himself as a pig farmer. I secretly laughed. A pig farmer?"

"Well? I'm holding my breath."

"He was good looking, a tall cowboy, hat and all. Probably in his sixties. I liked his Southern drawl, a bit brassy about his money, proud of his pigs which he said always earned the highest prices at auction. He wanted me to come to an auction and see how well they did."

Jill was attentive. She hoped it would work but probably could tell by the sound of tone I was throwing at her, it hadn't even come close.

I sipped my coffee before I struck her funny bone about what happened.

"He was nice enough, but listen to what he asked me during our lunch."

"Oh, oh, something's coming that's not so rich!"

"Well, honey, in a way it is rich cause he gave me a story I can tell other women." I sipped my coffee, deliberately keeping her in suspense.

"Well, go on, tell me."

"Well, he leaned over his plate of eggs and bacon...I thought that was going to kiss me…"

"Well...tell me!"

"Aneesa," he said, "can you tell me what your cholesterol level is?"

Jill leans back, her eyes wide and a smile creeping into her face: "You're not serious."

"Dead serious. Can you *believe that*? What in the world was he thinking? Or *was* he? Truth is, I don't even know what my cholesterol level could be. Not a clue. Anyway, I worked hard at not laughing in his face and then trying to be civil bidding him goodbye."

At that, Jill easily bursts into non-stop chuckling, tears and all. I joined her. The waitress come to the table, "More Coffee?"

"No more ads, please, Jill."

"I'm sorry, Aneesa. Forget it. We'll just keep praying."

"No. It's absurd. I've had enough praying for a soulmate."

"No, honey. It's the most normal desire in the world."

We finished up in friendly silence as the waitress delivered our check. I ended our meal with more doubts as I gathered my purse and began to rise.

"Maybe I never should have left the convent."

"Aneesa, damn it! Turn on your overhead lights! God certainly will keep the convent door open for you. As long as He's assured of your cholesterol level." She giggles again. "Meantime, you gotta know, come rain or come shine, I haven't given up on orchestrating your wedding.

We walk out together and she adds her comforting biblical reality: "Listen girl, in the gospel of St. Thomas, Jesus says, "what you seek, you will find."

I slam the car door shut. "I really want to believe you, honey but *Really?*

Like her amazing way of cheering me up, Jill sent me a poem that week.

Who is the third who walks always beside you?
When I count, there are only you and I together
But when I look ahead up the white road
There is always another one walking beside you
Gliding wrapped in a brown mantle, hooded
I do not know whether a man or a woman
But who is that on the other side of you?

~T.S. Eliot's "The Waste Land"

I'm out in the garden. At some point, I look up to see a blue sky hidden by gorgeous white puffy clouds. *Is that the way You deal with me? Keep me in suspence? Raise up my faith even more that someone is walking on the other side of me? …*

Oh dear God, Help me be patient, believe that You will bring someone in Your own time.

The sun is dropping. I sit for hours that feel almost solemn and watch the great work of the Florida sun. It covers an express line of rare bromeliad blooms sending to them their needed nutrients. The scene totally fills my senses, watching the red gifts of blooms raise their heads higher, God's genius working. Birds and a small bee fly close. Graham Greene's words float in. *There always comes a moment in time when a door opens and lets in the future.*

CHAPTER TWENTY-FIVE

Homeless

~Andrew~

new grounds

you call me homeless—is that what it is?
this homeless of yours—fits like ball & chain
i wish you'd find another name
wanna know about this place where i live?
plenty of fear and confusion, it's true
you wanna come in and save me from it?
please don't
much too long a haul to get here
and now that i've arrived i happen to know
deep down where no one else possibly can
and crazy as it sounds
here's exactly where i'm supposed to be
anyway where else would you have me
when circumstances grab the upper hand
and the glue holding it all together finally fails
and all always-supposed-was-me
flies off every which way
when fair to say meaning itself drops out—kaboom

wild free fall's all that's left to believe in
...yes i'd like your help
this new living room of mine is much too big
besides, who can take in cardboard this near?
the rain—the dirt—the shame?
yes, to be sure, when no one's looking
i do gotta admit—scared as hell!
but no thanks, i think i'll pass
on these rules of yours for decent behavior
your crispy projects and programs
your tidy schedules & pretend busy
most of all that cardboard god all your own
all answers readymade neatly from the page
so how do i say ALONE so you can hear it
and still not hold yourself too far away?
sure wish you didn't have to see me go through it
frightens you so. So why not try another name?
something like <u>explorer</u> instead?

I joined a labor pool and was stationed to mix concrete on the airport's runways, then to pulling heads of cabbage on sprawling patches of Palatka, Florida, "Stoop labor," bending over to pick abrasive prickly green balls. After only a day, my hands were bloodied from the dry sand caught in crouching leaves. That blood I could handle; scorching sun no way. It boiled my fair skin like paper to flame.

What about you homemakers at supermarket's cabbage bins? Do you ever think about us pickers? How bloodied our fingers? How hot the sun? Do you?

"Hey, man," one big guy black as I was red saw me struggling and reached to help. "Get your ass on the truck. I'll pitch my load to you."

After two sun-drenched weeks and a *"body all aching and wracked with pain,"* we lined up for our pay outside the farm's office. My friend ahead of me laughed as he walked away, check in hand.

"God almighty brothers! We ought to be grateful they didn't take off the air we breathed." Now there it was in my own dollars—rent deducted for that slab of mattress I slept on, the bunkhouse to sleep in, daily Kool Aid, morning cereals, evening bowls of burnt rice and beans.

> *sixteen tons, wha dya get*
> *another day older and deeper in debt*
> *st peter don't call me cause i can't go*
> *i owe my soul to the company store*

I hitched a ride with a Mexican truck driver back to Orlando, his truck bed piled high with tomatoes. He said not a word and I too said nothing, just too damn hot to talk. What could we say anyway after all that subtle stooping torture?

Back at the labor pool office, I cashed my check, money further diminished by boss-man's charge for check cashing. Walking out of his so-called bank door, it came to me again, this time good and loud...*sixteen tons wha dya get!*

I'm back on Orlando's streets, where generosity awaited us at the mission table, especially in homeless shelter places. As for a slab of cardboard I carried around I called my bed, the downtown Methodist church allowed us to sleep in their beautifully cloistered courtyard if we were out by 7:00 am.

In the church's parking lot, May and Doug Wilson arrived on their own by 6 a.m. every morning in their old Lincoln Continental, setting up tables for coffee urns, stacking paper cups and layers of boxed donuts no doubt begged from local merchants. When restaurant surpluses ran short, I heard our breakfast goodies were paid for out of pocket, by Doug, a retired Navy officer. In addition to food, this God-sent couple arranged with a local laundromat to donate coins and powdered soap for washing and drying street clothes. For me, clean clothes meant I could settle behind a library table without intruding on somebody's nose senses. For Doug and May it meant, in my book, the road to sainthood.

Most of the time I kept my feet going, ever observing newbies joining our cadres of street walkers, sometimes penning silent reflections about how they came to land there. Other times there was little left to guess. A few mouthed disregard for anyone but themselves, others painfully recounting their fall from society, stories that should have been listened to long before.

Often, I passed old Hungarian Louie pushing a supermarket cart around his sidewalks, his basket overflowing with kitchenware, draped clothing, and an odd potted dracaena plant balanced tall amid everything else around it. Police left Louie alone telling anyone who reported him, "Ma'am, he's in his own world and quite harmless."

I was lucky to meet teacher Sam living on the streets, one vigorous Georgia mathematics instructor let go because of budget cuts. Sam avoided the free meals at the Coalition, ordering his meals at a small corner cafe instead.

How do you do that Sam? Where do you get the moolah? That teacher was also a subtle entrepreneur, gleaning his day-to-day income from flashing a colorful poster at selected interstate exits. "Teacher Fired, Now Broke!" Handsome Sam prompted females to dig deep into their purses, often for as much as a ten or a twenty. One Friday, excited Sam found me in the library. "Andy, an old woman in a faded BMW tossed me a $100 bill. Talk about being at the right place at the right time. Let's dine in style tonight." And at the table, he proselytized, "Now there's one fine how-de-do, wouldn't you say, Andy?"

Life on the streets was surely less than rosy. Okay, where is it ever so? Still we were the easy targets. A guy could bluster from the window of his passing pickup, "Get a job!"

On our side, there was that young pretty mother with three kids trailing after her, who told us she'd recently found herself on the street, explaining she'd lost her job in Detroit. She looked us up and down, distastefully, added her own bluster, "I'm not like you people."

"You people?" What a line. Who are the "you people" she's talking about? People without virtue? Without a spot or a stain? People who preach to others? People who work in offices day after day, year after year? Are those the "you people" I really don't connect with those "you people" at all. Did this woman feel her disdain would help her feel better? Maybe. Three kids? Now that's a story to be told.

Merton said it well: *With all the noise that is being made on all sides about where we are supposed to be going, one tends to forget that people are not always willing to let others decide who they are and what they want—they tend in the end to decide for themselves.*

No telling what drove most of us to the street, what we're doing walking sidewalks up and down, the streets that became our place of passage for reasons all our own. I did meet a few interesting people, some more soulful than university-or business-engaged. Dear, old, black Billie slept curled up behind a grove of trees. Billie was a not-too-distant descendent of Alabama slaves, the skinniest woman I'd ever seen with the largest purple lips God ever put on a woman. Her eyes owned a look of ruin, most likely from early days of constant hunger. Longtime member of her hometown church choir, Billie belted out her spirituals like a Leontyne Price, singing as if she'd already reached the Pearly Gates. Her rendition of *Swing Low, Sweet Chariot* convinced impatient Sam to tune in, reach into his pocket to part with his hard-earned ten from a morning's compassionate female driver. "Billie, put this in your chariot for later."

Nobody could reveal more teeth than Billie's smile at that green bill.

"Isn't it risky, Andrew, living out on the streets?"

How could custodian John of the Homeless Coalition know this was nothing as bad as finding yourself stuffed into a ten-by-ten-foot cage for years on end with a bunch of noisy troublemaker inmates?

John, nothing speaks to me like an empty park bench at the wide foot of a sprawling oak, or raindrops rhythmically splattering on a dusty sidewalk. A kite sailing its way through inflated clouds touches my flying soul, a lone soaring osprey too. Breezes in pines under bowls full of stars? Ain't not riskier, friend, than sheer urban camping! Mother Nature whispers to me like never anything else.

What emerged was said a bit simpler. "No, John. I'm right here where I need to be for now."

What urban camping lacked even for me, was the very thing beginning to press its way home: misty hope this homelessness too was coming to its end.

God, anytime now would just be fine.

CHAPTER TWENTY-SIX

God on Sabbatical

~ Aneesa ~

My journal reminds me: *Growing up, I believed I was blessed with a brain and a heart. My mother's heart, my father's brain, although Mama's brain was pretty rich too. I also learned early that life could be challenging, but that I'd be able to handle whatever came along. What had come along in my past was the stuff that delivered me from the convent, delivered me from a priest's arms, and now delivered my soul to help others.*

I had volunteered to help feed the homeless every Saturday morning. Normal marginalized Americans were walking the streets. They suffered with no roof for shelter, no dining room table for rich cuisine, and no bedroom with a soft bed to call their own. Being at this breakfast called Grace and Grits, these homeless men and women were just what I needed to forget my own troubles.

For almost twelve years, my Florida home had been the scene of monthly Merton gatherings. I loved having these spiritually inclined folks in my living room. Nothing at those meeting ever seemed to go wrong, nothing seemed left out, everyone joined in discussions abounded around his writings. And sometimes that sharing could turn intense, even hot-and-heavy, but always a sense of full Merton will.

At some point, a few members brought up the idea of doing something for the homeless, "walk the talk" Jenny said. Some members rejected the idea and didn't join in. Okay for them. But most chipped in: I made my favorite home cooked vegetarian chili and carried the large pot in the car's back seat to the Coalition. It felt right that we were doing something like Merton himself would do if he'd been given the chance.

That Tuesday evening, most of us drove to the Coalition on the other side of Orlando. I'd never been there and certainly had never dreamt, probably would never consider hooking up with a man who lived out on the street, who had no income, and probably had no education no matter how desperate I could be for a partner. And yet, in God's strange way of doing most of our lives, one of those men walking through that food line could someday smile my way, eventually walk me into his future and down a Catholic aisle to the altar. Oh, what a story that would be.

But I'm getting ahead of my tale that all had started at one of Ronnie's breakfast tables with a man who was just that, who lived on the street and had no income of which I knew.

We happily fed men, women, and children, about a hundred or more who showed up for bacon and eggs, toast, fruit, mostly donated by local farmers and grocery stores. Ernie, former businessman in charge, sometimes forked over his own bills for the food, had signaled me, not to serve the meal to our ladies and gentlemen, but to get on the stage, "Play the grand piano while the 'guests' enjoy what we offer." That time at the piano was pure sunshine. I pushed my fingers hard on tunes the eaters recognized and whooped when they caught familiar lyrics: "To dream the impossible dream…" and "You'll never walk alone"…and of course, my old convent memory from Rogers and Hammerstein's *Sound of Music*: "The hills are alive…"

Our staff was loving toward the homeless, focusing on each as a real Christ coming through the wide doors. When those front doors opened and roofless men and women walked in, our staff was standing in a line, alert to clapping and singing the familiar lyric that I lustily banged out: "When the Saints Go Marching In."

These book pages do connect to my work with Jews and Arabs, and even with what it means to be a Christian. At a breakfast table one morning, I had a conversation with another volunteer before we opened the doors, a conversation that left me incredulous: "You know those Jewish buddies of yours are all going to hell."

"Bud, you don't believe that, do you?" He stood a middle-aged Episcopalian. He was studying for the diaconate. He had asked me about my work in Prejudice Reduction. Why he brought that subject up became clear when he exploded his historic bomb.

Again, I asked, "Bud, you don't really believe that do you? The substance of your Episcopal religion, and the well-known writer and biblical scholar, John Spong, doesn't believe that!"

"Sure does!"

"Well, I'm so sorry you hold to that. You must not have any Jewish friends!"

And at that, I got out of my chair leaving his ignorance, carrying my leftover eggs and toast and hurried back to the kitchen. I know the God I worship heard him declaring his silly stupid truths but the God I also know would just let him go on believing that…the way God always lets us hold on to some of our stupid beliefs.

I couldn't wait to share that story with Jill, the kindest woman I knew. How, I wondered, would she react to this prejudice thrown at her husband's and now her people. We were sitting out on her porch, and the Florida breeze was cool on our lunch.

She listened to my story about Bud. Like her usual self, she stopped eating that fruit salad I'd prepared, put down her fork and completely hooked me with a needed wisdom.

"Aneesa, watch how this Bud treats those homeless that you both serve. What's his behavior like with these down and out?"

I wondered why she directed me to observe Bud, what she might suspect about him and about me, and the why of it all. I followed her direction that next Saturday at the Grace and Grits breakfast.

I sat at the stage's piano, belted my tunes on the grand keyboard as usual, enjoyed the sound of men singing them. I followed Jill's advice, one eye on Bud. I watched how he smiled, how he moved from table to table chatting with a few, calling some by name. It was clear that he, not always them, was the one who picked up their trays after they finished breakfast and delivered them to the kitchen. He was the one who brought seconds available from the kitchen. He was the one who poured second cups, and he was the one who parked himself by the door to shake a hand: "Goodbye 'til next week."

Focusing on this man who believed all Jews were going to hell, I couldn't help but miss a few notes of the tunes I played. The guys looked up at me and raised a thumb of knowing I'd missed a melody key.

After that morning's breakfast, cleanup time had me standing at the kitchen sink wiping trays and some plates. I stored some and bending down then up, noticed that above hung a framed picture of the Christ on the Cross. I couldn't help but be caught up by that sight, that familiar image of Jesus, but somehow in a new way. Oh, yes, we're always learning something new.

When Bud walked back into the kitchen bringing the last of the dirty dishes to my sink, I realized we stood together under that framed Savior.

Getting into bed that night it grew even plainer. This man Bud asserts his religious beliefs completely out of whack with mine, so is God awful nice to every street-life client, with a heart bigger than my head, bigger than his own belief system? I do wonder if there is any homeless Jew that walks through our front door and that he wouldn't choose to chat with and serve?

Oh, what discoveries God forever has in store for me!

That night, in bed with me lay Mary Oliver's book of poems. One of her lines struck a chord: "If you are too much like myself, what shall I learn of you, or you of me?"

CHAPTER TWENTY-SEVEN

Hello, You!

~Aneesa~

"Go ahead, Jill, bring that guy you met at the Catholic conference to the Merton meeting. Didn't you say that he reads Merton?"

Jill squeals like a young teen.

"Oh, honey, stop with the matchmaking. I've tried to make a deal with God. Don't press the Prince Charming thing anymore."

"Okay. I'll pick him up. You just be there."

Meeting that Merton guy who owned a strange kind of story began weeks after the Rodney King beating affair in Los Angeles, California. Sometimes when friends ask how I met Andrew, I give them the background, "Because of the beating of Rodney King."

That tragedy convinced Orlando's bishops to energize better relationships between black and white Catholics, get them to talk to one another, stop even a bit of demonizing.

They sponsored a day's conference on race relations. Not too surprising, the only two whites who showed up amid a giant room full of blacks were Jill and this white guy named Andrew LeBouef. She liked him. They instantly connected. But that's always the trouble: Jill likes everyone.

She told me how easily she shared her beliefs with him: "Isn't it sad, Andrew, that we're the only two white people sitting at this table? I think that my favorite monk writer, Thomas Merton, whose written so much about race relationships might have asked his Abbot to be present here amid all these blacks."

"Merton?" Andrew instantly picked up.

"You mean *The Seven Story Mountain* Merton?" He shared his excitement, told Jill that Merton was also his favorite author. Had been his mother's as well. He used to listen to her reading parts of his numerous contemplative writing.

"A Merton group? You meet regularly?"

Jill couldn't conceal her delight about this man she'd met at the conference. "Imagine, Aneesa, the eagerness in his voice. Here's a guy who reads the very author that brings us together in your home!" I had to admit to her God-like amazement, a strange and surprising serendipity to that Rodney King affair. She sheepishly related her enthusiasm to me: "I think God remains present in everything about him, Aneesa. I think you'll like him. I really do."

"Okay, okay!"

"Well," she hesitated. I watched her confusion. Then she confessed a secret she'd been keeping:

"I have to tell you he's a bit homeless right now!"

A bit homeless? How can you be 'a bit' homeless? Live under half a roof?

Things moved fast after that breakfast. We all met at Ronnie's Cafe located in The Colonial Mall, an establishment that my father had been so excited to see go on the land across the street from his own.

Jill had picked Andrew up and was bringing him to breakfast. I sat waiting. I kept sipping my coffee as I checked the entrance. But for the reader, I was honestly fighting a flood of male images. My own prejudices completely surfaced. *Homeless? Oh God, Aneesa! So, he might smell. But that never bothered Sister Brendan who went down to the shelter weekly to feed the city's homeless, even gave one her own walking cane to one. And you, Aneesa? You've been serving breakfast to the lot of those homeless people. They didn't smell. Probably we could call Jesus homeless when he walked this planet.*

Ronnie's double glass doors opened and Jill and her companion navigated their way to my table. I looked hard. Jill was followed by a tall, wiry not quite gray-haired guy. She smiled expectantly as she noticed my stand up. I noticed the guy. *Oh, Deo Gratias, he looked pretty normal—no tattered shirt or ripped trousers, didn't look homeless like some of my breakfast people.* And as he got nearer? *OMG, those blue eyes!*

I extend my hand.

"Hi."

"Hi, yourself. Andrew here."

He puts a firm grip over mine, then helps Jill into her chair. The waitress stands by our table, pad in hand, and what follows is the normal ritual of taking our order. I continue to sip my coffee, looking to Jill to start some sort of conversation, help me pick up a clue of what to say. *Who talks first? Say something, Jill!*

Her warm gaze remains on him.

Out of the awkward quiet, Andrew reaches into his satchel, brings up a small steel kind of box, sets it on the table as he asks: "May I sit 'Woppity' here?"

"Who's this "Woppity?" I laugh at his naming a computer.

"A real buddy is this little guy. He's small, very portable, clicks down my words. Truth to tell, I'm never without him. We're together in the library."

This new person to my world was giving a machine gender, a male pronoun. I did that with my plants but never with a computer.

He opens this Woppity computer and what I see is a little keyboard with a tiny window, a kind of computer I'd seen in Radio Shack before Apple's laptops. My mind races about the cost. *Where in God's name did he get the money?*

Between bites, I watch his every movement, how he butters toast, holds a knife, sips that small glass of orange juice—behaviors suddenly inexplicably important, manners that belie his...*um*... unconventional situation.

"Aneesa," he smiled. "I hear we have a common friend in Thomas Merton."

Good Heavens, Aneesa, stop it. That face? Blue eyes.

"More coffee?" the waitress appears, interrupts the blue eye stare I couldn't help doing.

Jill holds up her cup and says:

"Honey, did you know that Andrew's family had an apartment on Park Avenue?" She forked another bite and said more: "He holds degrees from Georgetown and Columbia Universities.

God, Jill, stop the yenta. You're embarrassing him, I can tell. Me too. Filling my mind with questions I don't dare ask. My stomach was filling as well, not only with food but butterflies. I was plainly cuckoo at that point.

Feelings running up and down me wouldn't stop. What's up Aneesa? He's just a new member, I hope, for our Merton group.

"Really, Jill?"

I scrape globs of butter off my toast. Andrew spreads globs onto his.

"Yes, he's also done a stint as a Navy officer, then taught at City University of New York."

"So, Andrew," I leap into a boldness, a bite in my voice, a kind of meanness in me, my father? "Why on earth did you choose this vagabond existence?"

I could slice the entire country from that knifed look Jill threw my way. But she brushes away my question with a witted request.

"Andrew, how about giving us one of your poems."

His eyes brush hers fondly. He opens his Woppity.

"Well, I've got a signature poem, but hold it a minute. Aneesa. I'm happy to talk about that vagabond existence down the road."

I sit back, unfed by so much unanswered.

"Ok, I'd like to know, Andrew, how a man of your caliber gets lost like this, doesn't own a simple thing like a house."

I'm feeling mean.

"Okay, but how about hearing my poem for now?"

Whatever was going on in me, I wanted to know more about this good-looking muscular poet with a chest other women's heads would love to lay their heads upon. I simply could not contain my boldness. I didn't recognize myself doing it. *Why am I being so mean? I can't let go of his deep blue eyes. Baby blue.*

"Let's hear you, Andrew!" Jill pipes in.

He lays down his toast, wipes his hands on his napkin and half reads and half closes his eyes, knowing the poem by heart.

> *i'm just a poet don't ask for more*
> *don't look to me for the love of money*
> *or on these words erect more than their sound*
> *i don't try to be funny*
> *tho of late it's true, i do laugh alot*
> *what's more things strike me that way*
> *this taste of honey grows thicker each day*
> *with more new wrinkles*
> *to frame such disposition sunny*
> *than i had seen on a newborn laughing son*
> *more than drain tropical continent's countenance*
> *runny with midday's sudden passionate outbursts*
> *more than theatrical masks fashioned*
> *regardless of money*
> *i'm just a poet*
> *don't ask for more*

Hearing the rise and fall of his voice touches me. Too much! My heart beats and I'm taken in by everything going on at this table. A homeless man, Jill's friend, good breakfast food, poetry. It's like a story someone is writing, all three of us engaged in creating *another* story. We chat a bit more, our waitress brings more coffee and as she pours, someone at the next table leans over to ask who wrote that poem. *Talk about another story.*

But me, I'd had enough, fond of it all and scared to top it off. I know Jill just invited him to talk about the Merton meeting. I suspected she had more than that in mind. I pick up my purse, explore the whereabouts of my Visa.

"Jill, I have to go."

"Sure honey, let's all go!"

She let me move ahead, turning back to Andrew, in a voice I could well hear: "Andrew, I hope we'll catch you at the next Merton meeting."

Standing outside in a place free from his seductive poetry, his blue eyes, I breathe again. Jill gives him a hug.

"Andrew, don't worry about transportation. We'll pick you up."

I give her my meanest look: *Pick him up? Not me. Jill, not me.*

"That would be great." He brightens.

Jill got into her car and sped away quickly—too quickly—and I suspected she wanted to leave me struggling to find my keys, my words, my confused feelings about this intriguing man of so many contradictions.

He rested his foot on the fender of somebody's parked car and innocently requested, "Aneesa, would you like my post office box number?"

The phone jangles me awake.

"Are you up?"

"Now I am."

"Well, I just couldn't wait. Tell me, did you like him?"

"Jill, he did have smooth ankles."

"Oh, stop the jokes! When I told Todd where we'd met for

breakfast, he thought it was a funny, well, maybe not so funny, an actual coincidence that we had breakfast at Ronnie's Cafe."

"What's special about that?"

"Well, didn't your father own that piece of property just across the highway from Ronnie's? Can you believe we were having breakfast close to where your dad had sold that property to the furniture company? According to Todd, your dad made a bundle on that sale."

"Okay Jill, that was true. So, what?"

"Well, don't you think there's a bit of serendipity in that… Maybe your father's hand placed near the spot where you two would meet?"

"Jill, my father would never approve of anyone without resources. And a poet? No, no. So, stop the coaching. Andrew doesn't own a dime, no car, no roof. Well, maybe a dime because he bought that tiny computer but still, my father would never approve."

"Okay. Todd and I thought it might be something to think about, but I can see, you're not in the mood. Go back to sleep. I'll talk to you later—oh, wait, you should know Andrew's coming to the Merton meeting tomorrow night. I asked Kurt to pick him up."

I assumed that Andrew was at his first Merton meeting as I opened the door to this man. Oh, I was impressed. He'd shaved, wore a cool-looking green shirt and held a Merton reader in his hand. Kurt walked in behind him. *Where did he get that outfit?* I wondered. *Did he possess some hidden resource?*

From the kitchen and with my constant roving eye, I watched him choose the empty chair next to Jill. She'd saved it for him. Walking around to pour cups of tea, I peeked at the two of them chatting and I strangely felt left out, maybe jealous of her calm, her tightly woven marriage to a Jew whom she adored, and her ability to keep reaching out for me to find my own kind of Todd. Could it be that the handsome guy sitting next to her *was* because of her love for me, and that soon I could be convinced?

The bell struck and George Drake, a faithful Merton member sitting in the back who never missed a meeting, had volunteered to read the evening's text. I was listening carefully, wanting the discussion to stay alive, maybe a pride in me to produce a kind of performance for this new would-be member.

"What is a pilgrimage? A return to a place where there will be an encounter and a renewal of life; a humble, difficult effort to cross an abyss to achieve communion with people who, in such large measure, are deprived of identity and reduced to inarticulate silence."

Pilgrimage? Pilgrimage? Could this tall man sitting next to Jill be moving on a pilgrimage? A holy journey? My hand wouldn't stop shaking as I poured the last dregs of tea I'd prepared? *A holy journey? That's crazy. Hummmm, or is it?*

All discussions finally over, the cookie plate happily bare of a member's homemade gifts, the members leave one by one through the front door by themselves. Only Jill and Andrew are left, still chatting. Suddenly, he gets up, makes his way toward me.

"Hey Aneesa, I like the group…got me thinking even more about this man my mother read and adored. But now, how about lunch tomorrow?"

I look over at Jill whose head is bobbing furiously positive. "Thanks Andrew, but no."

I lower my eyes, hating the shameful feeling creeping through me. *Forgive me, God. Why not, Aneesa? Grow up!! This might be your chance.*

In bed, a quiet house was supposed to send me to sleep. Yet, under the brightly flowered sheets, I'm unable to get that Merton reading out of my head… *humble, difficult effort to cross an abyss, achieve communion with people?* I hardly slept the entire night.

The next morning after finishing the last of dirty dishes, I grab a towel, dry my hands to answer the ringing phone.

"Andrew here! Change your mind about that lunch?"

"Sorry."

"But Aneesa, I thought we were connected over Merton last night."

"Andrew, someone's at the door. I gotta go." I hung up, finished cleaning the kitchen, let my mind slump as outside, I hosed down my vibrant garden, every pot, every bloom. Something was driving me and I didn't like whatever it was.

Damn it, Aneesa, he's a nice guy. What's wrong with you?

CHAPTER TWENTY-EIGHT

Canoe Confession

~Aneesa~

A week later, Miss Perseverance telephones. I check the clock. *Good God, not even 7:00 am!*

"Please, Jill, too early. What's up?"

"Honey, I gotta tell you Andrew's living with the L'Amour family? They met him at church, heard his poetry, invited him to stay in their extra bedroom."

"Really? Gosh, that says a lot about their trust in him."

"Yeah, and it says a lot about his trusting himself, get it girl?"

"Okay, okay…so what else?"

"It was your secretary who knew that Mr. L'Amour needed help in laying tile and, and get this, he's installing a new toilet in the back bedroom. He took on this Andrew who seems to be quite handy. She told me he's even got Andrew reframing an old window. Our Andrew's pretty handy."

"*Our* Andrew? Jill, you're pushing again. I do think about him. And soon as I do, here's Dad pushing him away!"

"Listen, lady. I'm convinced your dad, even your mom, would have *handpicked* this guy. Besides, it's clear to me Andrew's no freeloader."

Next day, shopping at the grocery, deciding what yogurt will be best. *Does he eat yogurt?*

At the checkout counter, the memory of that tall guy, the guy I turned down. *So, the L'Amours trust him. Maybe I should invite them all to dinner?*

I shove my salted/peppered roast into the oven while beets cook and a chopped salad sits seasoned. Yes, it's true: my defenses are down. *Call him, Aneesa, no big deal.*

Just then that melodic voice of his rings out to my ear through my phone: "Hey, Aneesa. I'm living with Mr. and Mrs. L'Amour. They're inviting you for Sunday Mass and lunch afterward."

"Why *me?*"

"I couldn't stop talking about the Merton group."

In St. Stephen's Church, while waiting for Mass to begin, I'm a teenager sitting close to this former professor. The L'Amour family is seated in the same pew beside us. We're waiting for the celebrant to come out and do his Mass. But oh, no Mass had ever felt so good.

This new friend curls his fingers ever tighter around my hand, resurrecting upheavals of feelings more than skin deep. Above the altar, Christ remains nailed to the cross. He gives me the eye.

Okay, Jesus, okay! I think he's the one you've sent my way. But, really? A homeless guy?

After Mass and lunch, we leave the L'Amours, head for the old Canterbury Retreat Center where my Jewish-Christian workshops had taken place years ago—and now I find everything in that quiet setting: tall oaks swell as if called upon to do so. In a paddling canoe, this new friend and I will get to know more about each other.

Have I stayed close enough to You, God? Can I hope, in this familiar setting of trees and lake and bird calls, I will find myself really feeling that You never abandoned me? That the man of my dreams has finally come and all I had to do was wait for him?

We both shove the canoe into the calm lake. Andrew gently steers us forward under cypress trees and long waving oak branches, all that mercifully shades us from Florida's ever-exploding sun. God, am I truly here with this man-friend? It feels so good, so real, so okay.

There's nothing more I need than being here with a man I think respects me and I him, despite the homelessness bit.

The sound of a cawing osprey breaks the silence. Andrew holds the rudder but releases a laugh. "He's looking for his mate."

I ask, "Andrew, I'm wondering. What did you always want to be when you grew up?"

He laughs again that chuckle I was learning to like, and replies, "Well, I never dreamed of being a football hero, a war hero, or some wealthy stock broker. Nonetheless, I did some kind of dreaming and truth to tell, my dreams were all over the place!"

As he slowly directs the course of our canoe, out it comes. How our paths, no matter how seemingly off course, had led us straight into this undreamed present. My mind wouldn't stop trying to believe a new reality:

Dear lord, I have the feeling that this is the answer to my dreams. This man with the passage Merton talked about. This man with no home right now but a chuckle I like hearing, comments that make sense, that make me laugh.

As if in punctuation if not an answer, a mockingbird lets go a beautiful trill, tender and perhaps assuring me of a new story this man and I are beginning to create.

Unexpectedly, Andrew pulls the paddle ever slower toward himself until he finally stops rowing, stows it under the crossbar. He sits quietly, waits, looks directly at me. I was sitting backward facing him and suddenly, I became nervous. He says nothing, waits some more. I realize my mockingbird ceases to sing and at some point, the sun seems to grow shady.

I felt something dark entering our togetherness. Something foreboding and my toes begin to curl like they always do whenever something bad lay ahead. I cross my fingers behind my back and wait. I thought of Mike, and wondered if he might be telling me something I needed to know about this man. I pushed my hair back from my face. I thought of Jill, wanted her sitting beside me.

Dear God, pass the candy. Let this moment be one of renewal.

Andrew begins to share what I never expected to hear and never wanted to hear.

"Aneesa, it's difficult to say what I know I must tell you. You have to know that I once killed a woman." He reaches up to wipe his sweaty brow. "I took a knife, and plunged it into her and then into my own throat. I thought I'd be dead like her but somehow, it didn't happen. In all truth, I really should be dead."

Both my hands reach out to clutch the sides of the canoe. I don't think I can see anything, as if the eyes in my head had become frozen, staring, all of me trying to be with him, yet pulling away at the same time, pulling on the sides of the canoe, pulling at his sincerity, feeling his sincerity, craving to blot out what I was hearing, what he was saying.

God, am I hearing right? Help!

"Yes, Aneesa. I'm not even supposed to be here. Not a day passes that I don't live with that, still wondering why God didn't take me away."

His hands reach the sides of the canoe near mine, to steady it as a strong wind shakes the lake. Waves pick up and rock us together along with this stormy tale blowing from his lips.

I withdraw my hands, turn myself around toward the bow. I can't look at him anymore. I've been struck mute but manage to say: "Andrew, this is too much. I can't take anymore. Paddle us back, please, *now.*"

We approach the shore and neither of us talk. The air is thick, the birds are silent, and my heart beats wildly. *Turn your face to the sun, Aneesa.*

We reach the shore. He stashes the paddle away once more, and still wants to speak: "Aneesa, please, there's one thing I gotta say. Somehow, I'm trusting you to understand. As hard as it is to hear, this is a tough one for me too. I've only told a few; but listen to what I've never told a soul."

He gets out after me, stands in front of me and holds up his hand. "This hand that did it wasn't the me that killed her. I hardly understand how it all happened. Something or someone took over me, occupied me, something that wasn't me. I don't know how to explain it. I'm devastated by what I did, of course, totally confused by what I feel I didn't do. The court said I was plain crazy. I know there is so much more to it than what I'm telling you, what I'm even telling myself."

"Andrew, I've heard enough. Please. Stop! I don't want, just can't hear anymore."

I start up the car. I can't speak and don't. Words aren't there to describe what happened. Obviously, I'm in some sort of shock. Everything had seemed so perfect. Now?

I drive him back to L'Amour's home. My stomach rolls tight, the food in it doesn't want to go down. Upchuck? I can't look at those blue eyes anymore.

He leaves the passenger seat, shuts the car door, turns to stick his head into the open window: "Aneesa, its true I've taken a chance with you. I've gone deeper than I ever have with anybody. I hope I haven't lost you."

My thoughts drive me home. Mind races. I let it. *Gosh, God, it was such a lovely day. The Mass, the lunch, everything filling me with hope. Jesus hanging on the cross above the altar, the hymn, "Be not afraid, I go before you always, Come, follow me…"*

Now, I pass parks and businesses. Green lights all the way. The car drives itself, as if it knows I can't handle all that's required from it, as if it knows that I've just been slammed against a hard wall and stunned.

I make it to the front door. Company Cat is there to greet me, that familiar meow signaling that I'm home. *Gosh, Company, I made it back!* I bent down to his face: "Company, I was close to a murderer. *A murderer?*" My lips had trouble shaping that dark word. Company seemed to know.

I head for a soothing bubble bath, lose myself completely in the bouncing white foam, tangle with truthful prayer. *Help, help…dear God.* Can I make sense out of what's just come into my world, my heart? He destroyed my promising world. There's no sense to it. No, no sense. Nonsense!

Of course, we all make choices in life. The hard thing is to live with those past choices. Was he trying to tell me tht somebody stole his mind, that he didn't know how or why it all happened? That he wasn't in his right mind, the Andrew mind that I met and was attracted to?

Oh dear God! What's up with You? He seemed so nice, so intelligent, so right for me. Even the mocking bird thought so and beautifully warbled. I was deeply taken by the way he rowed, held paddles, smiled at me. I felt protected. And then…It wasn't supposed to happen that way.

I sunk deeper into the tub of bubbles.

I needed my friend, not Jill this time, but Mary, Mama's close friend, now my own. Mary Sissini and Mama were buddies just like Jill and me. Often, they'd complain secretly about husbands, how men easily enter the annoying stage.

At some point, they formed a sewing group for Syrian woman, and in that circle, shared hundreds of difficult afghan patterns. All were skilled women who designed and crafted sweaters, tablecloths, and blankets. Mama and Mary's colorful afghans still warm me on cold nights.

After Andrew's canoe confession and my continued, admittedly deep, attraction, I needed Mary's presence, her distinct way of seeing things that could really matter. She had always loved me, as a kid, as a teen and even as a nun. This friend would drive to the Novitiate to deliver her home baked nut and date-filled cookies called *ma'amoul*. The novices loved them and I was proud of her ability to show them her skills.

Now, arrived and welcomed, I happily sit at Mary's antique's green and red kitchen table and relay my entire story.

"Really! He took a life? Well, that's not easy to accept."

"Oh Mary, before that, I thought he was the one you'd been praying for, that he and I had something solid."

"Maybe you did, honey, sure could be you still do."

"But what if he does me in too!"

Oh God, Did I really say that? Me, after feeling so safe with him in that canoe?

"Mary, oh God, I didn't mean that. Down deep, I was never afraid of being in that canoe with him…. in any way. Something about him, his watchful eyes, his laughter assured me of protection, of caring, I felt special with him, really special."

"Oh, sweet child, he sounds authentic. I think you've got a man who's true blue. Goodness…growing up on Park Avenue, a Catholic. This might be a man who marched to a different drumbeat but let's keep up our hope."

"By the way, where is Eddy?" I ask.

"Where else? Out in the garage doing his doodling stuff. I think he's mad at me because I took up for my brother."

That was often the case. Mary and Eddy could easily fall into a squabble. I was glad he was out of the home so Mary and I could talk about Andrew. He often sat in our company without saying a word. It was always hard to know what he was thinking.

My gray-haired friend rises from the table, stretches her back, her arms high. "Let's keep looking at this, honey."

Then she does what Arab women can't help but do. They focus on nourishment.

She turns to the refrigerator, opens it where I see so many reminders of Mama inside: Tupperware's sealed containers, loaves of bread, a half cantaloupe, two oranges. She pulls out a container. "Food will help us make better choices."

Into a pot spills the cold lentil-spinach liquid. She fires up her gas stove, heats enough for the two of us, then joins me at the table with her steaming bowl offerings. We sip the lentil broth. I feel everything nourishing without talk, a friendship accompanied by sweet silence.

Afterward, she lays down her spoon and reaches for my hand the way she always does when something important has struck her. "You know Aneesa, not everybody travels the same path to God. Some fall into muddy waters, must dig themselves clean. We must keep processing this man. I know your mama would be very careful not to send him away too quickly."

At that, *whoa!* The roof bounces as it is pelted by hard dots of rainwater like ice. Were the heavens sending messages?

"Aneesa, listen to me...take it in. You believed in him, and I believe in you. That's pretty basic. So, let's be realistic. When I pray, I know all my petitions are worthy of God's promises but not always honored. I'd like to say we can be sure God is listening but only hope He hears our request. As Eddy always reminds me: 'Who can ever be sure of anything?' Remember Fatima, our cousin, the defense attorney, Kristina, who fell in love with her client before he even got out of prison? She'd visit his cell. They talked, found so many issues they believed in."

"I remember them. Are they married now?"

"They're now happily married and enjoy the blessing of two children. It can and does happen!"

It rains even harder as we sit in her mobile home finishing that soup in colorful bowls atop her humble red-surfaced antique table. Despite the pelting of the drops on her tin roof and the thunder and lightning shooting through every window, we are nourished in thought and deed. I search the window, one of Florida's heavy afternoon showers covering every garden. I am glad the earth is getting a good stiff drink and glad that her mobile home won't fly away, at least I hope so despite the kitchen wall shaking.

Mary's wisdom, her open life seem a strong defense against any mobile-home tragedy. And when she suggests we pull out our rosaries, I didn't think that extra precaution could hurt.

"Mary, I love you. You always bring me into a place where I feel I can handle what's on my plate."

She stands, leans to plant a kiss on my cheek, just like Mama used to do. She clears the bowls away while talking the wisdom I came to hear.

"Aneesa, listen to me: women are either beacons or dark clouds. By beacons, I mean the women who attract their man, marry him, and stay married. They don't regret their choice. By dark clouds, I mean the women who kick hard against their destiny. Every time they meet a man who might be the right one, they can't make up their mind, take a chance, press God to protect their choice and lose the opportunity to win what they so desire."

Dark clouds? Is that what I'm allowing to blacken my faith in this kind man? *He said he was deemed insane by the court at the time of the crime. It can happen, can't it? Jill had said that anyone who takes a life is obviously out of their mind.*

"Oh, Mary. Look at me. I'm still shaking, but feel kinda satisfied that I came, satisfied that you have given me what I needed to hear. I don't want to be a dark cloud."

We hug and she plants another kiss on my cheek while she hands me an umbrella. The visit gifted me a perfect connection. I plan to call this possibility of a soulmate, a man named Andrew and see what might be a solution to everything I have dreamed could happen.

I waited to call him.

A week later, Jill visits me, brings another African violet, this time, purple flowers atop its crown. Beautiful!

"Jill, admittedly he's on my mind despite the doubts." And then I said something that I've always regretted saying: "Could it be he needs a house more than he needs me?"

"God bless us, Aneesa, I can't believe you said that."

"Okay, okay. I can't believe I said that either. It's pretty obvious that I'm not liking the woman I'm becoming. All these doubts—of him, of myself— of my faith —pushing me to go low."

Jill sits on the back of my outdoor garden chair, lays her soft hand on my arm, locks her green eyes on mine.

"We've got to remember. From where I see it, the man is still coming from one hell of a breakdown. Sure, he's different. Taking a life's about as different as it can be. But honey, isn't he trying to get back on his feet for real? Could it ever be God's asking you to help him back up as well as fall in love with him?"

'Oh My God, Jill. What a question!!!'

That night before bed, I'm down on my knees and pray from that deepest question plaging me: *Oh, God, are you behind this? I guess it does look like something You'd cook up. And ask me to enjoy the imaginative food.*

Sister Brendan's words float back: *No coward's soul is your own.*

195

You will always do God's will. Now, in this time of pure choice, I have to really believe her.

Suddenly, I wake, check the clock. Midnight. I look around as if something or someone is in this room with me…And I'm not frightened as I pull the sheets tighter around me, but ask myself if I'm seeing things? Yes, I am seeing things…no, not things, but that beloved nun, that same beloved nun who never failed to teach me more about what it meant to be virtuous. It's my Sister Brendan! She points her long crooked wrinkled finger at my nose and speaks:

"For God's sake, Aneesa, it might not work in the long run, but you have to trust God. You must take the chance. Remember how you taught that black man at the homeless breakfast? You told him to listen to what the white redneck sitting at his table might have to say. And at your Prejudice Workshops, you dealt with all kinds of mistrust. Trust yourself, my dear! Trust! Merton's words to both of us. "Trust yourself" he said. Don't forget our convent years, our vows, Merton's words. Were they anything about nothing else but trust?"

I sat back in the bed and thought long and hard about moments when life sends its beams hard on our heart, transforms what had been there all along to push an opening to other possibilities, other directions. I was having such a moment, maybe even an entire morning before sliding out from under those cotton sheets. I felt a loosening of my narrow judgments to a roomier approach to this man Andrew inviting me to play house with him, this Andrew of the roofless identity. Could it be an approach that could let in barrells of sunshine, could deliver me to new heights of understanding, not only about homeless people but could lift me to find the kind of deep love that I'd always wanted? Sure *beats doubting, Thomas!*

Sun's beams stream through the bedroom's sliding doors, and I began humming Cat Stevens well-known Christian hymn, *Morning Has Broken,*.....

I aim for the bathroom, shower, shave my legs, comb out my curly hair, pull up tight blue jeans, wear my low-cut blouse, and now called this man called Andrew for our first real date. Then, afterwards, with coffee all drained, I telephoned Jill: "Honey, that sound I heard in the garden after my call to Andrew must have been God breaking into laughter?"

At that, my friend joined the Divine Him in the sweetest giggle I'd heard in a long while.

Going out the front door, I was launched. And of course, that other lyric came roaring in, Julie Andrews' lyrics when she walked out of the convent to be guardian to a Captain's seven kids: *What will this day be like? I wonder…What will my future be? I wonder….It could be so exciting, to be out in the world, to be free….*

I slammed the car door, and my Cadillac took me to the place I determined to go, to pick up a man called Andrew and begin the rest of my life!

CHAPTER TWENTY-NINE

Counting Courtship

~ Andrew ~

dare I believe again

dare i see the sun in more than darted glimpse?
rain—the laughter—all the in-between?
very occasional oh-so-precious hidden and guarded
become my breathing fare
again?
dare i?
dare i see you?
dare i swim in pools again?
dare i believe in what you dare to?
dare i touch again?
dare i awaken?
dare i?

~ Aneesa ~

Andrew and I walk Orlando's Greenwood Park, the very cemetery where my parent's lay side-by-side, where I had often checked on their graves when I needed a good cry. Talk about pure serendipity! This was his special place too? Never for the same reason.

I never saw this cemetery the way I'm privelged to see it today, never walked along the tombs and, for Andrew, telling me why it's special for him, why Andrew loves these groves of hidden pines, the pond that surrounds its winding paths, its few visitors.

He laughs: "It's my special place where I keep my stash, my books, few clothes, and computer." He was sounding proud that he'd found a kind of roofless home, a prayerful location.

"The Trappists wouldn't accept me, so here's where I made a silent monastery among these pines."

He laughs some more. *And oh, how I was learning to love that sound of his laughter*—a kind of low rumbling and tumbling giggle that can only come from a happy human being. I think I'm the reason he's become happy.

We continued walking and sharing thoughts.

"Aneesa, these trees are my chapel, the pond, my holy font, the big rock my pew, best place for praying The Hours."

"Did you really try to join the Trappists?"

I feel the smile on my face as we stroll the path of his private grove. Somehow, he can't keep his tongue still. And for once, mine is.

"I just wanted to see you, a former nun, along this ground that is so holy to me, so quiet, so right. Aneesa, when you live on the street, the maddening traffic sounds never stop."

His blue eyes dance as he talks about what matters to him. He makes me realize how homebound I'd become. I am a city girl after convent life, strapped in a moving car, always turning the key, going somewhere, here and there. But here, in his presence, I'm hoping this city gal can really connect with a nature boy. Sure, I love my garden, grow my green world, but he stands happy away from the crowd. Me? I love crowds, their diversity, their surprises. Could it be, as I feel my future growing under these streaming moving clouds a new life is being born, that this day has begun an unbelievably fresh start?

That I could trade my crowd sounds for something else...something much more soul-like, much more like this man who holds my hand?

On a bench nearby, we enjoy a simple lunch. Birds gather for the crumbs Andrew throws their way. We delight in their warbling songs, like Mama's own laughter coming from her underground resting place not far away. We finish and I pull on Andrew's hand, walk him across the park to exactly where my parents are curled up under that holy ground, maybe facing each other. What finer stillness for introducing Andrew to them? He stands silently beside me, a healing moment for both of us if ever there was one. In truth, we stand before everything ahead. Are we a new creation where God alone knows how to create things that matter? I look up to Florida's ever-bluing sky, still holding his hand.

So, this is what You had me waiting for all these years. And Mama, how like you to bring us together here at your burial place. As for you, Daddy, hang on: this man's so much more than a lazy guy lacking a home.

Love set in. We welcomed our two spirits vitally transformed. We hung out, shared journal entries, cooked up new hope, each of us stepping out of a story-grown-tale to create a new love story. No expensive dinners, cruises, or trips to Bali as Jill and Todd had taken. Just bubbling up tales on a back porch, like children at play, nighttime filled with delightful wet kisses, tossing under pink sheets.

With so much pleasure newly felt, I had to get out of bed while Andrew slept soundly, fall on my knees to thank the all-knowing God who finally accomplished what I believe He had wanted to accomplish all the while of my questioning, and only in His way, only in His time. What He knew was more right for me than living in that world where I had to hide my love for priest friend, Mike.

So God, really, there is never enough thanks, for it all. I'd become, like Mary said, a beacon, choosing the man and not waiting forever. I became what You, God intended for most women, to be in love and to be loved. Because of Jill's prayers, because of our going to St. Margaret Mary two times a week, of visiting Arab Mary to capture her wisdom, I'd finally found the man I'd penned on my "wanted" list. Sure, he didn't have his own resources but had so much more inviting reality. He was a man I could look up to, listen to, hold his hand, and feel joyful reality in his presence.

Dear God, I'd been happy as a nun, loved the kids I taught, loved working for Mike, knowing how he'd seen the unknown talents I possessed, but never, dear God, have I been as happy as I feel now. I owe You so much for your direction and wisdom a plenty.

Andrew moved in and in no time, like any married couple I suppose, we discovered inevitable differences. He liked sweet; I liked sour. I planted plants; he pruned them too much for my liking. I liked my own space to write; he pushed for closeness in everything, wanted his desk right alongside my own. A few choice words illustrated how easily tempers can flare. Finally, he recognized that having his own space was better for both of us. Our desks found separate rooms and they seemed happier as well.

We bought two Apple computers to write our story, which will be a tribute to God, to how we trusted the process, and to the value of so many friends' prayers. Along with penning its pages, Andrew will add artful photographs. We will call it "With This Story." It was our first joint project.

One day, in the company of a few Merton friends, he offered a prayer of tribute for the two people who had, as he said, brought him back to life: "In my book, the two are, one, my Aneesa, my lover, and two, Apple's computer whizz creator, Steve Jobs. If God were to ask me, I owe both my new life."

I had a dream one night, a dream that took me to a young Andrew running across the sweltering savannah, hungry for an animal playmate. A pack of friendly dogs circled around him. He laughed as they barked friendly. A black pony rushed close and his hand tenderly brushed its dark mane. Somehow, he began to weep over a dead rabbit lying in his arms. It was certainly a strange dream and at breakfast the next morning, it prompted a question, especially about who or what that dead rabbit could possibly be.

"Andrew, I had a strange dream last night. You were surrounded by dogs, a black pony, and a dead rabbit was in your arms."

"Probably being in a cell, noise upon noise. Oh, I really can respond to that."

'Well, what was the hardest thing about being in prison? How did you survive?"

"You don't want to know."

I waited. He didn't like talking about his messy past. Should I have asked him? I'm not even sure why I did. But he put down his fork, leaned back, and checked his watch.

"Like everybody knows, Aneesa, there's that freedom-lack. Nobody likes living under a razor-wire fence, cut off from Ferris wheels and cotton candy. You stand longingly at that fence gazing at nature's leafy green all around you, at open fields, wanting to feel your feet running on that grass, resting afterward in it, letting a towering grandfather oak shade you.

"Sure, I'd have given my right arm to see the curve of a woman's ankle, her swaying hips. But being confined from nature hit me the hardest."

I stared at this work of God, his eyes so glistening, so piercing at times. I thought about his take on prisoner's punishment, and was brought back to a passionate talk given by our parish's priest, Brian Farewell, what he had seen from so many encounters in his work with prison ministry, his words had never dropped from my reflection.

"Inmates are forced to steel themselves against being human.

They feel that denial every day. They've been robbed of their humanity, something going on in them that's always cold, unfair, intense." Andrew interrupted my reverie.

"But, sweetums, the last thing I want to do is drag you into that gated place. I'm done with it!"

I reached over, rested my hand on his long outstretched and warm fingers: "Isn't putting our stuff out to each other helping to heal it? I want to hear all the details, if you will."

"Okay, partner with all the relationship answers." He grinned his wry way. I loved that grin. We sat like that for a moment. Then he pulled his hand away, grabbed the glass to drink the last of his orange juice. Then he stood with outstretched arms. "Honey, let's do move on."

Years later when both of us attended that amazing movie, *The Shawshank Redemption* based on Stephen King's book, how could anyone forget that one prison-yard scene? Actor Tim Robbins had stolen into the warden's office somehow, and most likely would warrant a punishment, but he mischievously hooks up the outdoor loudspeaker to an old Victrola recording of an opera. I don't remember which aria but I'll never forget how the entire prison community stood frozen in the open yard, sun blazing on each head, mesmerized by the aria's free-flying soprano notes. That scene said it all about the denial incarcerated men are called to endure.

One day, driving to the grocery store, Andrew begins singing: "Come away with me Lucille in my merry Oldsmobile"

"Andrew, this is not an Oldsmobile."

"Aneesa, darling, I was born at night, but not last night! I know your car's not an Oldsmobile. Give me some room. Actually, I've come up with a name for your Cadillac."

"What now?"

"He's Carlyle."

"Carlyle? Where'd you get that?"

"Directly from the House of Lords on the Thames."

"Are you joking. Andrew, this car calls Detroit home, not London."

The man's still crazy and I love him for that off-beat thinking. Always making me laugh. Our friends, too.

"Listen, dear heart, sure your car's not exactly a Rolls Royce. But coming off the streets as I have, this car's still one upscale vehicle. He does deserve a good label. How about even *Sir* Carlyle!"

The name struck. I shared that story with Jill, and suddenly, she refused to listen to my objections to her suggestion that Andrew get a driver's license.

"Aneesa, have you thought about Andrew getting an official I.D.?

"No, what about it?"

"You know, a driver's license is like a passport. Without it, he's really a nobody."

"Forget it Jill. He's not going to learn on my car because nobody drives that car except me. Besides, how do I even know if he can drive?"

She rolls her eyes and looks out the window away from me: "Good God, Aneesa, he had a family, a job. I don't think I know you sometimes."

"Okay, okay, he drives. But, Jill, that Cadillac is my special car. My brother helped me pick it out at the auction. I know this sounds selfish, probably childish but hear me. This car has been my tutor. It became family to me.

"Remember how I was ashamed of it in the beginning?" *Me, behind the wheel of that one upscale sedan?* "I was a former nun, had taken a vow of poverty. I just couldn't accept an upscale car like my mother had. But I had to. I simply had to learn and it took a long while, to accept it as another gift from God. It wasn't easy. I had all this stuff in me, the convent's influence was still talking, deep talk, but to me, a car like that is pure luxury and a former nun can't go around showing off her luxuries. It was Connie, who continued to help me see it as a gift from God, that all material objects are gifts, and they all have a spiritual component."

Jill listened to me rant about my need to let Carlyle teach me what I needed to know about God's gifts.

"Now, I love that car. So, honey," I put my arm around her, and squeezed, "Nobody drives this luxury automobile but me. Okay?"

That next week, I found one of Andrew's poems by the window as I cleaned. My blooming babies were right outside that window.

and sun begins to peek through leaves now tentative
yellowing in a second rank behind this wall of green
i'm facing little white orchid and splashy purple of
bougainvillea outside both very expectant brothers &
sisters all so poised in prayer at this miracle dawning
you'd think we'd never seen and even if later we grow
jaded when caught up in the sheer business of living but
for now ever new just tots really here awe-stunned before
You creator with urging breeze and this perfect freshness

Time turns its wheel, as always it does and delivers enlightenment. Weeks later, I sit in the passenger seat as Andrew gets into the driver's side and smiles at me. And I take it in. We're doing something right, and it brightens my world. I felt my generosity, just like Mama always seemed to do. Andrew's smile signals a new and fresh adventure. *Like a husband and wife behind a car's dashboard. Husband and wife?*

"Don't worry, sweetums, at what you're about to see: I still know something about driving a car."

That may have been true, yet I still signaled the sign of the cross like Mama did, when at sixteen I first sat behind our old brown Plymouth's steering wheel to learn to drive. Daddy had given up trying to teach me. His impatience was unbounded. I kept crying and he'd yell even more.

Sure, Mama was nervous but hung in with my mistakes. For her, the sign of the cross was insurance that we'd both come out alive on Orlando's 17-92 four-lane trafficked highway.

Well, God did stay with my mother and I passed that driver's test. Now, with Andrew at the wheel, I couldn't help but pray another old call for mercy, *Kyrie Eleison.* Obviously, like Mama, I was the nervous one.

I watched closely—his movements, seeing him settle into the driver's seat. I liked the way he calmly adjusted the rearview mirror, pushed the seat back to accommodate his long legs, smiled sheepishly at me after he pressed the pedal too hard forcing us to jerk ahead. *Oops!* Carlyle... "Oh, Andrew, I think my car is telling you he wants me behind that wheel. He's not convinced I should be letting you drive."

But soon, we tool along and suddenly it's spring and I feel a burst of love as I watch him stop at red lights, make sharp turns onto a two-lane country road. Carlyle is adjusting to his new boss. I swallow a bit of jealousy.

A week later, we make it official and drive away for his driver's license. He takes the test, handling the car as if it were his own. The clerk delivers him his earned passport, and he, a beaming new driver, grabs the laminated entrance into a longshot world, shoves it into his old brown wallet, pushes it into his back pocket, his eyes sparkling my way. We hold hands, sail out the county's double doors into a world holding proof that he *officially* belongs.

Yes, Jill, he's got his passport and I've got a very proud Andrew who's just won back his public identity.

It was Merton time again. The 1993 annual Thomas Merton Conference would be held in Colorado. Taking that trip meant driving across the country. I was okay but—and that *but* was a big question mark. If we went, Andrew wanted us to camp on the way.

"I want to take you camping," Andrew announced. "You've never camped before. It's wonderful being out there without a roof blocking out nature's best scenes. And, Aneesa, we got a car that can tow a new pop-up, honey!"

"I'm not so sure. Carlyle wasn't made for pulling trailers."

"Oh, yes your Cadillac can do that, easily. The pop-up is not much heavier than a tent, the lightest one they make."

At some point, I wondered if I could be up for living with only one person to connect to for that length of time. I was in love with this man but I wasn't looking forward to long hours sitting side by side, don't ask me why. Maybe because friend Carol had warned: "Camping's a lot of concentrated coupling, Aneesa. If you two can survive that kind of long travel together, I'd say you're headed for the altar."

In the end, we bought and hooked up the pop up. Everything played fine as we tooled along America's interstates. If anyone saw us, we were two kids, relishing each other's presence, taking in America's sights flying by: old stores, national forests, and at that time, gassing up in cheap gasoline stations.

At one point, we broke into a harmonic rendition of *America The Beautiful*. Surprisingly, Andrew possessed the gift of perfect pitch, could make harmony with every song we attempted to sing. This new boyfriend had sung bass in the Paul Hume choir at his alma mater, Georgetown in Washington, DC. How amazing, the two of us. I had a degree in music education from Manhattanville College, this guy had a wealth of natural talent.

For the long car ride, we listened to John Gray's, *Men are from Mars, Women from Venus*. Little did I suspect how much I was from Venus, and that soon, Andrew and I would go to battle in our first fight.

We stopped to make camp. Andrew set up most of the stuff for the night. I pulled out the little Coleman stove we'd bought. It was delightful, I admit, eating our supper under the varied trees in one of America's national parks.

Yet, after even one night, I soon found camping too much. Too much to watch over, too much stuff to go back in a certain place, friends too far away. It didn't take long for me to start complaining.

Onward in the car, I reflected aloud on that joke some comedian had told: "Do you know why I don't like camping?" he tweaked the audience. "I don't like it because I have a house." *I had laughed but it proved true for me.*

Our first battle happened after the final Merton session. We got into Carlyle and headed for the Monastery of Christ in the Desert, located in the far dunes near Abiqui, New Mexico. I never, and Andrew probably didn't suspect either, the unapproachable dirt roads that lay ahead. This was the dessert. No interstate.

Bump after bump, sharp and unfriendly barren sand. My poor gentle Carlyle rode up and down and began fighting for his life, coughing more than I wanted to hear, rock after rock under his wheels until finally, my nerves let the horror be known.

"Carlyle is losing it, Andrew. We can't do this. We've got to turn back. This car is no Jeep. He can't take it any longer." Andrew just kept driving.

"Andrew, *ANDREW! Stop the car!*"

"Come on, he's a Cadillac, isn't he? He can carry us up this road."

"No, he can't.

"Aneesa, chill out."

"Chill out, yourself. Your pop-up's killing my car. You're supposed to know better. We're not going another inch." I reached for the door handle staring fiercely his way.

Finally, he pulled to a stop. I jerked open the door with more shouts at him. Now, looking out, it was no longer the car that got my attention but the barren desert I was facing. Could I even step into it, handle some of the low brush under my feet. No Florida land here but dry, prickly, uninviting ground, and probably hiding a poisonous snake. Scared and lost, I began to cry as I gingerly tread each step. A giant lizard crossed right over my foot. I screamed, jumped, danced away. What else was lurking to get me? *Oh God, get me home.*

Looking around, I saw Andrew finally letting himself get out of the car. His face granite, a face I'd never seen on him. This was hard, everything seemed wrong. Him, me, the desert, the car, even Merton. We'd never been so far apart, never propelled by such deep fury.

I had to leave Carlyle. Andrew was finding his way away from me as well. Was Carol right: this the sign that we were not to be together at an altar?

It must have been a while before somehow, I found myself bumping into him down on a ridge in the middle of this barren stretch of New Mexico. We were standing beside a bubbling stream running through rock and sand, my feet resting on the rounded pebbles, my heart literarily leaping with relief.

We stood together in the gathered silence. Finally, he reaches for my hand. I gladly snuggled it into his own, desperate to be back together as one. We embraced in a long hug…peace and love in that hug. I nestled onto his chest, happy to again be okay in his presence. How all that happened wasn't important now. What was important was that we were together once more.

As I pressed against him, I spotted an unusual stone below.

"Andrew, she's talking to us."

He sees it too: a small rock perfectly formed Madonna and child looking up at us. It seemed that nature herself had sculpted this religious stone relic by its eons of flowing currents. I grab it, brush off its wet sand, press it to my lips. "This Madonna is our sign, Andrew. We are okay together. We will make it, even if Carlyle can't stand these rocky paths."

We made it back to Carlyle, drove backward for longer than I liked, but finally free of the rocky road. Carlyle was still not the same but he got us back to Florida. Between us sat that Madonna where today, she graces our living room mantle, reminding us of that mixed Mars—Venus day of long ago, reunion that was so sweet.

When we got home, I had to call Carol, "Honey, we survived."

That trip to Colorado and a spirit-filled Merton conference dragging that pop-up didn't end happily for Carlyle.

"What do you mean his block is cracked?" I asked my Cadillac doctor.

"Aneesa, this car can't drive you anywhere anymore."

Standing nearby, after hearing my mechanic's diagnosis, Andrew turns away sheepishly, his head totally down as he disappears into the men's room. I let him. After all, he was the one who brought this onto Carlyle. I walk out to that dear four wheels of mine to say the goodbye. Tears wouldn't stop coming. I didn't try to stop them.

I stood at the window of the driver's seat and let him know my grief: *Of course, Carlyle, you couldn't last forever, despite my love for you. You carried me safely over 150,000 miles, your colorful dashboard always teaching me everything I needed to know. But you gave me so much more, just the one who showed me how prejudiced I'd been about the upper class, pushed my mind to climb the bigger places of God's abundance, reminding me of Merton's own perspective. "Possessions slip in and out with great frequency. In loving them, then letting them go, we experience the rich-sad tastes of life, the unavoidable price of soulful living."*

CHAPTER THIRTY

Wedding Bells

~ Aneesa ~

Months of constant togetherness obviously called for a wedding: big, ecumenical, culturally diverse, and grandly inspired. And Jill's planning helped make it that way.

For the music, there was no choice. "If ever I get married, that's gotta be my entrance," I informed Jill after once hearing the last movement of Saint-Saens Organ Symphony years ago on WMFE going to work on the Expressway, a morning I've never forgotten. I was about to drop my coins in the toll booth when that organ's thunderclap chord sounded, a majestic sound that pierced my soul. Saint-Saens, *Third Symphony, the Organ Symphony's Fourth Movement,* was pure orchestral bursts of joy. Its sequences flowed perfectly, one after the other, brass sounds layering on each other as if a grove of festive pine trees. I broke down, sobbed right there at the tollbooth, the coins still locked in my hand and which never found their way into the toll's basket as I drove off in a puffy cloud of reverence. Cops could have locked me up; I wouldn't have cared.

Now, wedding bells rang to that symphony in the very chapel where I had blamed God years earlier for taking a sabbatical. We were married on Thomas Merton's silver anniversary, December 10, 1993.

Mary Sissini sat in the chapel's front pew as a hundred friends reeled to that *Organ Symphony's* chord. I walked alone as that glorious sound filled the church. My white satiny palomino pants and many-buttoned white top looked as fresh as if right off the rack. I kept that smile on, as if I were Maria being married in *The Sound of Music*, walking up to my tall Captain Andrew in his white tux, preparing for his one-line vowing fidelity, no stuttering as he spoke his three words of promise: *I'm yours forever.*

Mary Sissini laughingly tapped my shoulder as I made my way, winked as did the whole world at this spectacular, how-did-it-happen wedding. Instead of rings, Father Kamide held high the pages of the short story we'd written together in preparation for this day. "With This Story" honored the miracle of how our monk friend Merton brought us together. Friends behind us put their palms together in resounding applause, followed by not a few giggles.

Special friends faced the two of us, offering diverse blessings in Arabic and Hebrew. Father Walsh's Gaelic blessing sounded as well, remembering how he had winked at me after Erica and I had spoken at St. Margaret Mary pulpit.

Oh, prayers had been more than answered. The world was turning beautifully on its axis and I floated hearing that resounding priest's—or was it God's?—declaration: "I pronounce you husband and wife!"

And then, the final direction: "Go, the Mass is ended." At that, the bellowing conquering alleluias from John Williams' resounded the *Empire of the Sun*. The assembly rose in a fiesta of joy, gathered in one bonding circle, held arms high, and danced an orbiting madness that sealed our future; NASA's climb to the moon couldn't have manifested its victory more explosively. In truth, Jill said, Andrew and I were bathed in God's goodness.

Late that night, I lay awake knowing my world would never be the same, that somehow, through the myriad paths of unpredictable chance, Andrew and I had met and everything changed. From my Catholic background and his as well, his divorce, to my leaving Mike…Endless *ifs*… If Rodney King had not been attacked, if Jill had not gone to that Catholic conference, if Andrew had not found work in South Florida, if Mike had left the priesthood to marry me…a thousand *ifs* of chance-like grace bestowed. We were destined to meet, God's odds of blessings pushing us to sit at the same altar and take in His grace of constant nourishment.

Later that night, I looked out the bedroom's glass door at the star-filled night. Grace had fallen over the disbeliefs and renewals, voices and faces, delivering sweet endings. *Oh dear God, You who made the world spin, You spun your little nun to this night of love. A huge thank you.*

~ Andrew ~

A year later, after times of more writing, Aneesa and I grew eager for a getaway loft, for me, another place of healing, where each of us could enjoy time alone. A place to meditate, yes, and write our stories away from phones and doorbells, even a partner's chatter.

We trailed a realtor into a small and simple Winter Park condo with combined dining/living room and a large bedroom, big enough to hold a desk and computer near a sunlit window. Reasonably priced, this second-floor loft was planted seven miles from our home, one perfect cycling spree.

The former owner's silver crucifix hung above the doorway confirming our choice and Aneesa dragged out her checkbook.

In the car on our drive home, I tell Aneesa "Buying this condo brings it up, honey, a prison dream of years. I gotta tell you, there was this place in my imagination, pristine and white, everything quiet, a place where choice words surfaced all by themselves." *And now it is ours.*

I record the many books I devoured in that loft: Edmund Dante, imprisoned hero in *The Count of Monte Christo, Etty* Hellisum journal, *An Interrupted Life*, how she sang on her way to the gas chamber. Books I picked up at bookstores, or were picked for me, fly me over my high walls, barbed wire, armed guards, detaching this heart of mine from its so long unbearable enclosure. Never have I felt so real.

Years fly by when one day I'm waiting in the Tampa's Crown's hotel lobby, large indoor waterfall gushes mightily behind me. The lobby ceiling must soar some fifty feet up. Three balconies arc their way around the lounge in bold, bulbous curves. A shiny grand piano begs for a player as undertones of soft jazz fill the space, masking the too-occasional MacBook keyboard clicks of my own. Bright spring greenery and luxuriant palms make themselves known on both sides of the tall encircling glass.

Next door, Aneesa is engaged with her speaker's academy, a monthly training ground for taking public her unique message about healing our relationship with money.

Truth is, I don't really know where to begin here. Our morning readings and prayers? Our drives in contemplative silences? Our music? Our jokes? Our wows? In such a moment, I have the chance to welcome words about an unlikely love, to say something upfront about my decade and-a-half of second-skin connection with this beautiful wife. With this wife, it's always like home, never a time when it wasn't. I've the feeling it's so with her too. It never mattered much just where—open park or woodsy nest, fancy hotels like this one, or a cozy bread-&-breakfast or cuddling up at home. We yak, we connect, we're present, we are one. From where I sit the way we are looks to have been downright ordained. Would it had always been so. (Would've saved heaps of trouble!)

~ Aneesa ~

Although Andrew and I launched ourselves into life's gorgeous cloud of love, we just as easily found our feet sloshing in old shit too. Andrew's unworthy feelings frequently surged and spread to all sorts of daily trials. If the rotor blade on the lawnmower broke, he'd slap his hand: "Bad boy. You didn't tighten it." When the front screen door wouldn't close tightly and let mosquitoes in, I'd hear him exclaim: "Damn, I didn't set it right!" The most disheartening of these outbursts happened when receiving a magazine rejection of his poem: "I thought this was a good piece. I guess not."

No Florida judge could impose such a never-ending low-lying sentence on this man who had come into my life with a chuckle and bright blue eyes.

Elizabeth Gilbert, well-known author of *Eat Pray and Love*, wrote somewhere: *"Oh my God, it is so hard. And we're the last person we can forgive. But it's so necessary, even more than discipline, even more than inspiration, we must be gentle with ourselves."*

Would it ever stop, this obvious lack of confidence, a behavior that concerned me more than it bothered him? Why was I scared about that? Was it just a part of normal fear, the stuff we always must deal with? Was I afraid he'd mess up someday? Tell off a cop? Get himself back in prison?

From the kitchen, I watched him make for his easy chair, grabbing *Cycle* magazine, hiding his face waiting for my call to supper. I put down the big wooden spoon. I saw a chance to get this worry off my chest. I walked up to his chair and he put down the magazine. I wanted to share what I'd read just that morning.

Outside, raindrops filled the opening moment and I took the opportunity to comment on his negativity: "Andrew, we've got to clean this up. You're always putting yourself down. What gives?"

He waited, and then out of nowhere, he brings me into to his childhood memories: "Funny thing, what I still remember so clearly was hoping to keep up with my father's tall stride when he held my hand. We were walking up Fifth Avenue to his office in Rockefeller Center. I can relish only a few precious moments like that."

"Oh Andrew, what must it have been at home if he was so absent to you?"

Andrew pauses even longer, rubbing his beard, and seemingly checking the laces on his shoes. Only the outside downpour filled the silence until he finally looks up to speak: "I'd say he was usually far away, except at the dinner table. It was there how easily he took over the entire meal. It was either Belgium's wonderful citizens, or his job in the Congo—and stuff like that. All I know is at dinner he was the full act, words and gestures, the entire table his drama. We sat mesmerized, even Mom tried to listen with all the attention she knew he needed.

In that breakfast morning of oatmeal and fruit, I asked and learned how Andrew's Mom, used to sing to him that famous Nat King Cole song.

"Andrew, I used to sing those lyrics myself as a teen. Let's sing it now…"

And we started in and I loved the music we were making.

> *there was a boy*
> *a very strange enchanted boy*
> *they say he wandered very far, very far*
> *over land and sea...*
> *and the greatest thing*
> *you'll ever learn*
> *is to love and be loved in return*

"Mom believed in me, wanted the best to come my way, was pained at seeing how Dad was so distant."

"Andrew, my own Syrian father eventually had his "never pleased with my kids" moments as well. He hated the fact that I became a nun. And as for the boys, they never seemed to bond with my father."

I loved those conversations Andrew and I began having at breakfast. This time about his negativity and how it may have begun. For Andrew, that poor relationship was capped by his bed wetting. His mom tried everything to stop it: "'Andrew, don't drink before bedtime,' she'd say, or 'Pray hard on your knees before sliding under the sheets.' But Anessa, I'd wake up on a cold morning, frozen in my own piss. I couldn't move in that unheated room in our country home. That uncontrollable wetting lasted until I was nearly fourteen."

"And your dad?"

"He'd stand there, watch Mom pull off the yellow soiled sheets wearing a scowl as long as Manhattan Island."

I got up, walked around the table to wrap him in my arms. I held him so close.

Out in the garden after he'd biked away, I reflected how my role might now be as a companion to Andrew: This is what I remember journaling:

Aneesa, calm yourself, and calm your mate. Remember to lay your hand on his knee when you're together, see how that hand always makes him feel loved. He's told you so. You've chosen this man, this new beginning. God wanted your love in his life, even if you never knew a thing in the beginning about his sad childhood, about the horror of his breakdown and about that awful prison life. It's all been part of his journey, and now has become part of yours. If you're smart, you know that illness of negativity has a purpose. And as Elizabeth Gilbert had said, it is so hard to believe that, to know a process to be true. And she said we're the last person we can forgive...we've got to be gentle with ourselves. And I have to trust you God, to teach me to be gentle with myself and with Andrew.

"Honey, after you left this morning, I read about a teacher who'd had it with a badly-behaved student. She took out a map of the world, tore it into pieces and handed it to the boy. "Go," she said. "Put this map back together," thinking it was going to take him days to complete the task, keeping him out of her hair—or black veil since she was a nun. In a few minutes, this kid came up to her desk, handed her the map pasted in one perfect piece. "How could you do that so quickly?' she asked. "Turn it upside down, Sister. On the back is the face of a man. I just put the man back together and that put the world back together too."

Andrew smiled into my face. But for me the conversation wasn't ended. I went on.

"Honey, you brought yourself around. Remember your countdown call in prison? Three times a day you prayed the Divine Office? My God, what grace you brought upon yourself, even in that place where grace could be so absent to inmates, although God's work is never absent, I know. But you! You transcended that line-up experience as if you were a practicing monk, you made the difference from being victim, giving that routine deeper meaning. If that ain't honest prayer, what is?"

"But you, Aneesa? Wasn't your Dad disturbing too?"

"Well, not like exactly like yours, but yes, somewhat unwelcome too. I remember as a kid having death dreams. I never knew where they came from but usually, I was in peril of some fatal event, usually falling from a high place, stuck in a house on fire, stuff like that. I'd wake up sweating. When I left home for college, the nightmares stayed home. To be sure, my father was no saint either. The American dream was his baby; he did little more than successfully nurture that. Mostly I suffered for my brothers and sister. I know Dad had something to do with their nightmares as well. But listen, with God's grace, most of us survive them. So, listen! I've heard enough of this 'Bad Boy' stuff. The guy I'm looking at is a good man and I'm so glad to be your lady of prison dreams, the woman who you dreamed owned 'the cottage by the sea, serving you tea and crumpets by her fireside.' So, Please. I'm the wife God has sent to you and you're the man that I dreamed would knock at my door, pull me into his arms, promise we'd always be wrapped close in God's love. We both have fought plenty enough for a life we prayed would be ours."

I put my head on his knee while silent Andrew rubbed his fingers through my hair, caressing my curls, leaning down to kiss my ear, his cycling magazine dropping to the floor.

Dinner dishes put away, the living room sofa turns into a relaxing bed. I had set down my wine glass as he reached for me, lifts hand to my breasts. Longing overtakes us.

"Mind if I eat you up! You're my woman, you! I'm your man."

He covers my face with kisses, desire furiously erupts, clothes fly off. I lay back in his arms, moans of pleasure erupting from us both, angelic, as if the whole world is spirited by this love making. Here works my man past sorrow and pain. Morning finds us curled still on that sofa, locked in each other's embrace.

CHAPTER THIRTY-ONE

Probation Sucks

~Aneesa~

Love, reverence, and even awe kept us together but the state had another idea for keeping him together with them: "Lifetime Probation." When it happened, that illegal sentence was foisted on my husband by a revengeful Judge despite Andrew's plea bargain. In our case, that judgment proved to be illegal as told us by our lawyer. Plea bargains, we learned later, cannot be altered and Andrew's plea bargain by his court appointed attorney didn't include monthly check-ins at a probation officer's headquarters plus monthly visits to our home, timed without our knowing when these officers would appear. We suffered through many a visit. What I have thus learned about probation officers is that they come in all varieties of gender, shapes, meanness, and kindness; you could say a comical array of law enforcers from The Department of *(So-Called)* Corrections as Andrew facetiously describes them. Truth to tell, these officers are rarely about correcting, or helping individuals fall back into living a full and honest life.

One early probation guy never failed to jump in with an almost laughable question: "Has Andrew done anything shady I should know?"

I was feeling mean: "Oh yes, he killed a grasshopper in our backyard."

He wasn't amused but truth to tell, I couldn't warm up to these people checking on my honest, well-mannered husband.

One month, a young probation lady rang the doorbell wearing a black mini-skirt and poured her cleavage into Andrew's face. I felt embarrassed for her and him. She stayed at our front door and whispered her questions to him, I swear a kind of Marilyn Monroe voice.

Later, I asked Andrew if the probation department knew she dressed and talked like that when calling on her "clients."

"They knew it, honey and liked the way she's dressed. A little perk in the office for them."

Then came Mr. Bumstead, a fat man with a protruding thick neck, always wearing the same green baggy pants, a lighted cigar clenched between his fingers.

"Mr. LeBoeuf, you won't have any problem with me!" That was what he offered Andrew the first time we met him in his office. It was simply a lie as we soon found out for when our permission papers spoke of a trip to an environmental conference we had planned to attend in Oklahoma, he phoned the administrator of that workshop and warned that Andrew was on probation; this officer who promised we wouldn't have any trouble with him. We couldn't even imagine the nervousness on the part of that conference leader when we arrived and how long it took to explain who we really were.

When a new probation lady came along, we thought this woman we'd seen at Mass plus the fact that her child was in one of my teacher's CCD classes, she certainly would go easy on Andrew. But she bluntly attacked him with this requirement: "You need drug testing, Andrew."

"What?"

"You got that right. I'm signing you up for it."

"Lady, I don't do drugs!"

He came home completely dejected. I sat with him on the edge of the bed for a long while, just holding his hand.

221

All that but we have survived. With God on our side, and with our belief in ourselves that all would eventually be well, life with probation officers was endured and overcome. A friend of mine laughingly commented, "That probation burden applies to that ancient 'monastic' concept, Aneesa. *Shit happens*."

The most disappointing weight in Department of Corrections' burden happened one memorable night, with a visit that both Andrew and I can and will never forget. My friends couldn't believe it really happened but I tell it exactly as I remember it.

It's 11:08 p.m. We're asleep, sealed away from the world or so I thought. But I'm roused by hard knocking, banging on the glass at the front door.

"Andrew, wake up! Who is there? They're breaking down the door."

He pulls on his robe, slides into his slippers, heads for the door. Outside, I can hear rain falling, hard. I trail behind, peek through the blinds. Three squad cars are parked in front—red and blue flashing lights, a crime thriller scene. *Oh my God! What can the neighbors be thinking?*

"Andy, unlock the door. Let 'em in—quick."

The lock is hard to turn but he gets it. A short, scruffy silver-headed man pushes open the door, shouting at us as he passes by us into our home: "Goddammit, what took you so long to open your door?" The man was shouting as if we were deaf.

At that, four young, armed police officers followed him in. They occupied every inch of our tiny living room. I stepped back near the piano aware that I could smell their sweat, pulled my robe tighter around me, tried to quiet my brain. *Dear God, this a scene out of a movie!*

The gray-headed guy shouts at Andrew, again as if he were deaf: "Where do you keep your guns?" Not stopping to hear me repeat, "Guns?" *Guns?* He heads straight for the kitchen, begins to pull open our drawers, then turns back, again barking at Andrew.

"Where does this room lead? We're searching every room. Who sleeps in that bedroom?"

I stood statue-like, my stomach feeling the shock of it all. Is this possible? Me, a former nun who had led a quiet life, now having an army of police invading my home.

Okay, there were times in my convent life when I didn't need the Superior going on a tirade the way this guy seems to be doing. And sure, I did have one that screamed at us before bedtime. I look at the four young guys standing there, somehow returned to that morning my nuns stood quietly as Sister Somebody began yelling at the four of us nuns living there with her: "Who kept lights on in the community room? I pay the bills around here, and you run up those bills." There we were, old and young nuns poised together like tiny waifs, eyes cast down, arms up our wide black sleeves, listening to her flapping mouth. I wanted to shout my own accusations: "Who do you think you're talking to? You're the one burning midnight oil."

But every nun knew that shouting at a Superior would never do, trained as we were, like infantry cadets to stand erect, to keep our eyes down—called modesty of the eyes—to keep our mouths shut. This was called Holy Obedience, taking it on the chin when scolding was thrown at you!

That night in the convent clings to my memory. Why? I can't say but I fell asleep connecting to the awful truth that even here in God's world, some Superiors could be, indeed, brutes, drill sergeants training us to obey every order. I call them marginalized worshippers, never really feeling at home. I had met only a few like that, who could frown and throw out orders, obviously testing our vow of obedience. And I thank God, in my experience, that there were only a very few.

Now, here in my own home, this callous uniformed so-called superior officer is freaking out, searching every room, yanking sheets off the bed—yes, doing that military thing—snapping open my purse, leaving it open, kicking a stool by the floor lamp on his way to the next room. A bully. *Call the police! But these are the police!*

The four city policemen shift back and forth, looking darn uncomfortable, avoiding my eyes. One lays his hand on his holster. I imagine these young minds might be asking themselves what the hell they are doing here. *These homeowners don't look like criminals or act like ones.*

Suddenly, I want to laugh; here we were, a week earlier at Pax Christi's conference on non-violence. Could anybody guess what lay in store for us two committed Pax Christi board members watching a bully search our house for weapons? *Hell, I can't even get Andrew to sharpen our knives!*

Suddenly, Jill's image on the mantle awakens me to my beloved being yelled at.

Look at this man of yours. A real man. Hadn't he confessed his crime to you from the start, hadn't he even tried to reach out to the victim's family? Always, in everything you both shall endure. It all shall pass.

I'm about to boil over as now the bully knocks into me coming out of our bedroom.

"Excuse me sir," I stand before his bluster. "*Why* are you here? Is there a problem?"

"There sure is, lady," he replies, and says nothing that indicates something.

I peek into our bedroom. *Oh, dear God!* Drawers pulled out, clothes thrown on the bed, papers strewn around.

Again, he heads for the kitchen. Andrew follows. Nothing of laughter left in me, only fear that Andrew won't take this brouhaha much longer. *God, come in here! Don't let Andrew explode.*

"Are you getting what you came for?" Andrew barks, *"Braves."*

Bully's face reddens, eyes bulge. He shoves his head under Andrew's chin, on tiptoes to look up at him. "Excuse me, what did you say?"

"Whatever you thought it was, it ain't here."

"You better shut up or you're coming with me back to lockdown."

God, shut him up! Shut up Andrew, too.

At that warning, Andrew hands him both wrists, challenges the guy to cuff him at once.

"Okay, take me back."

Oh Andrew, shut up! Yet, I'm proud of him too, staring up to this craziness.

I shuffle close to Andrew's side, take his hand. Then I'm eyeball-to-eyeball with this unacceptable superior, generating my meanest look.

"Are you scared of Andrew? Sir! Calm down!"

At that point, the youngest cop standing near clears his throat, steps up to tough guy, and lays his hand on his shoulder: "Okay, Crosby, let's go. Nothing here to worry about."

Locating his brain, bully brushes the officer's hand away, stomps toward the door and like a spoiled child who didn't get his way, grabs the last word: "Okay, mister, but don't you forget, you're on probation. Watch your step!"

The front door slams behind them all, and the weather adds a dramatic finish as a wild bolt of lightning flashes into the entire house followed by a giant thunderclap that shakes all our windows. I run to the blinds, peek out as the heaviest downpour slams into our uninvited visitors, scurrying them back to their flashing lights.

Andrew drops to the sofa. I drop beside him. Somewhere I read that only through overcoming an ordeal will we find meaning that touches our souls. But now we sit dazed, a pair of frozen kids wondering what we had done wrong.

Finally, Andrew barks, "Hell and damn fire! What now? Leave the country? They're never gonna leave me alone."

"Breathe, honey! Just breathe."

Through the night, we calmly relive every frazzled moment. The young cops, the bully, the knives on the counter, the clothes strewn everywhere, ringing of the alarm telling us to go to bed. Following a cup of soothing tea, we determine the work ahead. This burden of an unfair probation sentencing must go.

"By God, honey, we'll get off this damn thing. Badass Zero was infection enough. Now, this silliness. No more!" I pick up his hand, hold it to my cheek.

"I don't know how or when, but I swear by God, we're gonna lick it," sounding like Scarlet O'Hara rising from the Civil War ashes, determined that this will all be part of a past and we will be triumphant.

We slept most the day. Rain withdrew as an afternoon sun beamed alive throughout our home. I cleaned up the mess that brute of a guy had made. I wondered if our neighbors had seen those blue and red flashing lights. If they did, I'm sure glad they never mentioned it.

CHAPTER THIRTY-TWO

Dollars Welcome

~ Aneesa ~

Talk about the way God can surprise us, the very next week, Andrew comes jumping over a living room chair and completely startles me. I'm watering my African violets, an array of pink and white flowering blooms. I swear he practically shouts: "Honey, a certified letter from TIAA-CREF, my old teacher's retirement fund!"

Caught in his excitement, curious about what that letter might explain, I sit on the wicker sofa. Andrew rips open the envelope to receive whatever it might offer. He begins reading softly. Whatever that letter tells him generates an amazing wide grin, that kind of grin that easily takes me in.

"Honey, you're grinning. Is it from Santa Claus? Read it aloud." In the background, I can hear birds chirping, even an owl's hoot. Animals picking up on a human's excitement?

"Honey! It *is* from Santa Claus!"

I jump up, pull the letter from his hands and start reading it myself, but he grabs it back, shoos me away. Something is up. This isn't a bit like him.

"No, I want you to guess how much money they're sending me."

"You've got money coming? Really? Don't keep me in the dark."

My once-homeless husband was scheduled for a monthly Social Security check and even a Navy pension. Now, more money?

"Okay, big man, how much?"

"Guess, sweetums!" (I love how he calls me that, his own honeybun nickname for me.)

"Ten thousand?"

"Nope."

Was he kidding? The eagerness on his face fires me to play this money game with the man who came from having none.

"Okay, how about twenty-five-thousand? Is that stretching it too far?"

"No, go on."

"Andrew, are we really doing this. You mean enough money to take a trip, buy new computers? You're scaring me."

"Go on, guess again!"

I had it. Everything open? Feeling young and old, giddy and frenzied, I yell: "Stop! Tell me!"

He rubs his face, drops his head to eyes my level, then, in that deep bass voice of his, here comes the magic quote,

> *Mr. LeB, you have accrued a sum of one hundred and fifty-thousand dollars in your annuity account from teaching in New York. We've been searching for you. We checked your address. If this is correct, do let us know and we'll give you access to your account.*
>
> *~ John Jay Lipstrock*
> *Vice President of Retired Accounts*

I jerk the letter out of his hands again, check the letterhead, "Maybe it's a fraud?"

He grabs the letter back holding it high like a flag of waving confidence. *Oh Mama, I've a newborn on my hands. Wish you were alive to see who I married.*

I'm up, grab his hands between my own, and check the awe in his blue-green eyes.

"Damn it! Andrew! All those years thinking you had nothing? Walking the streets, picking up quarters, eating at the Coalition. Now, you have come through the wreckage and stand tall at the center. You are spreading God's amazing miracles. By God, your own bank account! I'm so happy. But scared too, I have to say."

"Why in hell would you be scared, lover-woman?"

"Well, maybe the worst can happen. You won't need me anymore."

"God, Aneesa, talk sense. Now I can support you, too. Take you shopping, lay down my own Master Card." He takes me close, grants me one his best kisses (which he calls 'thistles'), rubs my hair, then scoots. I hear the porch door slam behind him, hear his Al Pacino cry, WHO-AH!

I look up to the backyard's branches of grandfather live oak. Can it be? Has it gotten even better? Have I married a man who has grown more alive to the very bones under his skin? I recall George Bernanos who said: "To find joy in another's joy; that is the secret of happiness."

I picked up my watering can, thinking about the book I recently read. What I learned from all the women interviewed were stories of how money could create impossible yet happy outcomes, could do amazing things to a person's spiritual life, silver spoon it into new beginnings.

Now, here was a case of just how that could happen, my once homeless Andrew opening his own bank account. *Oh God, you're never finished with Your bombshell surprises.*

After all that good news-letter, I sat out under the gazebo, and began singing the song Andrew sang to me on our wedding night, the French lyric written by Rogers and Hammerstein from the musical, *Tales from the South Pacific*. He knew I couldn't speak French, but sang it in that French language, then in English. I found myself singing it more after my marriage to this unbelievable partner.

Dites-moi pourquoi la vie est belle
Dites-moi pourquoi la vie est gaie
Dites-moi pourquoi cher monsieur belle
Est-ce que parce que vous m'aimez?

Tell me why, oh why, life is beautiful.
Tell me why, oh why, life is gay.
Tell me why, dear mister beautiful
Could it be because you love me?

Alas, good as life was on that day, we were still in for more probation heartache.

CHAPTER THIRTY-THREE

Goodbye Freedom

~ Aneesa ~

Attorney Jose sits beside Andrew, leans close and winks encouragement. We chose him because he himself had exited a courtroom sentence and was locked up and disbarred for dealing in Mary Jane. I liked his honesty, telling us all that before we hired him. I took my seat directly behind the two men. I look over to see crew-cut prosecutor, Gilbert Jones, skinny bones, his fingers playing music on his palm.

Suddenly, I had to pee. I rush to the bathroom as the bailiff shouts: "All rise! The Honorable Judge O'Connell."

That morning, I had read a passage from one of my favorite books, *Spiritual Literacy.* Why I thought of it as I rushed to the ladies' room, I haven't a clue, but it came and I pondered it, wondering if it connected to what might be the outcome of this court decision, to be free from Judge Taylor's illegal sentence.

Once several members of a Hasidic congregation had become helplessly lost in a dense forest. They were delighted when unexpectedly they came upon their rabbi who was also wandering through the woods. They implored, "Master, we are lost! Please show us the way out of the forest. The rabbi replied, "I do not know the way out either, but I do know which paths lead nowhere. I will show you the ways that won't work, and then perhaps together we can discover the ones that do."

Are we to discover another way to rid ourselves of lifetime probation if this courtroom scene is unable to free Andrew? I was full of questions as I checked out the judge, a red-headed boyish looking countenance. I watched how he literally fell into that giant black leather chair, as if he were tired of all that was required of him, and then how his hands acted busy straightening a pile of papers before him. Somehow he honestly gave me an eerie feeling. Dear God, I recall Goethe's warning: *"Beware of those in whom the urge to punish is what powers them."*

The judge looks down at Andrew and begins: "Mr. LeBoeuf, I'd like to ask you a few questions."

"Yes, Your Honor."

And unbelievably this man in charge of the courtroom lets rip a set of silly queries, stuff all long-acknowledged on paper: "What was your work before the crime? Are you now married? Where do you now reside?"

I lean into Andrew's ear. "What in heaven's name do these questions have to do with Taylor's unfair sentence?"

At last, it's Attoney Jose's turn. He approaches the bench, reads each letter from our friends advising of Andrew's good character, letters pleading the judge to release him from all this probation stuff. Special letters from Jill and Todd, my secretary, Father Art, and daughter Kelly.

"Your Honor, in my hand is another letter from his state-mandated psychologist, David Levine, asserting that Mr. LeBoeuf is fully back on his feet, requires no more supervision."

"Let me see that letter."

The judge scans David's recommendation, hardly gives it a read, pushes it aside. I don't think he even read the first paragraph. Jose presses on.

"If it pleases the court, Mrs. LeBoeuf attests that her husband has no more need of state supervision. She does this up close and personal."

Finally, a smile appears on the judge's face. *Score one for me.* Walking to the lectern in my new tailored black suit that happily Andrew's credit card purchased, I stand confident knowing what I know and the best testament to my husband's character. I place the one typed sheet before me. My voice is steady, full of purpose and confidence.

"Your Honor, marrying Andrew in a Catholic ceremony before hundreds of well-wishers initiated the greatest adventure of my life, leading to untold, super joy. We are now married almost twenty years. My past had led me to the convent. A Sister of St. Joseph teacher for sixteen years, I instructed hundreds of college-bound kids along with instructing numerous adult education classes. Later I worked side by side with Jews and Arabs in Mideast conflict resolution and prejudice reduction, the kinds of diversity that poured great confidence in my character assessing. You must know that married to this man, an example of genuine resurrection, I assure you, your honor, Andrew does not require any more probation supervision. Please, grant him the freedom he's earned and deserves."

I had no clue if my words would work toward freedom. I prayed, but only the God that I prayed to would know if we'd walk out of here victorious.

He takes his time but finally, Prosecutor Jones rises, strolls back and forth as if to sound like a Clarence Darrow's summation. The skinny-nosed prosecutor points a long finger Andrew's way, opens his mouth in a deep theater voice as if the courtroom were crowded: "This man's crime was heinous, your honor. It doesn't matter what he's done since."

Doesn't matter?

This prosecutor was totally out of step with the reason for why we are here. Not once does he refer to the illegal sentencing. The judge doesn't stop him and by now, I hear the rabbi's answer that he doesn't know the way out of the woods. It's obvious that we are never to get out of this sentence, or to be released, no matter Andrew's rebirth.

I rub Andrew's back as this prosecutor goes on and on and the red-headed judge sits, as if enjoying a dinner he ordered. But me? The sounds of his words drum wildly in my ears:

"Judge, forgiveness? No, we cannot grant forgiveness!"

Oh, I felt the anxiety of any client waiting for a decision, hoping in his summation Jose might be Perry Mason, the TV kind of attorney who knew how to cleverly sum up a case in his client's favor. But I quickly learned Jose was no Perry Mason, the judge was not a TV personality, and the courtroom consisted of no actors, and God let whatever was to be happen.

Trial comes to a close. All hope disappears. There will be no change in direction. The gavel bangs hard on my heart and the judge's voice pierces it.

"No relief granted. Next case."

Even before we had walked into this courtroom, I now know the dice had been loaded. Andrew had always believed that South Florida would never forgive him. He had said it more than once: "That court will never realize I'm something more than my breakdown."

Outside, we stood in a sunny spot on the courthouse steps. I tiptoe up to Andrew, plant a knowing kiss on his cheek, then turn to tangle with our no-Perry-Mason lawyer.

"Damn it, Jose, this was about an illegal sentencing, not about the conviction. Why didn't you take it beyond that prosecutor's outrageous condemnation? Object? What did we pay our five grand for?"

"Aneesa, I had no control over this judge's decision."

His face was on fire. But I didn't care what he was feeling. He'd lost our case and we were out of that money and precious hope. He just turned away giving me his back, wanting no more of me or of this case.

Dear God, where were You?

Andrew and I stood together, while a Florida sun shone in full force. We plopped on the cold courtroom step. My teardrops fell and I didn't try to stop them as we rested on that hard cement, feeling that cement in our bones, two souls totally creamed. Cars whizzed by. It's over and all hope is blowing in the wind.

Some readers of this story might think we still deserved to be covered by the state. Prosecutors love that group of people who say, "Keep up the punishment." They believe a person should never be finished being punished. I've read numerous stories to that effect. But thankfully, there are others who know a person should be freed from constant supervision if their actions have proven they are leading resurrected lives.

-Andrew-

Rain pours itself out gentle, one of those long gray days like there used to be in the woods at Rippawam. A fire sizzles here in front, challenging greenwood to get bright. Apple's laptop balances on my lap, Aneesa's out on the porch just out of earshot. It's been some kind of week.

Today I won't take my position at church, nor migrate for my weekly constitutional to the Loft. Here and now's exactly where I'm called to be. Yesterday was for grieving. We talked about it this morning, how to let go of the dream. Get sensible? Fold. Prudence claims the last word. Accept what obviously is. Sure ain't comfortable…still learning, still angry.

~Aneesa~

The phone rings. I know it's Jill. I let it go. I want no conversation, need silence, completely drenched in a quiet that hurts. Jeans and sweatshirt cover my body as I rest under the backyard garden gazebo. A black snake crawls around the lemon tree; I watch it slither under my neighbor's fence but before it disappears, this black animal turns my way, lifts his head high. *What's up with you? What are you saying to me?*

Suddenly, I realize I'm not fearful like the days of my youth in St. Petersburg, terrorized in the undeveloped Florida home of snakes. I look over to my neighbor's house and remember the real secret of life: to put up with tragedies that befall us.

Katie, dear neighbor, you've got your own problems. You don't need snakes inhabiting your yard after thieves broke in a week ago, taking your mom's precious antiques. You suffered the loss.

We also suffered that kind of theft. Our cleaning lady betrayed our trust in her. For two years, she'd never missed an appointment, cleaned impeccably, yet, one day, she disappeared. I never saw her again. No phone number, no address, my fault for never getting those vitals.

Days later, I discover they are gone: Mom's diamond watch and gold fob. Stolen for good, despite police help, they were never recovered. Did she need that money that she'd get for them?

Sufis declare that what we lose is never ours to have. Somehow, it sits okay with me. I mull over that sort of twist, your thieves Katie, my thief, the black snake, severe lessons. How a known world can open into the unknown. And handle it? Part of growing? Learn to turn the other cheek?

The constant ringing of the doorbell drives me to open the front door. Jill's eyes shout her annoyance.

"You knew it was me on the phone. Okay, so that Judge let you down. I've researched it. There's still a thing called clemency at the other end of the state. I'm sure we've got another chance."

"Clemency? What are you talking about? Come in."

"No, I'm meeting Todd for lunch. But Aneesa, clemency means a governor in state convictions can pardon a person deemed guilty of a crime, commute the sentence or reduce it to a lesser sentence. Although you and I know Andrew committed the crime, the governor can grant clemency, grant it to anyone who demonstrates rehabilitation or public service. Your Andrew qualifies. Let's do it!"

I often reflect on my friend's capacity to make herself present to a person's needs. Jill is energized, climbs her appointed ladder to heaven, available on most days to whatever and whoever is coming up in her world. Her sensibilities are enormous, attending to Todd's mom, attending to Todd, her kids and somehow, to me whether we're to share joy or grief. I love the old-fashioned teddy bear she gave me for my birthday. It sits at the head of my bed during the day, and at night, I fall asleep hugging it. I've given Andrew instructions that my teddy bear will follow me to my grave, a possession I don't want to leave behind. Crazy, I know.

God's giving us another chance, a possible clemency hearing and release.

The sun had risen with us on that Thursday morning when as we drove to meet the court's representative.

The ongoing process of clemency required us to be interviewed by a court appointed representative. He'd been commissioned to locate fine details of background on my hero's life after prison. Drinking? Hoboing? You name it. He asked it. In a testy voice, totally unfriendly, this-no kind-word man sits behind his desk, pumping ninety yards of silly questions into the room, the silliest of all was this one.

"Now then, Mr. LeBouef, I see you got a ticket for failing to update your license tag. Correct? A policeman had to stop you to remind you to get it? Not good!"

Andrew agreed.

"Listen, Mr. Simons." I angrily piped in, "As soon as we got that notice, we renewed that tag the next day. Is that the only infringement you can find? Pretty normal infringement, wouldn't you say, Mr. Simons? Haven't you yourself ever been stopped for something similar?"

By then, my voice let him know I'm heartily and not quietly, pissed. His stupid attitude is bringing out the worst in me. "Mr. Simons, don't you want Andrew freed?"

Andrew delivers his hand to my knee and presses it...hard. I shut up for this man's next few comments, but his last question really sent me off: "Mr. LeBouef, are you on any drugs?"

"No, sir, I'm not on any drug."

"Oh, but, sir, he is. He's on a drug called "love." Our love has been his drug ever since we met."

At that, we were promptly dismissed.

Driving home on totally empty streets, I wondered why there were no passing cars, just us driving silently, sadly when suddenly, I couldn't help myself. I bubble over in feeling sorry for this guy working for the state.

"Andrew, that guy is really the victim, not us. He's lost his heart."

"Honey, he thinks he's doing his job. Being mean is part of it. I know how those guys work."

"Well, I wouldn't want to be his wife waiting for her driven man, a man who hates his job.

At home, Andrew disappears to his quiet place and I grab my garden shears to prune the giant bird-of-paradise. I went at the plant as if it were the State of Florida. This gorgeous high-rising plant probably doesn't like being pruned. Nature's call, not mine. Then I move to the lemon tree, badly in need of pruning too since huge amounts of Spanish moss had fallen from a neighbor's giant oak and covered its branches. I pull off the collecting moss that had made it hard for baby lemons to do their thing, to grant me the lemon juice I love squeezing into my guacamole.

Sometimes I wait and wonder what is it about gardening that captures me so? Was it my father's love of plants, his attention to the yard, his concern about too much rainwater on his garden. How many times I saw him full of reflection about his yard and his orange tree. And now, me too. Worrying about my lemon tree. And my gardenia plant.

I check my watch, Dear God, I've spent more than three hours in this Florida heat, repotting, pruning, then moving newly born cuttings to more beneficial growing places. Never is one day in the garden the same as another. And each day is like a credit card that frees me to help a dying plant or a bank account be nourished again.

That last hour, I opened the greenhouse door to see a tiny bird, a flying sparrow banging against the glass windows, trying to leave the prison he had found himself in. At the open door, I stand and this animal races past me and escapes. He had suffered enough. I close the door and make for the porch, all the while praying to God to also escape more probation visits.

God, tell me we're not finished, that no matter what decisions officials choose, there's going to be more to our life than some belligerent meanie knocking on our door in the middle of the night. Tell me!

~ *Andrew* ~

"Andy, your dad is dying. Come!"

Why did this ancient memory of a dying Dad flood back in my mind before our clemency hearing? Aneesa and I had just held a vigil the night before to fix on one sure release from this burden of state visits every month. And there it emerged, that entire scene of Mom calling me that night so many years ago. I let it bring me back, the details, the lack of understandings and most of all, the strangeness still existing between Dad and me.

The plane ride to their recently settled home in Ormond Beach was unsettling. I had no other thoughts except for this father. Were his last breaths to create a connection between us? That at his dying, our relationship might become alive?

Dad's ten years of cancer humiliated him. He, for most of his life, had bountiful presence enough to fill a crowded room every time. How he loved driving his Belgian business associates around to see America's accomplishments, especially the George Washington Bridge. That smile of his remained in my memory.

Mom's voice again rang in my ears all the way to the plane's landing.

"It isn't right that he should suffer this way."

In the cab, I considered all those generous birthday gifts of his to me: the top-of-the-line Schwin with the first derailleur anyone had ever seen in the area, the American Flyer railroad he set up in the basement with every bell and whistle. And mostly, my beloved mahogany, red-sail, gaff-rigged dinghy, days of glorious tacking and sailing alone on Lake Rippowam. But when it came to words, we— father and son—had so little to say to each other. It was his way, I had assumed, that his gifts would do his talking. He was choosing to come close with well thought-out suitable gifts.

Oh, how the unbelievable flood of memories that take over as I walk through their home's rooms. Each African memorabilia is framed as if in a museum. On one wall, hang the families' bright European tapestries. Mom had saved them that day we were forced to leave Brussels because of the Nazi invasion. On the room's long tables were displayed Dad's collections of ebony statues, spears, arrows from our post-war years in Leopoldville reminding me of my days playing with Moké, my Congo hero.

Now with silver glowing hair, Mom appears with that so familiar, so unable to resist wish for Dad and me to unite, a uniting which never happened and I suspect won't happen now.

"Andy, be with him. I know it's hard for you but this man was your father and you have no idea how you hurt him running off to elope like that."

She sobbed on my chest, took my hand, pressed it to her cheek. This woman had been my mentor, my dearest mother who fashioned me into her son, more than ever the parent I needed. We stood close for real golden minutes of togetherness but then suddenly, impatiently, she pulled me forward.

"Come!"

I stood by his bedside, hoping to feel something good. *Nada.* No shed of pity, no loving emotion that linked me to him, but like always, not a word out of either of us. Dad looked at me with only one blank stare. *Are you there?* I wondered. *Were you ever, Dad?*

Mom sobbed, her eyes focused on me.

"Look, Andy! That is no longer my beloved Jean Luc. Can't we make him look better? Please, give him a decent shave."

I pulled out his shaving tools: old-fashioned brush, shaving soap, razor, grabbed the towel, ran it under hot water, warmed his face, spread cream on his cheeks and neck.

"Get that part by his ear, Andrew. That's the part he always missed."

Strange that it was to be me, the one to begin shaving this

long-gone father in the final throes of his life. Was it a way of saying good bye, a good shave define how we'd always hope lived?

Mom stood close. It was like I was on a stage, she, the entire audience checking me out on how well I performed this personal service, whether from duty or from love. Love? I didn't know how to love this father, nor I suspect, did he know how to return his own love to me.

Following every wrinkle, my hand trembled as I pulled the razor down to capture each hair, like this engineer father I'm certain, would have done for his own dad. The last fold of his neck proved the hardest—dry, wrinkled, old skin. He'd grown ancient. This, the man I'd so very long looked up to, even if I could never reach him.

Finally, I cleaned up his face best I could.

In the end, this end of our togetherness, still not one goddamn word slipping between us. Those eyes did follow my every move, looking up to me, rarely blinking. As if Mom knew my indifference, she pulled at my arm as I washed up.

"Andy, what about that gift of his own treasured Rolleiflex? Dad watched you shoot those pictures, stood close, advised you on each knob and click to bring you to picture-perfect shots. Surely, you can never forget that? Can you ever forget?"

True, one kind day out of the ordinary, Dad stood right behind me along a quiet shoreline, watching me click an osprey dancing on skinny legs, and at one point I enjoyed his laughter, loved hearing it as he called the bird's dance an honest Bolero. We were standing under a thousand kindly suns.

It wasn't long after that shaving time when Mom's fingers closed his eyes, kissed his mouth, wept her goodbye. She had loved this man with every cell of her being, followed him wherever he took her and he had always raised her up as his queen, planting kisses on her in the silence of their togetherness.

Now, it was closing time, a misty dawn for a man who'd given the world a much-hallowed knowledge of how to...everything! How once upon a time, to run the Belgian Congo, and then back in New York to raise his family, bring us all to years of nature at Lake Rippowam.

How he built that rock wall, heaving giant stones up on it, high enough to keep any animals from entering our domain. Even so, with all these memories, I still, and must say sadly. I hardly knew the man.

The one biting thing that I did learn was how a man of such a large life, of such thriving business, could be cut down by mean-spirited cancer and forced to suffer the unfairness of it all.

Mom buried him at his precious Rippawam, down near the lake under his favorite birch, beside the stone wall he'd built, one boulder at a time. Dressed in her best black, Mom's tears streamed down as she held tight to my sister Penny, placing atop the mound a needlepoint cross she'd woven. I stood emotionless that day before my father's grave. I wish I could have cried at least one tear, but nothing was felt.

Never have I gone back. I expect I never will, settling at last on that long-trained absence of his own, or was it my, creation.

CHAPTER THIRTY-FOUR

Paris Bienvenue

~ Aneesa ~

On the night before departure to Paris, Andrew's hopes run high regarding our clemency hearing. "You gotta know, honey, traveling to Europe feels like freedom already given. Clemency's freedom will be next. I really believe it."

To make that Paris trip, my husband was required by his probation officer to jot every planned visit: who, when, and where, phone numbers, addresses, details beyond imagining.

"Honey," I asked sarcastically, "Did they give you permission to breathe while you are there?"

Despite the weighty overflow of people and baggage, we're finally airborne, pushing the sky's vaporous clouds aside with our Paris magic carpet. I witness each cottony puff we nudge away and thank it for moving aside, thank TIAA-CREF's college retirement for that surprise to my man who never had run after money. And to Jill, big thanks for twice a week praying with me, delivering this male dream to my single world.

Sitting back, we both put earplugs in and chose Beethoven's

Ninth to play through the plane's headsets, the famous ending chorus and happy to discard them when the blond stewardess's silky voice announces:

"*Bienvenue à Paris!*"

Charles de Gaulle International bustles with crowds of babbling greeters. Magic market posters wave names colorfully scribbled, and sweet shots of hugs everywhere! Finally, cousin Monique and hubby Louis see us, pull us close, babbling delight at this long-awaited reunion, a new chapter for memories that will always lift our spirits. I smell Monique's Chanel—I think it's Chanel—and I watch and love how she and my husband walk ahead, arm in arm, love Andrew's wink at me as he babbles so easily in French with her. He's home, the land of dreams for us both. For me France stands tall as the land of Merton's birth, land of visionary artists, writers, poets, composers, Joan of Arc, Eiffel tower. I'm overwhelmed, feelings of awe and love for the present gifts being granted to my spirit.

Paris is like a dream, brings beauty, reverence, and awe. In the weeks that follow, we leave Monique and Louie, walk its streets alone, merge into two kids smelling every flower's scent, paging in old bookstores, nibbling on freshly baked croissants, holding hands everywhere, giggling, and trusting each day to spoon fresh nourishment.

All old Europe reveals an Andrew on his own. I don't get enough of him, like actor Gerard Depardieu's voice tossing commands to ticket folk, hotel clerks, waiters—a long way from slump of negativity, from a church's barking dogs and growling cops running up the stairs to clasp his wrists, and worst of all, Father So and So—*a priest*—telling the police to "Take him away."

Here Andrew celebrates his powerful poetic self-born creature in a culture best known for creativity. He doesn't pull out his pen as often as I'd like him to. I give that wish up. As for me, I take in Paris' delight myself, especially the day I kneel in Notre Dame Cathedral under a giant statue of St. Joan of Arc as soldier pinned high on the stone wall, sword in hand and who wasn't canonized until May 16, 1920 in St. Peter's Basilica by Pope Benedict XV. I stare at that blazing sword, her young but piercing eyes set my soul afire, jerking me away from old silly faithless moments I once agonized over.

I'm free under her, Andrew observing me kneeling, my quiet smile, and chuckles. "You glow like you're serving cookies and lemonade to that saint!"

At some point, Monique and Louis drive us north through lovely Brittany, across the Belgian border to ancient Bruges. We stroll one lovely moment after another on picturesque bridges built over charming rippling canals. And what a remarkable sight. Our Lady of Bruges cathedral where under a towering ceiling sits Michelangelo's white stone Madonna cradling her infant, sight of which somehow causes me to stop my approach, drop to my knees up close, linking me to that spirited presence I'd read about, never known, truly visceral first beyond anything ever experienced in my nuns' chapels. Now, in that cathedral I am alive with wonder at all that past primed for this moment. In my mind, my heart, I sing Maria's hymn from *The Sound of Music,* because for this moment, yes "I must have done something good."

At a Belgian restaurant of her choice, Monique excitedly blurts out how thrilled she is to sit next to Andrew and share their past. She's simply unable to stop her stream of memories tumbling out in English.

"Andrew, recall how both of us at sixteen, climbed that peak in the Italian Tyrol? You cleared the top, pulled me to your side, and there we stood breathless, surveying that unbelievable landscape spread out far as we could see. You knelt, wrote a poem to some girl back in the States. I was speechless, and dreamy, so happy to be far from my own 'bossy father.'"

*Ah…*Belgium, and its remarkable food! After only a few weeks in that historic land I'm gaining weight as never before. Weight Watchers decrees are far from my table in these restaurants where every main course is unique.

We are both drawn to visit cathedrals, our capacity never strained or burdened by our walks in their direction. In Brussels, Andrew's birthplace, there exist so many, never-to-be-forgotten, huge cathedrals. One day, we found ourselves on a street in front of a giant synagogue, probably a main street. This day their Sabbath. We both saw its giant front doors were closed. No one was coming to it. *What gives?* We both stand wondering as a Brussels's sun streams over us like grace that awakens the reality of why this synagogue is empty.

Yes, yes. I get it; few Jews are left after the Nazi occupiers determined to route them away. The Nazis even grabbed Andrew's Brussels home and used it for one of their headquarters, forcing his father to get the family out of the city. If you were Jewish, you would have been trucked to some camp far away from home. The horror of the past reality hits us both. I grab Andrew's hand, squeeze it as that painful truth hits my thoughts, my heart, my eyes that fill up as I hear German guns shooting and running tortured Jews forward: men, women, and children crying aloud, Christians standing by unable or not wanting to stop them.

I don't know how long my husband and I stood in that place. At some point, as I look up, I notice the large engraved French words high above its enormous fat cement pillars, reminding me of my Jewish friends, Michael, Enid, Erica, Jill, and Omar.

Andrew interpreted the quote above: "Aren't we all children of the one God?"

"Honey, let's get back to the hotel, try to forget what we've just seen."

"Aneesa, maybe we're not supposed to forget what we've just seen. Maybe we're to carry these memories back home, share how we saw the Holocaust up close and personal. And right here in the place where I was born."

I sprinkle sugar on Andrew's cocoa at the hotel's cafe, sip my coffee. Jill's comment uttered to me so long ago in the kitchen one Shabbat night floats back as I let it in:

"Becoming a Jew broadened my life, Aneesa. Singing and dancing at Jewish weddings, every happy face is an angel throwing beams of love out to everyone. Jews know how to dance, how to stomp passionately their heels because, I believe, they know how to suffer. I've never been sorry the Holy Spirit led me to Todd's religion, despite so much anti-Semitism that still swims naked in our world. I'm actually happy now to be called a Jew."

A week later, we board the high speed *Train de Grande Vitesse* for Provence. Andrew's sister Sarah and husband Bernard live in a small French town she'd written about and we planned a week's stay there. Their home was right out of the movies, an ancient old renovated circular *pigeonnier* that Bernard had remodeled.

A few nights later after arriving, we're sitting in one of Bernard's favorite restaurants. We are four, the only guests in that place of unique French tastes. Sarah's husband simply winks at the chef who came out to greet us, and soon, a magical meal begins to appear without menu, course after course, taste upon new taste, one of the chef's engineered work of art.

There was only one drawback that next morning. I couldn't fit into my jeans.

"Andrew, tell me about Robert. How's your son doing?" Sarah had asked.

"Sis, Robert and his brood are all well. We talk by phone weekly. He's an account executive, grown so smart, able to see life in ways that helps me know I didn't do such a poor job with my kids."

Sarah throws Andrew a high-five.

Back at their home, Sarah grabs my hand, rushes me to her bedroom, pulls out a gold necklace, fastens it around my neck.

"Aneesa, this was Mom's. You alone have fashioned my darling brother into the happiest I can ever remember seeing him."

Before drifting off to sleep, Raymond Carver's poem comes floating on a cloud, a poem of his I'd copied down somewhere in a worn journal:

Late Fragment

And did you get what you wanted from this life, even so?
I did.
And what did you want?
To call myself beloved,
to feel myself beloved on the earth.

Gorges de Verdon? Let's do it, Aneesa. His eyes radiate excitement.

"No, I want to pack, rest before tomorrow's flight back home. Anyway, Sarah told me about that Gorges. You get dizzy just looking down from its canyon."

"Come on, sweetums. I've got to hike it!"

I looked closely at him, reminded myself that it was God who wanted this man in my life. Shall I surrender, be grateful that he even wants to take me on this adventure, to explore France's high pastures of awesome view?

This is the husband who has dedicated his life to planet earth or "Ma" as he refers to her, recording issues online that raise reader's consciousness to help preserve her future. Climate change is his major issue and he never tires of shining light on what everyone can do for our planet home. And now he wants to hike a piece of her beauty and surrender I must regardless of inclinations of my own.

I follow him on that rocky upward path, fascinated as my father would be, by the rows of wild fig trees sprouting everywhere on the steep climb. But niggling needles pinch my feet and body, making me complain more than usual. The strangest sight of all?

"Andrew, what in heaven's name is a donkey standing there doing nothing that I can see. Up here? All alone?"

That isn't Andrew's concern and after a few more uphill climbs, terror strikes. It is so true. I'm caught scared, totally terrified.

"Andrew, if anything should happen to you! Well, what will I ever do here? I can't speak the language if someone came along."

He pushes ahead as if he hadn't heard me.

"Stop! Listen to me! You're moving too far ahead. I can't keep up. What if I lose you? Even if someone finds me lost, I told you before, I can't explain anything to them. I want to go back. I have to pee."

He turns, as if staring at a strange woman he doesn't know any longer. I'm sure by the look in his eyes wondering who is this woman he's married to? Somehow, despite that look, he finds his sweetest voice despite undertones of guilt.

"Aneesa, I've dreamed about hiking this range ever since I was a kid, read about it in French magazines, and now's my chance. I'm going on. You stay here, pee. Nobody's around except that donkey and he doesn't give a damn, probably pissing plenty up here himself."

Laughing, he points to a boulder by a fig tree.

"Wait for me over by that rock. You'll be okay."

The excitement of his moment smells like fear to me, especially if I look down on that tiny raft sailing on the river below, that raft about as big as an ant. My knees wobble at the sight. *Get me outta here, God.*

I hear a voice that tells me: *Well, stop looking down.*

Suddenly all is quiet. Andrew is gone, totally out of view and I'm in view of everything new and strange. In the silence except for the incessant droning of homebound insects, comfort is not an option. Too much fear lives in me right now, a strange kind of fear that I've never known.

I rest my butt on the giant rock that he had pointed out, a giant rock near the precipice with nothing to offer me except the fact that I must pray, and pray hard. I fold my hands under my chin, close my eyes and aloud let the words come: *Dear Lord, I'm mad, isolated, and need your calm. Take this fear out of me.*

I focus on a spider weaving a wide web near the side of my face. *Oh God, so true that insects and animals live in the moment. You can too, Aneesa. Keep your eye on that spider.*

How long I sat, my hands still in prayer, when suddenly, not knowing why or what, but I felt a strange kind of restlessness, a push from above, as if something apart from fear was pushing at me, as if something or someone was there. I turn all around.

Oh my God. Is it really? Are my eyes deceiving? No, it can't be! But it is.

What I'm staring at is hanging on an outstretched dead branch, and it stares back at me. It is that familiar cap of blue and white, a logo on the ordinary gray baseball cap that is totally familiar: *The Orlando Magic!* I cry out: "Mercy, Mercy!" I keep staring. This is Orlando's basketball team and Andrew and I loved its players. We have rooted for them more than a dozen times—whooping and hollering for their newbie fine player, Shaquille O'Neal, even as he failed his free throws. I could do nothing else but grab that hat and press it close to my beating fast heart. That magic is here and it is talking peace of mind to me.

Dear God, you are something, sending me a message of faith from my Florida. A baseball cap! In France? How could it be out here in the middle of nowhere, grabbing both my attention and my gratitude. Maybe it doesn't even matter how it got here. I turn it over and over in my hand. It's clean, almost like new. What am I learning? What could this cap be telling me?

Andrew returns and as I guess I really knew he always would return, full of excitement, describing his colorful hike. I felt his happy feelings and was glad he'd done what he wanted. But me, I couldn't hold back my own blessed discovery. I jumped up, wearing the cap, hugged him long and hard. Let it be known: I was a completely changed woman from the one who had lost her faith.

On our plane ride home, Andrew breaks into one of his huge grins. "I bet I know what that cap means."

"Okay, spill it."

"That cap is spelling out our victory to come, achieving clemency at our hearing in Tallahassee just around the corner!"

At that, I pull out the now crumpled gray hat from my purse, rub it, thank the Magic genie as much as God for what I hoped would come.

How strange, an Orlando cap called Magic.

CHAPTER THIRTY-FIVE

Clemency

-Aneesa-

A balmy Florida morning greets us in Tallahassee. The sun shines like it never has before, puffy clouds signal nothing can go wrong on this gorgeous day. We had ignored the letter sent by the Department of Corrections telling us our chances were minimal. With Andrew's fine and noble behavior, I believed we could overcome all obstacles.

Jill and Todd follow us through the State's giant mahogany doors and another set of double glassed security doors. The large courtroom is abuzz, claimants' voices murmuring expectantly. We settle in a middle pew-like bench, me between Jill and Andrew, Todd on the outside.

It's now or never.

Bushy-haired Florida governor sports a blue shirt, twirls a white pencil, and with his cabinet sits on the dais in a stretched row of black plushy leather chairs facing all of us. Cabinet members swivel their chairs to face us. Obviously, we sit as a group of anxious men and women hoping to push against so much state law. My thoughts sprint up and then down the ladder of hope. I watch cabinet members whispering to each other, some laughing. Will we ever be able to join in laughter?

Though I walk through the valley of the shadow of death, I will fear no evil: for Thou art with me; thy rod and thy staff they comfort me.

I squeeze the Orlando Magic cap hidden in my purse. Andrew holds my hand and sometimes squeezes it. He leans to me and whispers: "We'll be okay, honey, I feel it."

He's riding high. Come on, Aneesa, get your own wings flying.

I turn my heart to see good results from this court of…let me call it mercy.

"Good morning!" The governor's bass voice quiets the room and the process of granting or not granting clemency begins. Overhead lights focus on a short-bearded attorney representing woman imprisoned for five years. He steps to the microphone.

"Governor, Melissa Melgen operated a friendly bar, with no trouble until this guy, Jeffery Conway, appeared regularly. Whenever she served him, he'd grope parts of her body each time. Slapping him to stop didn't work. To really stop him, she obtained a restraining order yet, he continued to follow her around that bar. She called the police, but nothing was done. A friend lent her his gun, told her when he does it again, shoot him in the leg. The result was that she, the victim, received a sentence of twenty years. In fairness, governor, we believe the state should definitely reduce that sentence."

The attorney sits back down and suddenly, the wife of the groper rushes to the microphone. "Governor, my husband lives in a wheel chair for something he did not do. That woman doesn't deserve a reduced sentence. She's a bad person."

The governor bangs his gavel.

"Pardon denied."

The room buzzes. The wife returns to her seat with a smile.

My heart grows heavy. *What does that verdict say about what's coming up for us? Do we have a chance? Is the governor always prone to honor the victim? Hasn't Andrew become a victim too? Don't let Gerta's family be present.*

Suddenly, I catch the granite face of that Clemency Board Administrator woman up front, the one who sent us that depressing letter: "A pre-clemency hearing of your case does not look favorable. However, you are of course legally entitled to plead your clemency in person."

Something about her presence signals a fixed arrogance, a mean-spirited bony attitude. Andrew's face plays rigid. He sees her too! I squeeze my Magic cap. *Will it take a miracle? Then give us one...please!*

A short African-American man stands at the lectern. "Governor, I've spent twenty-three years behind bars for a rape I didn't commit, locked up on the basis of no evidence. DNA finally cleared me. I demand my record be expunged."

The gavel slammed down without any hesitation: "Pardon granted!"

The man's head drops onto the lectern for an understandable long sigh, a long-sought relief! *How awful. Locked up for a crime he didn't commit?* Sometimes life can be so unfair. Back down the aisle, numerous television cameramen envelop his dark face into their lenses, a photo to appear in Florida newspapers the next day.

Andrew leans over to me.

"That guy should sue the state for that time served. He was innocent but forced to endure steel bars staring him in the face!"

Suddenly, we hear Andrew's name called.

Here we go! The final touchdown? "Sister, what's a touchdown?" That was what my little fourth grader Bunny asked me to explain the meaning of a football touchdown. 'Bunny, a touchdown is when a team makes seven points added to their score. And when the game's finally over someone with the highest points or touchdowns has won.'

Jill, Todd, and I follow Andrew to the lectern, stand close as he faces the governor. He begins his testimony and I love hearing that deep voice of his, not a bit of stuttering, no holding back, only pure truth.

He concludes with: "Governor, I have paid my sentence behind bars. Lifetime probation was an added but illegal punishment. If you think about that, additional supervision provides no benefit to the state or to myself."

Bravo, Andrew.

I step forward. I start with a quick version of the ancient story of St. Francis and Brother John standing outside in the rain, barred from their monastery, despite their incessant knocking. Finally, some monk douses them with pails of water—monks who are their brothers and are standing on the balcony above.

" 'Francis,' Brother John shouts out to the saint. 'The monks don't know who we are.'

'Yes, Brother John,' St Francis replies. 'But we know who we are.' "

"This is what I need to say about my husband, Governor. You don't know who he is." In my heart, I appreciated the somber silence as I told that story, not a sound could be heard in that courtroom.

"Governor, my husband knows who he is. He wasn't this guy then. He had a massive breakdown that he lives with daily. He has regretted that terrible crime all his life, and knows, as hard as it is to understand, he was never really the man who did that horror in the first place. Please, Governor grant us relief from this unnecessary lifetime probation."

I step back as Jill approaches to speak. Madam Arrogant stands up to say to her: "That is enough, Miss. He's had his time." *No, no. Jill and Todd must speak.* I rush back.

"Governor, our friends traveled miles to be with us today to support my husband's belated freedom."

The Governor nods. Jill begins her plea to the governor in her strongest voice:

"As a therapist, I recognize Andrew's integrity. I counseled him for months before his wedding, witnessed his civic actions, his caring for the homeless. He visited nursing homes, listened to the elderly recounting their difficulties. It's time, Governor, for the state to recognize this man's contributions."

Surely, Todd's eloquent witness to Andrew would do it, wouldn't it, God?

Todd wasted not a minute, approached the lectern to speak. "As a medical doctor, I honor my instincts. Andrew's ground is fertile, Governor. After knowing this giver to so many causes, your instincts for justice will compel a pardon."

Todd winked as we all walked back and dropped into our seats. I clutched Andrew's hand hard. It soon became clear: state had informed her of our wish for clemency. And so, Gerta's sister, though not in person, had written to this clemency hearing. Would Gerta's sister now speak? I didn't see her, but hadn't a clue what she looked like. Now, I knew what was coming as a six-foot, crewcut frame in business suit moved to the lectern. He pulls out her presence written on legal yellow paper:

"How dare this man ask for clemency. He showed no clemency to my sister."

Not true.

"He slashed her neck, her blood flowed. He served only five years."

Not true.

"He's still un-remorseful."

Not true.

"He traveled to Paris."

With all kinds of needed permission!

"Governor, this reprobate has done nothing to warrant any pardon."

Doesn't anyone fact-check her lies?

It became horribly clear that we would always carry this disappointing scene with us, the shredding of Andrew's character, the lies that would deny us clemency, the lack of forgiveness from all who heard the story.

His gavel banged and Governor Crist sentenced Andrew to live with this life-time punishment: "Clemency denied!"

I shot up like a lit match. "Kids, let's go!"

CHAPTER THIRTY-SIX

So Be It

-Aneesa-

Andrew's unfolding story began decades ago as advised by therapist David and is now concluded, or probably will never be concluded, as his children will add truths to his redemptive life, in touch favorably, lovingly. Eventually, I'll send the entire pack of his journals to Kelly, who will share them with her young twins when grown adults. Kelly now lives in New York and no longer limps. Her medical doctor referred her to a surgeon who could and did extend her shorter leg. "Such a blessing," she told her father.

At some point, Andrew's Mom had changed her will, since sisters Sarah and Penny were happily provided for. Penny lives in California and Sarah, with means of her own, left Kelly the New York home including the summer place in Rippawam which never was sold to a stranger. She and Ron spend weekends there walking its trails, picnicking down by the very lake where the boy that was Andrew sailed his favorite father's gift, that gaff rig yacht tender.

-Andrew-

It's early morning. Coffee is ready, Abby cat comes in, goes to his dish. This male cat, a Maine Coon and I connect on the sofa, our morning moment alone, something like an hour, candles flickering. I like this cat guy, independent as hell, helps me connect to what's real. After a while, Aneesa delivers a breakfast smoothie after watering her planted green kids in the blooming courtyard. We catch up—*Your tummy? Your feet? How'd you sleep?*

Time for morning chores. I make the beds, pull up the curtains, same for the day's air-conditioning setting. Two years ago, about this time found me pedaling around our lake, ahead of sunrise and the day's fierce heat, back by nine, exhausted, energized, brimming over with endorphins. That was before arthritis took over my flat feet, shoving me into surgery, where last winter the left one was fused. Today a new tadpole recumbent has me moving again.

Because morning is for work, indoors or out, we get it done. For lunch, kitchen-soup, veggies, crackers from that creative pallet of Aneesa's, then always some home-baked goods to follow. Netflix movies wrap us together, especially our many BBC friends. After that, things slow down; before you know it, night time again, iPad, emails, array of pills.

That's how it looks day to day. Life turned simple enough, gently aging our couple-hood, breathing together moment-to-moment.

When it comes to Mother Earth, a few years ago, I took off from our closeness, pedaling from NY to DC with a group committed to our planet's survival. Two years later, again oldest rider, we peddled down California's coast. After that, I initiated a blog writing details of what we all must do to protect this mother home, life's very story here on our gorgeous living planet. Regular online postings from a wrinkled dyslexic of Mother Earth's "*beauth & trutti*". As my license plate itself proclaims: 1-GAIA!

One can guess I often ask how to live after what I'd done, plus how to repay all I've been given. Well, the first question mostly fades from upfront view, especially since I published my tragedy fifteen years ago for my first grandchild. The second does draw me in plenty these days.

~ Aneesa ~

I hold his last journals in my hands, delighted that he agreed I could scan them before mailing them to his children. I loved reading his cryptic style...

> *reflected on my failures, my tunnels, my remorse, my passing tableaux of ruin and wreckage, the mountain tops, the deserts a plenty...was a time when the world was where it was and imagination what was left of it in my case could freely take off to fantastic places but no more of a sudden i'm glued to here-&-now turned fantastic and nowhere left for roaming...when the walls broke down, the light broke through...and i found empathy for my fellows.*
>
> *i snap albums of mental pictures anyway, can't fight the state anymore, accept the authority of a lifetime penance...the horrible images persist...mom's early call to her nature boy, he forever awed at nature's lushness, "how'd you do that?" i ask florida's stately palms, giant oaks, pelicans, osprey wandering over land and sea as i myself had wandered...it rains four days of this gray but no one complains relieved of the sun——who could take it...streaks of light again just now break through.... pick my pen up,...accept whatever had happened in my lifetime, on my knees to mercy and love. that dark period determined my transformation, lines and more lines burst in my heart...edge of the st. john's rippling water...midnight times on back porch,*

muse in these remaining years...lie in green grass,
work for fragile planet, something special for ground
i breathe above, sit sentry to it as hero, john muir. the
sun is setting, clouds hover out here near the st. john's
river that flows north... water heals my wounds... as
for the others who pulled me through, this journal isn't
big enough to mention them all

Before dawn breaks, Andrew and I are up riding along the St. John's flowing, glistening moonlit water. He peddles his tadpole and I, my hybrid bike, lovely to be with the early day's natural rhythms. I ride along the river's edge, and for a few minutes, a nameless white bird follows at my heels. All nature seems alive as now a bevy of newly hatched ducks waddle into the street quacking near the bike. I make room for them. I listen to the robin's song saying not to worry.

Long strands of moss hang from celebrated giant oaks that line our quiet street, oaks gown tall, fed and watered by Nature herself offering everlasting shade under fiery sun. Beyond them that hundred and twenty-year-old red-brick schoolhouse surrounds itself with a colorful garden blooming white and pink roses, dewdrops bragging of last night's watering. Robin's serenade reminds me that love has been good to me. That God has been there whether I recognized Him straightaway or not. That because of Him, here was this Andrew come into my life. That we've lived our vows since that Merton day in December over twenty-five years ago.

Cup of coffee in hand, I gently rock on our front porch, happily living in this old Florida northern town. I try not to mind the wrinkles coming on my arms and hands aware that life is a gift and I've lived it, and it's okay to someday not exist here anymore. I've done enough.

In truth, sometimes I wonder why I'm living a long life. Often, my past becomes my present. I hold dear the young girl who still lives inside me. The girl who for sixteen years dressed in black, stood before groups of kids in a grade school classroom and with them laughed at their antics, loved their stage presence as they sang out in St. Juliana's numerous musicals, still the girl who fell for a dedicated priest and how he graciously lifted her awareness of having talents she hadn't recognized, the girl that led a choir of loving adults, the girl who never despaired of life, and thankfully saw all of it as gift. Yes, yes, she still lives in me and her faith dictates she will live beyond her last breath. I raise high my cup. It overflows and I overflow holding a giant *thank you!*

EPILOGUE

~Aneesa~

It's a quiet afternoon. Someone knocks on the front door. There he stands, grinning from ear to ear, this dark-skinned man with piercing blue eyes waits.

"Is Andrew here?"

"Who is calling?

"You must be Andrew's other half? I'd been looking forward to meeting you."

He extends his hand.

"I'm Sergio Gomez, Andrew's new probation officer. Is he here?"

"Oh, Mr. Gomez, Andrew has been bragging about his new officer. He came home a week ago after so many visits with you, sharing how different a watchman he has this time. I hope you can stay on the job for, well...maybe forever."

We enjoy a laugh.

Yes, Sergio is a real human tutor who knows how to smile every time he calls on us, who respects my husband's talents, who allows Andrew to be flexible with his appointments. I send Sergio back to Andrew's studio, my "ex-offender" safe at last.

"Honey, this man treats me as if I were a friend, not a criminal. He jokes with me, takes time to ask how my life with you is going?"

"Did someone in Tallahassee direct him to you...maybe?"

Sergio, the human correction officer, appears monthly at our front door, always with that bright Latino smile, remaining with us both for only time to share a few greetings. Soon I begin to welcome him like family, walking him often into our vegetable garden, since he too is a gardener.

A few months ago, Sergio reminds my husband: "You always show up on time. You never miss an appointment. You have no need to be here. Go get your wife, I'm making a call to the judge."

We sit before him in total surprise as he phones the very judge who had ignored our petition for relief from lifetime probation. I cover Andrew's hand that he presses against his thigh, a tiny smile creeping over both our faces.

"Have I got the third district judge? Your honor, I have Andrew LeBouef sitting before me with his wife…" Sergio pours out about Andrew's fidelity to the rules. "He sees me on time, every time. I visit his house and every thing's in order…This man leads an exceptionally productive life. I recommend we take this man off a monthly schedule."

Silence.

We get a gesture from him for us to keep quiet. He listens and smiles our way. "Thank you, your honor. A quarterly schedule will make a big difference to us both."

Genuine Thanks

- to my healthy, close loving Syrian family who got me started into spirit and music;

- to so many generous Sisters of St. Joseph of St. Augustine helping shape my early spiritual development and musical education;

- to former, lovable students of mine, many of whom are still in touch online and in person;

- to so many of today's close friends continuing to hear my own takes on the Aneesa and Andrew that take up these pages, beginning with longest friend Georgia and new neighbor, Diane;

- to this regular writing group family of ours in Mount Dora, often listening to my pages and offering thoughtful advice;

- to poet and writer, Bernie Welch, who gave of his time to offer Nun and Bum its first edit

- to favorite priest Father Steve Bauman, generously editing and writing extremely helpful comments;

- to professional Brooklyn editor, Alice Peck, taking my manuscript to professional book level, who in the process became a warm friend;

- to Anita Moorjani, whose recent memoir, <u>Dying to Be Me</u>, calmly spiritualized my soul to accepting my current diagnosis of breast cancer graciously not just as an illness but as God's loving gift of self-discovery.

- most of all, my deeply felt thanks to beloved husband, Jim Rucquoi, for his constant support, his speaking for Andrew, his own poetry & photos, his own edit here & there. Best of all my companions, I stand grateful to God for sending Jim to me.

Adele Azar-Rucquoi obtained her B.A. from Manhattanville College in New York and her Masters in Religious Education from Barry University in Miami, Florida. Raised in a Syrian-American family, Adele entered the Sisters of St. Joseph and worked as a teaching nun for sixteen years. Afterward she directed the Central Florida Chapter of the International Thomas Merton Society. With poet-husband, Jim, Adele taught courses in creativity at Florida's Rollins College. Her articles have appeared in Spirituality and Health, Orlando Life, America magazines. Adele is an active member of the Mt Dora Writers Guild. The Nun and The Bum is Adele's first foray into fiction.

Jim Rucquoi was born in Brussels and raised in New York. He holds degrees from Georgetown (BS) and Columbia University (MBA), and has been a Naval Air Intelligence officer, Madison Avenue account executive, and professor of marketing and advertising at City University of New York. Later, after leaving professional work, he devoted his life to performance poetry. He now spends time creating videos and photography for mother earth and friends at shemovesme.com

Printed in the United States
By Bookmasters